DOING RIGHT

DOING RIGHT

A Practical Guide
to Ethics for
Medical Trainees
and Physicians

SECOND EDITION

PHILIP C. HÉBERT

OXFORD

UNIVERSITY PRESS

OXFORD
UNIVERSITY PRESS

8 Sampson Mews, Suite 204, Don Mills, Ontario M3C 0H5

www.oupcanada.com

Oxford University Press is a department of the University of Oxford.
It furthers the University's objective of excellence in research, scholarship,
and education by publishing worldwide in

Oxford   New York
Auckland   Cape Town   Dar es Salaam   Hong Kong   Karachi
Kuala Lumpur   Madrid   Melbourne   Mexico City   Nairobi
New Delhi   Shanghai   Taipei   Toronto

With offices in
Argentina   Austria   Brazil   Chile   Czech Republic   France   Greece
Guatemala   Hungary   Italy   Japan   Poland   Portugal   Singapore
South Korea   Switzerland   Thailand   Turkey   Ukraine   Vietnam

Oxford is a trade mark of Oxford University Press
in the UK and in certain other countries

Published in Canada by Oxford University Press

Library and Archives Canada Cataloguing in Publication

Hébert, Philip Charles
Doing right: a practical guide to ethics for medical trainees and
physicians / Philip Hébert.—2nd ed.
Includes index.

ISBN 978-0-19-542841-4

1. Medical ethics. I. Title.

R724.H39 2008   174.2   C2008-903599-2

Cover image: Bart Sadowski/istock

CONTENTS

PREFACE TO THE SECOND EDITION

It has been 12 years since the first edition of *Doing Right* was published. The reasons for a second edition were many, but prime among these was to update the book with what I have learned about healthcare in being a doctor, a parent, and a patient myself. If you have read the previous edition, you may note that my discussion of some of the older cases will be a little (or a lot) different as a result of these intervening experiences.

The book has been completely rewritten from start to finish. In this edition I have included cases that affect all healthcare professions, not just physicians. It is still heavily weighted to the medical profession (for example, I use the term 'patient' rather than 'client' or 'consumer') but, to some degree, this is inevitable because I am a physician and experience these issues from that perspective. Nevertheless, many of the lessons learned and the directions taken would be the same for any healthcare professional.

The perspective, then, is that of the healthcare professional in general. Although different professionals will have different degrees of agency and responsibility for handling ethical dilemmas in clinical practice, the 'right way' of doing so should reflect a common 'professional point of view'—best arrived at by consensus and critical interprofessional discussion. There is an ongoing revolution in medical education, in favour of patients and multidisciplinary teams, which this book is meant to mirror and encourage. This interprofessional cooperation only emphasizes what I wrote in the preface to the first edition. When a troublesome decision must be made, two nostrums can be recommended: *Use the wisdom of others* and *Try to find someone to help you.* Medicine is a difficult enterprise but rarely a lonely one.

Another major reason for this new edition is to capture recent developments in our understanding of capacity assessment, informed choice, new reproduction technologies, resource allocation, and end-of-life care. Many of the cases are new and the discussions have been updated with current developments in ethics and jurisprudence. The focus, it is true, is often on Canadian law but, quite frankly, developments here may be found elsewhere.

I do refer to Anglo-American law and legal precedents, but this brief book cannot be comprehensive in that regard. Readers in other jurisdictions must familiarize themselves with their local laws to see how they could impact the cases we discuss.

Interestingly, there is a developing international approach to professional medical ethics. Despite many large differences in culture, religion, and politics (differences that should not be minimized), the healthcare professions throughout the world share similar goals: the prevention and treatment of illness, human suffering, and premature death. These goals unite healthcare professionals across the globe and have done so ever since humans have treated illness. Modern medicine would not be possible were it not for inventions and advances in various cultures and religions—from Islam to Judaism, from Europe to India and China—all have contributed. *Dialogue and progress in ethical matters do not require a common ethical language.* But they do require allegiance to a value requisite for all the healing professions: a respect for humans and human dignity. It is the commitment to this value and its implications for healthcare that we will explore in this book.

ACKNOWLEDGMENTS

The second edition of this book is long overdue—unpredictable events affecting my health are largely responsible for this. Oxford University Press has patiently tolerated my recurrent failure to meet deadlines due to conflicts with the surgeon's knife and my constitution's inability to cope with certain rigours of middle age. I owe a debt of gratitude to Pamela Erlichman of Editorial Services and my editors at OUP (most latterly, Dina Theleritis) and their reviewers for this edition of *Doing Right*.

Equally supportive were my colleagues in the Department of Family and Community Medicine at Sunnybrook Health Sciences Centre, University of Toronto, who made every effort to accommodate my periods of disability. And just as patient were my patients who have graciously adapted to my long absences. In helping them I have learned better how to help myself and have in turn learned better, I hope, to help others.

Being a patient has made me appreciate all the more the importance of caring healthcare providers. There are many people whom I can thank for putting back together my body and soul, but special thanks go to David Juurlink, an exemplary physician who embodies the best aspects of medical professionalism (competence, caring, and respectfulness), Michael Ford and Michael Fehlings, surgeons extraordinaire. Special thanks also go to Karen Kaffko, Louise Bailey, Lorne Zinman, Jim Todd, and Gary Opolsky.

This edition could not have been completed without the insightful feedback and help from a tremendous number of wise and supportive friends and colleagues. Thanks to those who read and commented on portions of this book: Yusra Ahmad, Peter Allat, Rob Buckman, Lisa Burzillo, David Carr, Nancy Carroll, Eoin Connolly, Rocco Gerace, Kathy Glass, Laura Hawryluck, Hannah Kaufman, Michael Kaufman, Nathan Kaufman, Ann Munro, Janice Newton, Alison Organek, Linda Sheahan, Laura Sky, and Shawn Winsor. Tracey Tremaine-Lloyd and Audrey Karlinsky provided cases used in both editions of this book. Special thanks to my lifelong friend, Kristine Connidis, who took time out from her own writing to encourage mine when I was still recovering from one surgery or another. There are many other friends and relatives who have provided support over the years, too many to mention individually. They know who they are and how grateful I am.

Not surprisingly, however, the biggest debt of gratitude I owe is, once again, to my wife, Victoria Lee, who has scrupulously read and commented on every word in this book—not that she necessarily agrees with everything that is written. How it is written (and, dear reader, how short it is . . .) has depended largely on her editorial efforts long into the night, burning the midnight oil. Without her unwavering support, this book never would have been written or revised. Saying thank you would never be enough, no matter how many times I would like to say it, so to Victoria, the love of my life, I will say it just once: thank you from the bottom of my heart. My two boys, Matthew and Neil, now teens, have put up with their Dad's work, always knowing it would eventually get done. It did—just in time for spring training and a new season of baseball.

Philip C. Hébert MD, PhD, FCFPC
Sunnybrook Health Sciences Centre
Joint Centre for Bioethics
University of Toronto
Toronto, Ontario, Canada
philip.hebert@sunnybrook.ca
August 2008

INTRODUCTION:
A REVOLUTION IN LEARNING

Now, what I want is, Facts. Teach these boys and girls nothing but Facts. Facts alone are wanted in life.

Charles Dickens, 1854[1]

Schools for healthcare professionals have traditionally emphasized the technical side of medicine and the multitude of facts students must know. So many facts were planted in the student's brain that they threatened to choke out everything else. However, once out in the real world looking after patients, the novice healthcare trainee, as well as the seasoned practitioner, faced other less factual—but no less important and often even more important—issues, such as ethics. Ill-equipped to deal with such issues, healthcare practitioners often managed these in ways that reflected their personal or professional biases. Such attitudes and practices may have been acceptable in the time of Dickens but they will not suffice for the twenty-first century when we are able to do so much more for patients and are indeed expected by the public to do so much more.

A new medical curriculum

In the past decade since the first edition of this book was published, the traditional curriculum of all the healthcare professions has undergone dramatic changes.[2] New pedagogies of medical learning stress critical reflection and lifelong learning, rather than rote memorization and regurgitation of facts. Trainees no longer wait two years to see patients. Instead, they are in the trenches almost from day one, learning how to listen and talk to patients. Rather than days full of tedious lectures, there are subject-integrated problem-based cases of the week whereby students learn to appreciate the many-sided aspects—physical, psychological, and social—of illness. They learn what many clinicians in previous days did not: of the patient as a person, not as Disease X in Bed 2, but as Ms Brown, a retired teacher with no living relatives who has been admitted to hospital because of cognitive decline and poor self-care. Healthcare trainees still learn anatomy and physiology, pharmacology and cardiology, but they also learn about empathy, communication skills, organizational aspects of medicine, and the social determinates of illness. Compared with the traditional curriculum, this has amounted to a revolution in learning. This is a revolution of which many are unaware, not everyone has accepted, and is far from completed, but it is a revolution and one, I believe, that will be irreversible.[3]

As part of this revolution, entire new cadres of teachers have entered the healthcare schools: philosophers, lawyers, theologians, sociologists, anthropologists, even poets, to name a few, in efforts to 'humanize' medical teaching and care. Medicine is a human venture. Becoming a better medical practitioner may be achieved not only by learning the treatment of rabies or how to recognize geriatric depression but also by reading a novel such as Camus' *The Plague* or understanding how participants in medical research should be treated. This has been generally all to the good, although seen as a threat by some. The new teaching and teachers have helped make the healthcare professions more willing *and more able to listen to patients and to each other*.

Aim of book

This book aims to provide a readable introduction to modern professional medical ethics that befits the new pedagogies and curricula of healthcare. The twentieth-century Austrian philosopher of science Karl Popper held that anything important could and should be said clearly without obfuscation or technical language.[4] An aim of this book is to make the complex topic of ethics more accessible to, and usable for, medical trainees and practitioners.

One problem with this endeavour is the disarray of bioethics and the apparent diversity of moral views and practices across cultures and across history. Although bioethicists may differ and morality may not be the same the world over, increasingly, professional medical ethics may be. Medical regulatory authorities now meet internationally and medical graduates everywhere must pass similar exams of which ethics is now core material. An international code of healthcare ethics also seems a long way off in a world rife with assassinations, brutal wars, mass starvation, and widespread denials of basic human rights. Nonetheless, steps in the right direction can be seen in, for example, agreements on an international code of medical rights for patients, on rules for the proper conduct of medical research, and in widespread opposition to physicians participating in torture and state executions. The diversity in modern bioethics may be a sign of its youthful exuberance, not a mark of medicine's irreconcilable moral differences.

Ethics is about right and wrong and the reasons that we give for our choices and actions. This is clearly central to medicine, since doing the right thing for one's patients—minimizing suffering and treating illness—has not only a factual but also an ethical dimension. Clinical ethics—the subject of this book—is concerned with ethical problems arising out of the care of patients. We must often make decisions on problems that go beyond the facts at hand. *Ethical decisions* appeal to *what we may do, should do, or ought to do.*[5]

For example, should practitioners always inform patients fully about their condition? May confidential information about a patient be disclosed to a third party? To what extent should the odd views of an eccentric patient be respected? May desperate patients be offered medically risky research? Do parents have the right to refuse medically indicated treatment for their children? Are religious objections to brain death valid? To how much of society's resources may a patient lay claim? How far ought clinicians go in helping their patients die? As we will see, many of these dilemmas have been subject to probing thought and gradually a consensus of professional opinion concerning how to approach some of these has developed.

What ethics offers

In tackling an ethical problem, if it were simply a question of the right and the wrong path to take, there would be little doubt as to which path a morally acting person should take. Unfortunately, it is not always that easy. *Ethical dilemmas arise when there are good reasons—at least at first glance—for different ways of proceeding.* Further complicating this, their resolution sometimes requires choices involving better and worse solutions, optimal and less than optimal solutions.

What medical ethics can and should offer is an expanded set of considerations to take into account when making a difficult decision. Ethics does not offer a solution but an approach. It does not replace all the other important elements—such as discernment, sensitivity, compassion, common sense, and good clinical reasoning—that go into a wise and right medical decision, the decision that seems to be the optimal one for the individual patient or practitioner to make. Some have argued that ethics may not be the only source of values and factors to take into account when attempting to make a decision.[6] There are, for example, professional regulations, commitments to families or friends, availability (or not) of real alternatives, financial issues, all of which can have an impact on the decision as well as on the decision makers.

Professional ethics is different from ethics as a philosophical discipline. In the real world of healthcare, we rarely have the luxury of time for considered reflection and armchair theorizing. In caring for a patient, no matter what the uncertainties, we must have a plan of action. Resolutions to moral dilemmas are frequently tentative and uncertain. The wise clinician understands the importance of 'triangulating' his or her decision by obtaining input from various sources. Here lies one value of interprofessional cooperation and team-based medicine: to ensure that contentious decisions, if later called into question, have had the benefit of more than one opinion and do not invite charges of unilateral, high-handed, ham-fisted, or paternalistic decision making. Professional ethics is really interprofessional ethics.

Two trends in ethics

One of the tools needed to manage ethical problems is ethical theory. There are two broad schools of ethics in Western societies: deontology and consequentialism. This book comes down squarely on the side of *both*. Deontology deems certain duties and/or rights to be fundamental, whereas consequentialism makes certain consequences or outcomes (either to be avoided or sought after) to be basic. Deontology treats rights and duties as the foundation of ethics, regardless of the state of affairs that results, while consequentialism treats the resulting state of affairs as the yardstick for ethics. Thus, for example, a deontologist would say it is intrinsically wrong to tell a lie, no matter what the circumstances and results. (The Bible's Ten Commandments are an example of a deontological view.) A consequentialist would say it is wrong to cause suffering and right to relieve it, no matter what act leads to that result. Thus, for some, one does right by following certain rules, laws or duties; for others, one does right by encouraging or avoiding certain states of affairs.

Deontology is best represented by the eighteenth-century Prussian philosopher Immanuel Kant and consequentialism by the nineteenth-century English philosopher John Stuart Mill. Mill's philosophy of utilitarianism is the most famous form of consequentialism. In his wonderful 1859 book *On Liberty*, Mill explained: 'I regard utility as the ultimate appeal on all things ethical, but it must be utility in the largest sense, grounded on the permanent interests of man as a progressive being.'[7]

By contrast, Kant saw ethics as arising out of self-set universal laws (maxims) of reason. To wit: 'A deed is right or wrong in general insofar as it is in accordance with or contrary to duty. . . . The categorical imperative, which in general only expresses what an obligation is, is this: Act according to a maxim which can . . . be valid as a universal law.'[8]

Duty or consequences? Which theory gives the best account of morality? There are many, many theories and approaches to ethics that combine, modify, and even claim to overthrow these basic approaches, but no one theory predominates. The ethics decision procedure described in Chapter 1 includes the two key perspectives. The following four principles of ethics are part of a kind of ethical toolbox that is used to analyze ethical quandaries:

- (1) The autonomy principle (acting on the basis of respect due to persons: what does this patient need and want?)
- (2) The beneficence and (3) the non-maleficence principles (acting in the patient's best interests: what can be done to avoid harm and provide help to this patient?)
- (4) The justice principle (acting on fairness: to what resources may this patient lay claim?)

The autonomy principle is largely a deontological principle; the beneficence principle is consequentialist; whereas the justice principle contains aspects of both (the basic notion of justice or fairness could be considered deontological, while distributive justice could be deigned utilitarian). The toolbox approach to ethics is admittedly eclectic, preferring usefulness over theoretical consistency, but it does depend on one core commitment: that a respect for humans is required in everything that we, as healthcare providers, do.[9]

Cases and law

When it comes to responding to moral problems in medicine, the prudent clinician also does not ignore the lessons from other well-known cases in modern law and ethics but learns to apply them for the benefit of his or her own patients. Important legal cases, which are typically interesting, often crystallize society's sentiments concerning medical morality. In any event, when faced with a moral question, practitioners do often ask: what does the law say?[10] We may not agree with legal rulings, but they are always relevant to what we ought to do, and they form part of the professional's problem-solving toolbox. We ignore legal rulings and other ethical precedents at our professional peril.

However, what the law says should not bring the discussion to a full stop. Medicine is about doing what is best for patients, whereas the law has a whole range of social interests and concerns to balance. Practically speaking, when a dispute comes to court, the law *does* have the last word about morality in the strictly clinical context of medical practice. Nonetheless, the law itself is in constant evolution, as evidenced, for example, in the current debates about euthanasia. One cannot be endlessly self-reflective but the law changes in part with input from professional ethics. Thus, where a clinician disagrees with existing law, taking a judge through one's considered ethical opinion is a way of helping the judge see how 'the reasonable standard of professional care' (such as that regarding truthtelling by clinicians) is changing.

This is not a source book on the law and so cannot be comprehensive. Nevertheless, I have tried to present the most important legal cases—largely Canadian, but also some from American and British law, with which the clinician needs to be familiar. Whether a judgment cited is the right guide in any particular case will depend upon the reader's considered moral judgment. The core moral principles and their reflection in law and public sentiment are not unique to one country or to the calling of the physician. They apply, albeit with different force and intensity, to all healthcare professionals and healthcare trainees.

There is not one medical morality for doctors and one for everybody else. Ethics is for everyone—professional, patient, and public alike. This does not mean that each has the same duties, but the *professional's* duties ought to reflect society's expectations of medicine. Society must understand and endorse what healthcare professionals do and are expected to do in carrying out their healing mandate, otherwise the trust between healers and patients may be lost and the whole healthcare enterprise is threatened.

Book outline

The plan of the book is as follows. Chapter 1 sets out a way to approach and manage ethical problems in medicine typically encountered when conflicting responsibilities must be balanced, and it serves as a useful summary for the book as a whole. Chapter 2 examines a crucial principle of contemporary medicine, patient autonomy. Because this principle engenders duties regarding confidentiality and disclosure, these are presented next in Chapters 3 and 4. Chapter 5 looks at informed consent, while Chapter 6 considers the ethical problems involved in incapacity and substitute decision making. Chapter 7 examines another fundamental principle of medicine, beneficence. Chapter 8 discusses the new professionalism and the issue of medical error—when medicine goes astray. Chapter 9 examines justice, a less familiar principle for many but one recognized by Hippocrates and now of increasing concern in everyday healthcare practice. Chapter 10 looks at new life issues and the new reproductive technology. Chapter 11 is concerned with care of the dying and assisted death. The Conclusion contains suggestions for further reading and web-searching.

Throughout this book I provide cases followed by a focused discussion of each. Many of the cases are taken as-is from real-life dilemmas that have arisen in clinical practice. None of this case discussion should in any way be taken as legal advice. Nor should my opinions be taken as the 'right answers'. In the ethical problems of real life—as in medicine generally—decisions are fraught with uncertainty and even the seemingly best choice may have reasonable alternatives. I encourage you to develop your own opinions on the cases.

By the end of this book you should be able to analyze and manage ethical problems in medicine in a reasonable way. Although there can be no guarantees that you will have done the best thing in responding to an ethical problem, you should be satisfied that you have tried to solve the problem in a comprehensive and careful fashion.

Many healthcare professionals view their future—and their patients' futures—with dismay, feeling that theirs is a profession under siege.[11] Patients and families, too, are restive and critical, and know all is not right with healthcare. Dickens' book title seems apt for our times: *hard times are here and are ahead*. Nonetheless, hard times can be catalysts for development and improvement. In any times, an emphasis on the key ethical principles and values—such as trust and mutual respect—enhances the relationships between practitioner, patient, and other healthcare workers, and makes for a more satisfying practice.[12]

Studies suggest that healthcare professionals experience less burn-out and cynicism if they remain in touch with the meaning and significance of what they do.[13] Ethical sensitivity can help patients and clinicians alike by enabling them to recognize and strive for the best possible outcomes not only in good times but also in hard times—when resources are scarce, practices criticized, and outcomes uncertain. Effective attention to ethical concerns can help those involved do their best to do right—and feel confident they have done so—and this enriches us all. Hard times—perhaps—but also exciting times when we are able to combine science with humanism to renew medicine, 'the greatest benefit to mankind'.[14]

ETHICS MATTERS: PRINCIPLES AND ETHICALLY SOUND MEDICINE

The mental and moral, like the muscular powers, are improved only by being used.

John Stuart Mill, 1859[1]

. . . the foundations of moral motivations are not the procedural rules on a kind of discourse, but the feeling to which we can rise. As Confucius saw long ago, benevolence or concern for humanity is the indispensable root of it all.

Simon Blackburn, 2001[2]

I. ETHICAL REASONING AND PRINCIPLES IN MEDICINE

As a healthcare professional, you will frequently encounter ethical dilemmas in your work with patients—especially in situations where you will have to make a decision about what to do when there are conflicting alternatives. Although you will want to do the right thing, just what that is may not be obvious. How do you assess what is right? Is it what is best or right for your patient? For his or her family? For yourself? For your co-workers? For your profession? For society?

In this chapter you will be introduced not only to the basic principles of medical ethics, but also to an analytic tool to help you manage moral problems effectively in healthcare. The best way to learn about medical ethics is to consider cases and how healthcare professionals should respond to them. I begin with a case that is familiar to clinicians and patients. I then consider two other cases that illustrate troubling ethical dilemmas. I will end with a deeper exploration of a more challenging case.

CASE 1.1

TO PRESCRIBE OR NOT TO PRESCRIBE

You are a young primary care practitioner in the downtown core of a large city. You are seeing a new patient, a 32-year-old factory worker who has been unwell for 24 hours with a runny nose, aching muscles, a dry cough, and hoarseness. Apart from some tender muscles, his physical examination is normal; indeed, he barely seems ill. You tell him, 'You likely have a viral illness and antibiotics will do no good. We can get men to the moon, but we cannot cure the common cold. It will get better on its own.'

Unconvinced, the patient requests an antibiotic because he 'always got one from the clinic down the road.' He then, rather loudly, voices concern that you do not really have the experience or skills to make the proper diagnosis. 'I felt so under the weather today that I couldn't go to work! How do you know I don't have one of those new superbugs I heard about? One of my buddies at work picked something up. He went to see his doctor who said it was nothing and the next thing you know he's almost dead in the ICU.'

Is there an ethical issue here? What should you do? Should you do what the patient requests or what you, the professional, think is appropriate?

DISCUSSION OF CASE 1.1

There is a conflict here between what you believe is the right treatment for the patient and what the patient is requesting. The choice is either to prescribe the antibiotics or not to do so.

In this case there are some pros for prescribing antibiotics:

- The healthcare practitioner may be mistaken about the nature of the patient's illness.
- The patient may benefit because of a placebo effect.
- They can be prescribed quickly and the patient will not go away disappointed.

However, there are many cons to prescribing unnecessary antibiotics:

- They drain away scarce social resources.
- They may cause side-effects.
- They may allow resistant organisms (superbugs) to grow.
- They perpetuate the idea that there is a quick cure for every illness.

Although patients have the right to voice their wishes, not all such wishes are appropriate. Practitioners should provide only the care that is likely to be helpful and not harmful. Every time clinicians give in to inappropriate demands for tests or treatment, their ethical

fibre is weakened, making it less likely they will act properly in the future and hold the line.[3]

Rather than a blanket refusal, you should take the time to talk with the patient regarding his expectations and to explain the reasoning behind your refusal to prescribe the requested antibiotic. If the patient remains unconvinced, you *might* propose a compromise: offer to call his pharmacy in a day or two with a prescription if he is not improving. If the patient is reasonable and your communication skills are good (for example, you sympathize with his concerns, listen well, address his fears, and don't appear to be dismissive), the patient may be swayed to accept this. Some might argue that even this degree of compromise with the patient's request is inappropriate, given the contemporary concerns over antibiotic overuse.[4]

Principles

Doing right at a very basic level means treating people fairly. Fairness can be considered both a principle (fair play) and a process (due consideration) (see Chapter 9 for more on justice). Giving patients their due—moral due care—may be fulfilled by attending carefully to your basic responsibilities as a 'moral agent' in your role as a healthcare professional. Patients are, first of all, due proper care—care that will be helpful to them: treatment that will, for example, alleviate suffering or prevent disease and its sequelae. This task can be captured as the moral obligation of healthcare professionals to act 'beneficently', that is, to act according to the principle of beneficence. But, there is in modern healthcare an equally compelling obligation—the principle of respect for persons. By this principle of autonomy, healthcare providers ought to provide care that patients will want and find beneficial according to their own values and beliefs. Ethical principles may conflict and one task of bioethics is to help healthcare professionals recognize and manage such conflicts.

Conflict resolution

A conflict between such opposing principles or obligations is the most common sort of ethical dilemma in clinical medicine. Trouble lies ahead for the clinician and patient if such principles are not adhered to or if the conflicts between them go unrecognized and are not properly addressed. The first step is to recognize and acknowledge that there is a problem—often it is rooted in an apparent disagreement, or 'dis-ease', between clinician and patient.

An important aspect of Case 1.1, for example, is the patient's direct criticism of the clinician's expertise. Although it might seem easier to ignore this and simply get on with treating the patient, an adversarial relationship has already been set up that may hinder good patient care. The patient may view the clinician as dismissive and uncaring, which does not augur well for compliance. The practitioner might write the patient off as difficult and demanding and then ignore legitimate concerns. Addressing the patient's criticism, if done in a respectful manner, will set the stage for a cooperative therapeutic relationship.

Beyond principles

Real life is complicated—emotions, suffering, and troubled relationships make many moral problems difficult to manage. A knowledge of ethics does not provide an answer to every clinical dilemma. We may not have an agreed upon ethical perspective or there may be other factors that are more important than ethical concerns, such as the patient's family relations or the professional's self-survival. The modern philosopher Frankfurt has argued that in real-life dilemmas there are other evaluative concerns—aesthetic, cultural, or religious—that may be more important to a person than ethical considerations in deciding what to do.[5] (For example, a 'good' picture is not made so by any notions of right or wrong except as these apply to artistic techniques. As well, what makes a person 'good' from within a particular religious tradition may be different than the criteria for 'being good' from a secular ethics perspective.) Thus, a knowledge of ethics may help the clinician identify the moral implications of making a certain decision, but it will not compel him or her to act on those moral considerations. However, in the modern world of medicine, ethical values *should* outweigh other values in most instances. Today, the institutions of medicine—universities, hospitals, regulatory colleges, and so on—are there to ensure that clinicians act on professional moral concerns and not on those of self-interest or other values.

An example of ethics versus survival applies particularly to healthcare trainees who are in a subordinate position in the hospital and uncertain of their rights.[6] In hospitals, power and prestige traditionally held sway over sense and reason.[7] Doctors were at the top of the heap, other professionals next, and, of course, patients and families at the bottom. This hierarchy continues today. Junior medical trainees are still particularly subject to intimidation by their teachers and other senior trainees.[8] For example, a survey done by a class of medical students at the University of Toronto revealed that about half the class had experienced or witnessed ethical misbehaviour, such as being asked to do pelvic examinations on anesthetized patients just prior to surgery.[9] Such infractions are common and not unique to one medical school.[10] Here is one such case.

CASE 1.2   A RISKY TEACHING TOOL

A clinical clerk—a fourth-year medical student—is doing a two-week elective in anesthesia. He is observing a patient being intubated in preparation for surgery. Suddenly, the staff anesthetist removes the patient's endotracheal tube, asking the student to show him how he would re-intubate the patient. Not surprisingly, the student cannot do so and the staff person must eventually do the re-intubation himself. The student feels embarrassed about his failure and does not mention the episode to anyone until much later.

What should the clinical clerk have done at the time?

DISCUSSION OF CASE 1.2

This situation is unacceptable for many reasons. It is inappropriate because the student is unprepared and the patient's well-being is endangered.[11] As well, such action is an assault upon the patient, unless the patient had given prior consent to this teaching lesson. The student feels overwhelmed by the situation and unable to see past his own embarrassment to do anything about it. Is the staff physician simply mistaken about the clerk's capacities? Or is he in the habit of challenging novice learners? Such pedagogic practices are liabilities, whether or not this particular patient suffers some tangible adverse outcome related to the failed intubation.

Although he is intimidated, the clerk could tell the supervisor how difficult the situation is for him (this is not a realistic option, however—a clinician who teaches in this way is not likely to let a trainee question his pedagogic technique!). Failing an adequate response from the staff physician, there should be another hospital or university resource for the student to access, such as a student advocacy office.

There is no easy way to overcome such roadblocks to acting ethically in practice. If you are the person who encounters them, you should not ignore your feelings of outrage, disappointment, and sadness. In such situations, it would be best to have a tactful discussion with your peers—fellow learners, other clinicians, sympathetic teachers, members of the healthcare institution's administration. If you are a patient, talk to other patients and/or your family.

The institutions of medicine *are* changing in dramatic ways. Many have complaints processes, patient advocates, patient safety offices, bioethics departments, and so on—all of which can lend sympathetic ears to disenchanted staff and learners, not just patients. Many medical schools also now have resources to help trainees, troubled by the medical hierarchy, to raise issues without fear of reprisal. By candidly acknowledging the situation, not only is remedial action sometimes possible but also a troubled conscience can be relieved ('It was a tragedy/terrible what happened, but I/we did the best that could be done in the circumstances.') Following the law seems the route sought by many, but it is not always a solution to difficult moral issues.

The role of law

Established legal precedent—the kind of law that healthcare professionals like to know—seems to set the floor if not the ceiling for appropriate professional practice. The dictates of prudence suggest it is better to respect the devil you know than follow a more perilous—even if more ethically defensible—course. Nevertheless, it is problematic to accept the law uncritically, as if it were a gold standard for ethically exemplary practice, because the law can itself be immoral and unjust. Law and its framers must be subject to ethical scrutiny—not an easy task for anyone.[12]

A healthcare professional's critique of law should derive from the intrinsic values of medicine—in particular, the healthcare professional's devotion to the patient's best interests and service to the patient's wishes. Laws, for example, that may interfere with offering proper care to patients are ethically questionable and deserve attention from healthcare professionals and their medical societies. Just as medicine must learn from the law, so too must law learn from medicine. For example, in 1994 the voters of California approved a law that would deny healthcare to illegal immigrants and require physicians to report them to the government. An argument has been made that physicians should defy this law on the grounds that it is incompatible with medicine's traditional professional ethics.[13] From that point of view, a law should not be followed if it undermines the physician's role as the patient's advocate. The laws and legal judgments referred to in this book are, I believe, more morally defensible than this.

II. THREE ETHICAL PRINCIPLES AND QUESTIONS

How can you prepare yourself, as a healthcare worker, to exhibit fairness and provide moral due care in healthcare? One way is to be familiar and comfortable with the previously alluded to duties of healthcare professionals to provide beneficial care and show respect for patients. These responsibilities are always relevant to medical practice—thus they are 'prima facie' duties—and should be followed unless there is some stronger reason not to do so. Certain authors have analyzed these duties as deriving from the key moral principles of medical practice and it is their analyses that I use in this book.[14] The principle-based analysis has its limitations, as it can fail to capture the ethical complexity and nuances of real-life cases.[15] Nevertheless it is a very helpful way to become familiar with the ethical responsibilities of healthcare practitioners generally as well as the ethical expectations of the public. (It is also true that eschewed principles often remain implicit in the case discussions that critics of 'principlism' use.)

The fundamental ethical principles of healthcare are: autonomy, beneficence, and justice. In later chapters I will discuss each principle in greater detail. For now, it is helpful to ask and answer three questions corresponding to those principles (see Box 1.1).

BOX 1.1

The core ethical questions

1. What are the patient's wishes and values? (Autonomy)

2. What can be done for the patient and what are the harms and benefits? (Beneficence)

3. Is the patient being treated fairly and are his/her needs able to be satisfied? (Justice)

These questions lead to three basic duties that are almost always relevant to every healthcare practitioner's everyday clinical practice:

- Clinicians should listen to patients and respect their wishes and values.
- They must seek to prevent harm to patients and serve their interests.
- Clinicians should also strive to ensure patients get treatment they are 'fairly' due.

The last two duties are recognized in the traditional Hippocratic Oath.[16] What is new in modern medicine is the importance attached to the patient's perspective.

The principle of autonomy

What are the patient's wishes and values? Consider, for example, the competent patient's wishes for treatment. So long as these are informed wishes that do not contravene any other important moral principles, the patient's wishes should guide his or her treatment. If the patient is incompetent (for example, in a coma), you should try to determine what the patient would have chosen when capable. This is where knowledge of the person's values and prior views come into play. A 'proxy' or 'substitute decision maker' for the patient—someone who should know the patient well and has no conflict of interest—will usually be called upon to make decisions for the patient, taking these prior-expressed views and values into account. We discuss autonomy in greater detail in Chapter 2.

The principle of beneficence

What can be done to help the patient? Medicine is most concerned with attending to the patient's well-being. How can harm to the patient be avoided? What are the various medical options, and what are the burdens and benefits of each alternative? How much uncertainty attaches to the patient's diagnosis, and what can be done to lessen it? To help the patient with the risk-benefit analysis of any proposed medical intervention, the clinician not only needs to share his or her professional expertise but must also take into consideration the patient's values and beliefs. Problems can arise when healthcare professionals make assumptions, without much discussion, about what their patients should do.

The principle of justice

This principle is that of fairness. Is a person receiving his or her fair share of scarce resources? Will other persons, such as the family, other patients, or professional staff, be unduly burdened by the treatment chosen? The job of the clinician is to try to access appropriate, not inordinate, care for his or her patients and to attempt to balance the needs of patients with the interests of others—not an easy task.

Non-maleficence: 'Above all, do no harm'

I have not made non-maleficence a fundamental principle. This is the Hippocratic principle of *primum non nocere* ('above all, do no harm'), the oldest and seemingly least controversial moral rule in medicine. For our purposes this principle can be included in the principle of beneficence. Other things being equal, the wise practitioner would, of course, recommend the intervention that would result in no possibility of harm to the patient.[17]

Unfortunately, truly non-maleficent interventions are pretty rare in medicine these days. Simple interventions, such as taking a venous blood sample or discussing a diagnosis with a patient, involve some small risk of harm, even if done well. While many healthcare professionals refer to the non-maleficence principle, it rarely serves as a guiding principle for medical practice—otherwise, therapeutic nihilism (the view that medical treatment is worse than the disease) would result.[18] Although this certainly is sometimes true (maybe more often than we would like to think), it can hardly be helpful to the practitioner in the trenches who must use the therapeutic ammunition at hand. Of course, sometimes it is better to take a wait-and-see attitude to illness rather than to intervene with risky or uncertain measures.

It is better to think of 'do no harm' as an ideal to be incorporated into the principle of beneficence. The best choice is the option where the benefits outweigh the harm. Although there are evil clinicians about (such as Harold Shipman in the UK who killed several hundred patients before being arrested), most clinicians do not go to work with the conscious intent to harm their patients.[19] They can act maleficently, however, as a result of ignorance, incompetence, or mental illness (not always mutually exclusive categories). They can also do harm by being overly aggressive and excessively risking harm to patients with unproven therapies.[20]

Patient-centred harm and benefit

In general, harm and benefit cannot be purely objective notions. They must be defined with some input from the patient and tailored to that patient's situation. What might be a great harm to one patient might be relatively no harm at all to another. Lack of awareness of a patient's values is one factor that can lead practitioners to inadvertently act in a maleficent manner (see Chapter 7 for more on beneficence).

CASE 1.3	DESPERATE HOPES

A 46-year-old man, dying of multiple myeloma, has fought the disease every step of the way with a remarkable determination to live. He has undergone every known treatment—bone marrow transplantations, experimental therapies, naturopathic remedies. He is now thin and wasted and on dialysis. The disease has, it seems, finally reached its terminal stages, and he has but a few weeks to live. He recognizes he is dying but refuses to agree to a 'palliative care only' order. For him this would mean giving up. He wants any extra moment of life that aggressive interventions might give him. His treating team wants to transfer him to a palliative care facility, which could better serve his many needs. The patient refuses this.

This patient seems to be asking his caregivers to break the *primum non nocere* rule: he is asking them to do something that will almost certainly cause him more harm than good.

Can this ever be acceptable?

DISCUSSION OF CASE 1.3

Desperate situations can lead to desperate hopes, and this is probably one of them. If we strictly followed the non-maleficence principle, we would not agree to the dying man's request. On balance, however, it is his life and his death. On his scale of values it would be better to try likely futile end-of-life gestures than none at all. This is an important wish for him; therefore, I think it should be respected—or at least, for the time being. There are limits to what patients can ask of healthcare professionals, but this is one circumstance where one could defer to the patient. It would be difficult to feel as if one were pushing the patient out the door. His belief may be that palliative care means giving up on him. He would have to be reassured otherwise by deed and attitude of those looking after him that this was not so.

Empathic communication, such as the questions and comments given here, can enable care providers to understand the patient's perspective and resolve the moral impasse.[21]

- What do you understand about your health situation?
- What are you hoping for?
- How do you want things when you die?
- Tell me how you feel about all of this.
- It sounds like you are worried we will give up on you. We won't and we will do everything we can to help you in your illness.

This conversation tries to close the gap between patient and care providers by acknowledging the patient's perspective and assuring him that he will not be abandoned.

III. 'RESOLVING' ETHICAL DILEMMAS

Various formal approaches to resolving ethical dilemmas have been developed by a number of authors, such as Lo, Thomasma, Siegler, and McCullough.[22] All use some variety of the 'ethics principles' approach and all presume an organized approach to understanding an ethical dilemma in medicine is helpful to its appropriate resolution. Thomasma deemed such an organized approach an 'ethics work-up' to make it seem familiar to medical students used to 'working up' the causes of a patient presenting with new onset heart failure or fever of unknown origin. Since then, some people have worked themselves into a tizzy assuming the use of an 'ethics work-up' implies that moral decisions can be made mechanically. This misunderstands the purpose of such a procedure.

The procedure reminds medical practitioners and students of the fundamental moral issues and principles that need to be considered in the adequate resolution of a moral quandary. This approach enables practitioners and trainees to ensure they have addressed the most important moral elements of troubling cases they encounter. The exact interpretation of the issues may depend upon aspects of the particular situation (such as the conscience, thoughtfulness, and professionalism of the participants) that the procedure cannot capture.

The importance of the circumstances

In ethical matters, as in other matters, it is important for good decision making that the right people are involved. It is not surprising to find great variance in ethical decision making. The people involved, the circumstances of the case, and the milieu will often help to determine the 'right thing' to do. Doing right for a particular patient will mean being aware of such circumstances as

- institutional regulations,
- laws,
- attitudes of peers, and
- emotions and cultural background of the patient and his or her 'significant others'.

I cannot stress enough, however, that knowledge of rules and context is singularly futile if not accompanied by common sense and a sensitivity to the needs of others.

Really hard choices

The decision procedure cannot be a moral algorithm that will churn out right answers like a sausage-making machine. As well, the procedure cannot always make you feel good about your decision—some dilemmas about patients are so problematic that any choice seems less than ideal.

Unfortunately, we have to make do with such decisions. The most heart-breaking example I can think of is in the movie *Sophie's Choice*, based on the book by William Styron.[23] This movie is absolutely heartrending to watch, particularly for parents, because the mother is forced to decide which one of her two children she must give up to the Nazis and certain death. There is nothing that philosophy can do that could ever make such a choice acceptable at any level. The distress accompanying some moral dilemmas is inescapable. What a good practitioner can do in such circumstances is listen to and bear witness with the patient and/or family. This compassionate presence is always appreciated, making patients and families feel supported and cared for.

IV. 'DOING RIGHT': A DECISION-MAKING PROCEDURE FOR CLINICAL ETHICS

The procedure for analyzing and resolving ethical problems in the care of patients (clinical ethics) has eight steps (see Box 1.2). Keep in mind that case resolutions do not always follow every step. In some instances it will be obvious how to proceed after a few moments' reflection because one ethical principle or the context may suggest the best way to proceed. The full procedure is most helpful for deciding difficult cases or when you wish to ensure that your decision is backed up by careful reflection.

Step 1. Recognize that a case raises an important ethical problem.

Ethical problems arise, as suggested earlier, when there is a conflict of values and when there are different ways to proceed. For example, the relatives of an elderly woman with dementia wish to have her placed in a nursing home, something she refuses to consider; a patient does not want his sexual partner to know that he carries the hepatitis B virus; a 15-year-old girl, 16 weeks pregnant, is resisting the abortion her parents insist she have. In all these cases clinicians must make a difficult decision about what to do. Open and direct communication with patients and their families can help you understand alternative ways to proceed. Don't rush this step. The too-hurried health professional, treating a delicate and unusual case as if it were unremarkable, can run into moral trouble.

It is important to be as knowledgeable as possible about the case. You should know the most relevant aspects of the patient's life story and family context, his/her medical condition, the working diagnosis, and the various treatment options as well as their associated burdens and benefits. A true ethics consultation for a case will usually not rest content with the kind of 'thin' case studies used (due to space limitations) in this book. The devil, they say, often lies in the details, but sometimes in the details is the angel, the best solution to the case.

Step 2. What is the problem that has to be solved?

State what you take to be the central problem. This is often the most important step. Should the woman with dementia be institutionalized without her consent? Should the partner of the hepatitis patient be informed of his partner's condition? Do parents have a say over their daughter's abortion?

Always be clear on what needs to be resolved. Seemingly intractable ethical problems can arise when the participants are not asking the same question. For example, a family resists for some time the transfer of their cognitively impaired father to another ward. Consultation reveals the problem is not that the family wants something inappropriate; the problem is a disagreement among the siblings. What they need is help as a family in resolving their differences. When this is achieved, a solution to the ward problem is found. Sometimes an ethical dilemma turns out to be a communication problem or a family concern or an issue for psychiatry. Once the problem is precisely identified, you will be better able to decide what resources you'll need to resolve it.

Step 3. Determine reasonable alternative courses of action.

Asking what is the right thing to do for the patient presupposes there are alternative procedures—usually two or three—for this patient. The list of options need not be exhaustive, but clear alternatives should be given. They may be quite simple: for example, either the woman with dementia should be placed or not; the partner should be told or not; the parents should have a say in their daughter's decision or not. The final resolution of the case will probably be one of these options or some compromise among them.

Step 4. Consider each option in relation to the three fundamental ethical principles.

This is a critical and difficult step. The ethical healthcare practitioner or trainee is expected to utilize and consider the three fundamental ethical principles of respect due persons or autonomy, beneficence, and justice. One problem is knowing just how to interpret the principles in light of circumstances and the agents involved. What to do when the principles seemingly conflict is another problem. As well, as mentioned earlier, the weight of the principles will often change with the case and its circumstances. Thus, using the 'decision procedure' will not automatically give you the right answer. Broadly speaking, the patient's wishes come first, but the acceptability of these wishes will sometimes depend upon the medically possible options. You need not agree to the patient's wishes if they are illegal or unusually burdensome to others. For example, in the case of the woman with dementia who refuses to leave her home, you will want to weigh the importance of her wish against its effect on her well-being and the safety of others. Does she pose a risk serious enough to outweigh her wish? What if she is a smoker—in bed? What if she is prone to leaving the stove on? Or wanders in the snow shoeless?

Step 5. Consider who should be involved and other circumstances.

Clearly, you must ensure the right people—family, close relations, other health-care providers, and clinicians—are brought into the patient's circle of care and consulted. If the patient is not capable or is doing something potentially harmful or out of character (such as avoiding needed medical treatment), you must attempt to contact the patient's family or substitute decision maker. You may also have to involve others, such as a public guardian or public trustee, who may have been appointed to look after an incapable person.

You should also consider other circumstances, such as institutional policies, professional guidelines, cultural norms, and personal or emotional factors. In deciding what to do for the woman with dementia, for example, you will have to take into account specific factors such as legislation that might allow an incapable person to be removed from her home. You may also wish to take into account how strenuously she would resist being 'placed' without her consent.

Step 6. Decide on a resolution to the problem.

You must take a stand as to what you think is the right course of action. Try to follow your best guess as to the right thing to do, all things considered. Your conclusion may be disputed, so you should be able to justify your choice as the best one.

Step 7. Consider your position critically.

Before and after the decision, keep an open mind and consider what you could do or could have done differently. Are there circumstances in which you would advocate a different course of action? It may help to formulate your position as a general maxim or principle, as Kant would have recommended. For example, if you decide the woman with dementia should be allowed to stay at home, you might generalize this into a statement such as: persons with dementia may stay at home providing they are not putting others in danger. The next step would be to consider the limits of such a principle. What if the impaired person refused any help or monitoring of his or her condition? What if, say, she didn't smoke but had weak legs, which could result in a high risk of falling down the stairs?

Also, ensure that you can live with the decision you make. At the end of the day, ask yourself: will you be able to sleep soundly given your decision? Would you be comfortable if your decision were to be made public?

One of the most common errors made by practitioners is to make contentious moral decisions on their own. Have you discussed the case with colleagues?

Will your colleagues stand behind you? If they will not step forward to support you, this may be telling you something you should not ignore. Consider that you might be wrong. If you or others feel ill at ease with the decision, carefully reconsider the main features of the case. Of course, in difficult cases where no option seems a good one, not everyone will agree, and sometimes your feelings can be mistaken. Nonetheless, do not be pushed by abstract ethical principles to do something that your conscience or emotions tells you is wrong. Emotions can be a helpful corrective to reason.[24] Sometimes such emotions can be important indicators of the better thing to do. Remember, it is you (and not the moral rules) who must take responsibility for the decision.

Your own conscience and emotional reaction to a case can provide reasonable brakes on action. They can represent your deepest values, identity, and integrity as a professional. For example, you can in good conscience refuse to go along with a practice, such as abortion, that you find morally objectionable (but in consideration of concern for the patient, you may have some obligation to refer her to another doctor).[25] Not all moral disagreements can be readily settled and, in the end, people in moral disagreement have to learn to work with one another.

Step 8. Do the right thing!

This step should go without saying but there are many roadblocks to acting ethically in practice. Doing the right thing may be difficult because of conflicting loyalties, cultural differences, survival needs, and extreme circumstances like war and disasters. Professional ethics may seem a slim reed to grasp onto in extreme situations. Those who do cleave to the moral route in such circumstances may fare better in the long run than those who shuck their ethics, as if it were a mere moral carapace, for the 'easy' thing to do. Doing the right thing is sometimes the hard thing, but you learn by attempting it and by the perseverance it requires.[26]

A note on the cases

In this book I use many clinical vignettes to illustrate typical ethical problems in medicine. My discussion tends to be brief and pragmatic, using the ethics decision-making procedure as a template only. This procedure is assumed in many of the discussions; I do not pause to make each step explicit. This is how to proceed in real life as well: slow down enough to consider only the most relevant moral aspects of the case. It would be pedantic and unnecessary to consider factors carrying little moral weight. Of course, knowing when you can cut short the moral discussion comes with time and experience. When it comes to moral discussion, novices may be wise to include more, rather than less, in their case considerations.

BOX 1.2

The ethics decision-making procedure

1. *The case:* Express simply but with pertinent facts and circumstances.

2. *What is the dilemma?* What decision needs to be made?

3. *What are the alternatives?*

4. *How do the key considerations apply?*

  (a) Autonomy: What are the patient's wishes and values?

   Consider the patient's capable wishes, beliefs, goals, hopes, and fears. If incapable, look to a substitute decision maker.

  (b) Beneficence: What can be done for the patient?

   Consider the benefits and burdens of the various alternatives from the perspective of the clinician, the patient, and possibly the family, and the probable result of each one.

  (c) Justice: Is the patient receiving what is fair?

   Consider the patient's fundamental right to his or her fair share of medical resources as well as the interests and claims of the family, other patients, and healthcare staff.

5. *Consider involving others and consider context:* Are there other situational factors that are important? Consider others who ought to be involved. Be familiar with institutional policies and guidelines, professional norms, and legal precedents.

6. *Propose a resolution:* Weigh these factors for each alternative; then say what you would do or recommend.

7. *Consider your choice critically:* When would you be prepared to alter it? Consider the opinions of your peers, your conscience, and emotional reactions. Know your resources. Formulate your choice as a general maxim, suggest cases where it wouldn't apply, decide if you—and others—are comfortable with the choice made. If not, reconsider key considerations and consider consultations with specialists in ethics, law, administration, or other specialists.

8. *Do the right thing—'all things considered'.*

V. APPLYING THE ETHICS DECISION-MAKING PROCEDURE

Now, let's consider the use of the decision-making procedure in a rather complicated and controversial real-life case with which I was involved many years ago.

CASE 1.4   TO FEED OR NOT TO FEED?

Ms E, a 22-year-old woman ill since age 14 with severe anorexia nervosa, an illness of self-starvation, is brought into the emergency room in cardiovascular collapse. She is extremely emaciated, weighing less than 60 lbs., and is virtually unresponsive. She receives a bolus of intravenous glucose and perks up long enough to pull out her intravenous line.

The patient has been admitted numerous times in her starved state and has spent most of her previous eight years in hospital. She has been considered one of the most 'difficult' patients by specialty units of various tertiary-care hospitals. All corrective therapy has so far failed. Drug therapy using antipsychotics and antidepressants has been unsuccessful. Different psychotherapeutic approaches over many years—including 'paradoxical' therapy (admitting to the patient that is she is going to die and hoping she will struggle against this pessimistic message)—have also been unsuccessful. On previous admissions she has been force-fed which has required restraints and caused major disruptions on the ward. She had expressed a wish to die but not consistently so. She had recently told her family doctor that she wished her suffering would soon end and at that time requested no forced feedings in the future. She is unhappy with her weight (she thinks she is always overweight) and does not believe her refusal of food endangers her life. The various tertiary-care hospitals now refuse her re-admission because of her previous extreme resistance and disruptiveness.

What should be done on this admission? The clinicians involved in her care consider the option of providing her nutrition through a gastrostomy tube (a tube inserted directly into her stomach through a small incision in the abdominal wall). This would entail a surgical procedure and putting her in restraints.

DISCUSSION OF CASE 1.4

1. The case
The first step is to acknowledge there is an ethical dilemma here. Sometimes, we become so focused on what we are doing in

medicine that we fail to question—wait a minute—what are we doing here? Are we sure about this? Should we be doing something different? Once these questions are raised, the ethical moment has been recognized. The care providers for this patient felt it was their duty to feed her but were troubled by its *consequences*—for the patient primarily, but for everyone else as well.

2. The problem
This case contains a number of problems, but the central one is whether the patient should be force-fed or not. The standard of care for such patients is to re-feed them by any means possible but does the standard of care require you to do so again and again with a protesting patient?[27] When might not feeding a starving patient ever be appropriate? How important are the interests of others when it comes to re-admitting her?

3. The alternatives
Obviously, the central immediate problem of starvation poses the alternatives of force-feeding her once more or not force-feeding her. What is the status of her recent wish not to be force-fed? Or her action of pulling out her IV? Are these simply the products of a mind unbalanced by delusions (firm, fixed beliefs unamenable to criticism or evidence) and starvation? What if she were force-fed long enough to be conscious again? Would her wishes then be any more reliable? Not re-hydrating her and not re-feeding at this point will result in her death.

4. Applying the principles
As feeding and not feeding her are two sides of the same coin, let us consider the problem from the 'not feeding' side. What are the pros and cons of not feeding her?

Autonomy
PRO: Not force-feeding is what the patient has previously requested, so this option accords with her wishes.[28]

CON: While it appears to some that this patient seems to understand, when not in a starved state, what she is doing and the risks she is taking, it can be argued that this understanding is in fact not competent and therefore not authentically autonomous (and therefore quite distinguishable from that of a person on a hunger strike). Following her wishes will result in her death by starvation, an outcome she has not consistently or clearly requested. Perhaps her request for her suffering to be over was a wish for healing and not for death. Her failure to truly appreciate the consequences of self-starvation and refusal of force-feeding, as is the case for many anorexic patients, makes her views incapable and therefore unreliable.[29]

Beneficence

PRO: The benefits of not force-feeding the patient include not prolonging her suffering and not having to restrain her to maintain the feeding. There is also an implicit recognition that this patient is terminally ill and cannot be rescued—it might, therefore, be a 'mercy' to let her go.

CON: The most important harm in not feeding her is fairly obvious: the patient will die. This patient is delusional about her weight and engaging in self-destructive behaviour as a result. In most jurisdictions, healthcare professionals are obliged to intervene when individuals place themselves at risk in the context of a mental illness.

Justice

PRO: The patient's care *per se* is not expensive but the demands on others are high. The family and healthcare staff feel quite burdened by her care. Letting her go would relieve them of the emotional burdens of looking after her. As well, if treatment is truly futile, then we are wasting precious resources in keeping someone alive who is doomed to die anyway.

CON: As she is the patient, the focus of care must be primarily on her, not others. She deserves her fair share of medical resources. One standard for this would be the treatment that other patients in her situation would receive from a 'reasonably competent practitioner'. Most starving anorexic patients are force-fed and a lack of resources is not an issue; thus, this intervention is due to her unless there are good countervailing reasons.

5. Context

Contextual factors include the possible negative emotional reaction of staff to a difficult, 'unlikable' and so, in their eyes, 'untreatable' patient. By contrast there are fears of legal liability—such as negligence—if the patient were allowed to die. Courts have generally ruled against forced feeding but that has usually been in the context of competent refusals of food, such as by prisoners who go on hunger strikes.[30]

6. One resolution

Autonomy triumphs—usually. On the other hand, when autonomy is thwarted by illness, we, as care providers, must try to rescue those in harm's way. It would seem to be in the patient's best interests to force-feed her because she will otherwise die, something she has not consistently verbalized as her wish (although her body language speaks otherwise). This may burden the staff and her family, but it is not clear that such burdens are as yet intolerable. Their emotional reactions may indicate that the limits to their tolerance are being reached, however. Finally, while there is no legal duty to force-feed starving patients, there is an obligation to rescue patients who are in imminent, perilous danger.[31] Weighing these factors together supports the position that this patient should be force-fed.

The options as to how this might best be done should be discussed with the appropriate substitute decision maker, because the patient is currently incapable. If and when she ever seems to regain capacity over nutritional matters, the patient needs a careful assessment of the ability to authentically make a 'food and fluids' decision. If she is found capable of making such a decision, her most authentic wishes ought to be explored: does she want to be saved again should the need arise even if she insists the opposite (a 'Ulysses' contract) or is she suffering so much that she does not wish resuscitation (a 'reverse Ulysses' contract)? (In the ancient myth of Ulysses, the Sirens were sea nymphs whose singing could cause mariners to throw themselves into the ocean. Ulysses ordered his crew to stuff their ears with wax and to bind him to the mast of his ship and not release him, no matter what he said, until they passed safely by the Sirens' island. Indeed, as they sailed by, the Sirens' song was so sweet and attractive that Ulysses struggled to loosen his ropes, begging his men to release him. They ignored him and bound him even tighter until they were able to safely pass by.) It may seem odd, but if she could be found capable of making such a decision, her wishes ought to be respected. It is, however, unlikely she would be found capable because patients with such severe anorexia are delusional about sustenance.

7. Critical considerations

This position could be generalized into a principle such as: 'Incapable patients in danger of dying from self-starvation should be force-fed.' When might this be unacceptable? It would certainly seem so when the patient has a *competently* expressed wish not to be force-fed. It would also be unacceptable when it is clear that further force-feeding can no longer benefit the patient. In other words, if the patient is going to die anyway, further feedings would be futile and should be withheld.[32] This might be the case if the patient had, for example, a terminal illness such as cancer or advanced amytrophic lateral sclerosis. One need not give treatment that cannot achieve any reasonable medical goal (see Chapter 11 on End-of-Life Decisions). It may well be that the patient has already reached this near-death stage in this case. Although not suffering from a recognized terminal illness, it may be that she is so emaciated and so intractable in her belief that she is overweight that she cannot be rescued. The duty to rescue should be a proportionate one and not an excuse to torture the dying with extravagant therapy.[33] The care providers in the ER might win today's skirmish, were they to re-feed her, but the war is being lost.

8. Action required
The physicians should proceed to give this patient whatever nutritional support is required, at least until a further assessment can be done.

FOLLOW-UP TO CASE 1.4

This patient was, in fact, not force-fed. After meeting with her family and obtaining consultations in hospital with the departments of psychiatry and internal medicine and the hospital ethics committee, her physicians deemed her terminally ill and, on grounds of compassion, did not force-feed her. She died shortly after being admitted. A more detailed description of this case is available elsewhere.[34]

Of some concern is the possibility that the decision to limit care in this case was due to an unexplored animosity of the healthcare providers toward a seemingly hopeless and demanding patient. Did they give up too soon because she seemed incurable and imposed such a burden on others? (Some hold that *no* patient with anorexia should be considered hopeless but this may be overly optimistic.)[35] Needless to say, such cases are very troubling for all concerned.

My own views have evolved in the years since I was involved in the care of this patient. I try to guard against negative reactions to patients that might lead to under-treatment while not ignoring the emotions invested in a patient that can lead to over-treatment. Emotions have an important role to play in healthcare—they cause us to *care* about what we do, as reason alone cannot. Arguing for the importance of feeling and sentiment to judgment, the Scottish philosopher David Hume wrote several centuries ago, 'Morality, therefore, is more properly felt than judged of.'[36] Feelings of benevolence—caring about our patients and a concern for humanity—ground and stabilize our ethical judgments.

This kind of case demonstrates how difficult the resolution of ethical dilemmas can be in the real world of everyday medicine. Eternal ethical truths may be hard to come by but we should not cease seeking for the truth in our ethical deliberations as so much turns on what we do.[37] While a complete ethics discussion may help participants feel everything appropriate has been done and aid them in arriving at a shared solution, it cannot erase the feelings of guilt and sadness that the death of such a young patient can have upon caregivers.

CONCLUSION

Ethics is a complex and sometimes confusing field. In this chapter I have presented an approach to sorting out and addressing ethical dilemmas in medicine—a kind of ethics toolbox. It is a method of analysis to introduce some consistency in how healthcare professionals should look at and manage moral questions in medicine. Clinicians using the ethics toolbox can arrive at ethical solutions that are comprehensive and well organized. Later I will examine in more detail the ethical principles that form the foundation for the acceptable professional practice of modern medicine.

2 | THE ALMOST REVOLUTION: AUTONOMY AND PATIENT-BASED CARE

Autonomy, the liberty to live after one's owne law.
Henry Cockerham, 1623[1]

Every human being of adult years and sound mind has a right to determine what shall be done with his own body.
Justice Cardozo, 1914[2]

The concept of patient autonomy has almost revolutionized healthcare over the past 50 years—at least, in much of the Western world.[3] It has changed in an irreversible way how clinicians, patients, and the public think about acceptable medical care. In modern medicine, the right thing to do now requires incorporating patient values and wishes into medical decision making. The question is not *whether*, but *how* best to do so.

I. THE AUTONOMY PRINCIPLE

CASE 2.1   THE PATIENT'S AGENDA

You are a family physician looking after a 49-year-old man who smokes, is overweight, and has poorly controlled hypertension and mildly elevated serum lipids. He also has a family history of heart disease: his father died at 52 of a massive myocardial infarction. You have worked a year with this patient to try to get him to change his ways, but to no avail. Weight loss is followed by weight gain, exercise by non-exercise, periods of abstinence from smoking followed by chain smoking. (The patient quips, quoting Mark Twain, 'It's easy to quit smoking, I've done it hundreds of times!') His blood pressure today is 190/110.

Despite being cautioned about the threats to his health, he refuses for the umpteenth time to take any medications. 'Doc,' he states, 'I gotta do this on my own! I swear, see me in six months, I'll be a new man.'

You consider your options as to how you might manage this patient. Should you threaten to terminate the therapeutic relationship if the patient continues in his self-destructive ways? Should you try to browbeat him with the cudgel of evidence? Should you sound the panic alarm?

DISCUSSION OF AND FOLLOW-UP TO CASE 2.1

This type of 'non-compliant' patient can make health professionals think about changing careers! It's patient autonomy versus beneficence, right? The patient is an adult, possesses decision-making capacity, but exercises it in a seemingly self-destructive way. It would be easy to say he's mature, he's autonomous, let him be, or to see his decision making as the product of some mental malady. One author, commenting on this sort of patient, writes: 'The physician should do more than consider whether there is something wrong with the patient; the physician should ask what might be wrong with the doctor-patient communication.'[4]

Indeed, communication is a root issue for many non-compliant patients. Rather than acting out of alarm or abandoning the patient, the clinician needs to try to better understand what his fears and concerns are. As it turns out, the patient, like many others, is worried about side-effects from medication. His previous doctor had put him on pills two years ago that gave him erectile problems and swollen ankles, making him feel like an old man, he says. He stopped taking them and never went back to the doctor. He is in a new relationship now and wants nothing to do with pills that might interfere with his sex life.

Once these issues were addressed, the patient was willing to work at lifestyle changes and to try some alternative medications. Recognition and management of the ethical dilemma, by incorporating the patient's wishes (autonomy) with best-evidence care (beneficence), resolved the problem. While simple, there is something important in this kind of reasoning: it does not rely on the autonomy principle or the beneficence principle alone. Rather, the physician strives to do the right thing by taking into account the patient's preferences and experiences but does not forget the professional responsibilities of minimizing harm and maximizing a 'good outcome'. Just what is a good outcome will, in turn, depend on the patient's perspective.

Patient-based care

Patient-based medicine is intimately bound up with the ethical notion of patient autonomy. Simply put, autonomy means that patients' views and aspirations are the central foundation of good healthcare. As regards *capable* persons, autonomy means two things:

(1) having the right to decide what they want when it comes to healthcare, and
(2) having the right to be treated in respectful ways by healthcare professionals.

Expressing these notions as 'rights' implies that healthcare professionals have corresponding duties towards patients. Indeed, they do. If clinicians are to help patients live their lives in ways they want to—and they should do so, if the ends are reasonable ones—then this means respecting and, at times, helping to promote the choices and values of capable patients.

As regards *incapable* persons, autonomy requires:

(1) showing fidelity to patients' prior capable views, and
(2) treating those patients as individuals with inherent worth and dignity (see Chapter 6 on Capacity).

Autonomy is about privacy, 'the right to be left alone', but it is also about the limits of choice. Informed patients have an almost unlimited right to *refuse* therapy and a somewhat more prescribed right to *choose* therapy. Autonomy has been a long time coming to medicine. For centuries, medicine's ethos was that of benign paternalism: the doctor was viewed as a 'father-knows-best' figure who always knew and did what was best for his patients. This role is not without its defenders: when ill, one hopes and wants to be looked after—especially by a kindly professional who knows what to do. There is still an important role for this type of medical paternalism—especially where the patient's capacity is compromised or where the patient wants the clinician to decide for him or her—as we will see.

Autonomy has been supported for decades in judicial and ethics writings and has been established in American, Canadian, and UK legal systems—albeit with various nuances and cultural differences. Entrusting patients with the responsibility for decisions concerning their healthcare is now the law in other countries, such as Germany, France, and Austria, as well.[5] Western societies express a democratic ethos—the right to self-determination—that may be contrasted with the therapeutic ethos—the obligation to treat and ameliorate disease. Modern jurisprudence has strengthened the hand of autonomy and the democratic perspective in medicine, to the chagrin of some clinicians who simply want to get on with the job of healing.

Although autonomy as a decision-making principle in medicine may appear to have been imposed from the outside, by judges at the bedside as it were, this is only partially true. Patients have often been active participants in their own care.[6] The difference today is that scientific medicine has made it possible to treat and prevent certain illnesses effectively in different ways, so patients now have real choices to make about what kind of treatment they would prefer. The respect due humans naturally leads to respecting and promoting the choices patients make.

Although some countries in Europe and in Asia place less emphasis on patient autonomy than we do in the West, this may change with time as the notion gains a foothold in their courts. There is evidence that patients in widely disparate countries wish to be involved in decisions about the treatment they receive, especially if seriously ill.[7]

The meaning of autonomy

Autonomy is derived from the Greek '*autos*' meaning 'self' and '*nomos*' meaning 'rule' or 'law'. *Autonomous* patients are those capable of exercising deliberate and meaningful choices, choices consistent with their own values—making their own laws, as it were.[8] They are persons with the cognitive and emotional 'competence' or 'capacity' (in this book, I will not distinguish between these two terms) to make decisions for themselves (see Chapter 6 on Capacity).

Heteronomous patients, by contrast, cannot make decisions for themselves. They may exhibit 'decidophobia'—an inability to compare alternatives and make decisions 'with one's eyes open'.[9] This may be because of familial, cultural, or social factors that encourage an inordinate (or *appropriate*) dependence on others.[10] Heteronomy may also be because of a lack of certain mental capacities, for example, as in a newborn or a comatose or severely demented patient or to a seeming 'lack of will', as in depressive or compulsive disorders.

However, autonomy does not mean one *must* make all decisions by oneself.[11] An autonomous individual—capable, rational, well-informed—can relinquish or 'waive' the right to make his or her own decisions in favour of a spouse, family unit, community, or the like (see Chapters 4 and 5 on Truthtelling and Consent).

Autonomy as used in this book simply means being true to one's self. How one experiences and achieves this has much to do with the local culture and mores. However, once the self is recognized as the fount of decision making and the locus of certitude, certain ideas naturally flow from that—ideas about independence of thought and action, idiosyncrasy of interpretation, the right to be 'wrong' and not be sanctioned for this, and so on.

In the West these ideas all flow from the Enlightenment. Seen against the background of religious fundamentalism and the Inquisition, the seventeenth-century philosopher René Descartes' argument that the only statement of which one can be absolutely certain is *cogito ergo sum* ('I think, therefore I am') was a remarkably novel and radical departure from the punishing conformist attitude of the time.[12] This idea was one of the foundations for the Enlightenment. Just think how radical Descartes' dangerous idea still is: only the individual can decide what is right and true; everything else—Family, Society, Religion, God—is uncertain. He was lucky not to have been burned at the stake for this philosophy!

Respect for autonomy is not just a fine moral sentiment. The idea of autonomy backed up by the force of law has transformed healthcare; however, modern courts do not see autonomy as the only principle or as an unfettered right. The courts will infringe upon personal autonomy if the latter threatens important social interests (see the Rodriguez case in Chapter 11 on End-of-Life Decisions). Moral complexities do arise in considering just how far patients may go in asking for care and as to how clinicians should respond when patients make choices, such as refusing life-sustaining care, that clinicians find unacceptable or less than optimal. We will return to these matters throughout this book.

Autonomy as the patient's preference

Autonomy as a principle makes the patient's 'own priorities and aspirations' the focal point, although never the sole point, of medical care. A healthcare practitioner cannot in general substitute his or her wishes and preferences for those of the patient's, even if what the physician wants seems more likely to promote the patient's best interests. A successful medical encounter may largely depend on the practitioner understanding and working with the patient's wishes, perceptions, and beliefs.

CASE 2.2   THE PATIENT KNOWS BEST

A patient had undergone menopause at age 54 in the mid-1990s. At the time she had significant menopausal symptoms (flushing) but was otherwise healthy. Her mother had died in her early sixties of heart disease. Her primary care physician, following well-established 'evidence-based' guidelines at the time that recommended estrogen replacement therapy (ERT) to both alleviate menopausal symptoms and to lessen the risk of heart disease, suggested she start ERT soon. This the patient adamantly refused to do, believing that menopause was a natural process and should not be 'medicalized'. In their discussion it was apparent she was well informed and certain of her choice and elected not to go on ERT.

How should a practitioner evaluate a patient's refusal of evidence-based 'best care'?

DISCUSSION OF CASE 2.2

From a strictly physiological and scientific point of view, this patient's refusal of therapy might have seemed less than optimal at the time because the substantial benefits of ERT seemed so well established. As it turns out now the patient was quite prescient: the 1990s evidence was flawed. Not only does ERT increase cardiovascular risks but it also increases the risk of breast cancer. Obviously, this patient was not irrational (far from it); she simply had different beliefs from her clinician. She preferred her symptoms and the risks of future illness (such as osteoporosis) over taking any hormonal therapy. (How right she was!) Abiding by the patient's choice was the right thing to do. Despite guidelines, the right of patients to refuse recommended therapy ought to be respected and other ways to help them achieve the medical outcomes they have chosen (that is, to alleviate their symptoms and reduce the risks to their health) ought to be pursued by their clinicians. For some clinicians this may be the problem of patient 'non-compliance', but this term is less helpful because it dismisses the patient's own expertise as a patient and an adult.

In retrospect, this patient was quite right to refuse hormone replacement therapy; ERT is, on balance, harmful for most women. Clinicians may overrate the success of new and approved treatments while patients, generally more risk-averse than clinicians, may be more skeptical of the latest medical fashion. The principle of patient autonomy entails respect for patients' decisions even if thought sub-optimal, and it expects clinicians to provide patients with information and guidance needed to empower them to make authentic choices. Clinicians should approach this task with the appropriate caution and humility.

Patient-centred care

According to the autonomy model of 'patient-centred care', the encounter with a patient in day-to-day medical practice is best carried out if the clinician knows not only what disease the patient has, but also what the patient's beliefs and feelings, hopes and fears are. What effect the patient's state of health or unwellness has had upon these beliefs and upon his or her functioning should also be considered.[13] In other words, any healthcare professional ought to approach illness from the patient's point of view as a whole. Some have called this 'narrative medicine'; this patient-based understanding is what good clinical care is all about.[14] This model attempts to ensure that the medical encounter serves the needs and interests of patients as defined by them. Although patients do not and cannot have a full say over their care, they have a very important voice that must not be ignored. One can only know what a patient wants and expects if one takes the time to ask.

The principle of autonomy can create special dilemmas for clinicians when the evidence for what the patient has chosen is less than clear. In cases where the patient's choice will result in death or serious injury, the usual advice is to err on the side of life. This is an extension of the 'do no harm' rule. Unfortunately, this rough guide may not result in non-liability because exactly what is viewed as 'harm' may differ between clinician and patient. A case in point is the well-known Canadian case of *Malette v. Shulman.*

II. THE CASE OF MRS MALETTE AND DR SHULMAN

This Ontario legal case shows how far law is prepared to go in terms of respecting a patient's freedom of choice. Even in life-threatening circumstances, the autonomy principle can supersede that of medical beneficence.

In 1979 Mrs Malette, a 57-year-old woman, was brought, comatose, to the Emergency Room.[15] She had been in a severe motor vehicle accident in which her husband was killed, and she appeared to be bleeding to death from a head injury. Dr Shulman, the Emergency Room physician, believed a blood transfusion had to be given to save her life. However, Mrs Malette had a signed card in her wallet, albeit neither dated nor witnessed, stating she was a Jehovah's Witness and would never want to receive blood products. Despite knowing about this card, Dr Shulman ordered a blood transfusion. He would later justify his actions by stating that because of his uncertainty about the patient's true beliefs and the dire consequences of not treating her, he had to treat her. In my mind this was a reasonable calculation to make (see Box 2.1).

BOX 2.1

Where a patient currently cannot express his or her wishes, the patient's previously expressed (capable) wishes—whether written or verbal—regarding therapy should be followed.

Reasonableness and beyond

A later court settlement found that the transfusion, although it had saved the patient's life, had been given against her known wishes. Dr Shulman was found guilty of battery and ordered to pay $20,000 in monetary damages. In commenting on religious refusal, the court reasoned that 'if the objection [to treatment] is on a religious basis, this does not permit the scrutiny of "reasonableness" which is "a transitory standard dependent on the norms of the day". If the patient's objection has its basis in religion, it is more apt to crystallize in life-threatening situations.'[16] In other words, deeply held views, such as some religious ones, are enduring and should not be treated as irrelevant or untenable even if they put the believer in harm's way. One wonders why religious views are so privileged—would the court be so accepting of non–faith-based idiosyncratic patient views? Perhaps so (see Case 2.4 later in this chapter).

The crucial finding of this judgment is that Dr Shulman's care, from the judge's point of view, was substandard because it ignored the prior expressed wishes of Mrs Malette. A higher Ontario Court of Appeal later upheld the earlier judgment: 'A doctor is not free to disregard a patient's advance instructions any more than he would be free to disregard instructions given at the time of the emergency.'[17] So, while medicine's goals are to ameliorate suffering and prevent premature death (the beneficence principle), in general, these cannot be achieved at the expense of the patient's preferences (the autonomy principle). Competent patients have a right to reject any and all medical care—and courts countenance this when the decision to refuse care reflects what a person wants, even if such preferences are far from mainstream thought: 'If [the doctor] knows that the patient has refused to consent to the proposed procedure, he is not empowered to overrule the patient's decision for her even though he, and most others, may think hers a foolish or unreasonable decision.'[18]

With all due respect, the court's remark seems a little off the mark—it is not that Dr Shulman *ignored* the patient's wishes—he seemed genuinely *uncertain* as to what they were. It is difficult for doctors like Dr. Shulman to know how good the evidence of a patient's prior wishes must be to require abiding by that individual's apparent refusal of emergency treatment. Should Mrs Malette's wishes have been respected—and she be allowed to die—even though her signed card was neither dated nor witnessed?[19] (What would you do, if on a dark and stormy night, a patient came in, alone, to your ER with a lethal, but treatable, injury and she had on her person a vaguely worded card refusing a life-saving intervention?)

Dr Shulman's position was thus an unenviable one. Where the basis of treatment refusal is unclear and the patient will certainly die without treatment, you should, in general, treat that patient until the wishes are clarified. In the court's view, if patients leave home with their vaguely worded living will refusing treatment, then they take upon themselves the risk that they will not get that treatment. Easy for the courts to say—they're not at the patient's bedside!

Bottom line: *clinicians ignore even uncertain evidence of a patient's wishes at their peril.* (It must be said, however, that while Canadian courts have been fairly consistent in recognizing the primacy of patients' wishes, the same consistency cannot be said for US courts.)[20]

In another case, concerned with the right of mentally ill patients to refuse antipsychotic treatment (to be discussed in Chapter 7 on Beneficence), the court wrote that the best-interests standard (the patient's 'well-being' from the medical perspective) cannot be used to overrule the patient's wishes to refuse treatment (see Box 2.2).[21] If that were allowed, best interests would take precedence over the patient's wishes, violating 'the basic tenets of our legal system' and would not be in accordance with the 'principles of fundamental justice'.[22] The court assumes that the patient is competent until proven otherwise—the patient may be mad, bad, or just plain ill now, but it is the patient's prior expressed preferences that must guide care.

BOX 2.2

'The patient's right to forego treatment, in the absence of some overriding societal interest, is paramount to the doctor's obligation to provide medical care. This right must be honoured, even though the treatment may be beneficial or necessary to preserve the patient's life or health, and regardless of how ill-advised the patient's decision may appear to others.'

III. CHOICES: THE GOOD, THE BAD, AND THE UGLY

1. The good: the right to choose

Patients, by the principle of autonomy, have a right to make choices about the kind of healthcare they receive. The right to a second opinion is an important corollary of this, as is the right to information (see Chapter 5 on Consent). Patients, too, can choose to have or forego tests or surgeries. They can choose what kind of dialysis to go on or choose not to go on it at all (and risk imminent death). They can ask to see the best surgeon for brain or heart surgery—provided they are willing to wait in Canada or to pay big bucks in the US. Patients can ask for almost anything. Whether they will get it depends on the urgency of their problem, where they live, what the alternatives are, and whether they can afford to wait—in short, it depends on supply, availability, and the standard of care (see Chapter 9 on Justice).

Reasonable choices by patients are still sometimes thwarted by physicians who find paternalism an attitude difficult to forego.

CASE 2.3   LIGATION LITIGATION

A 24-year-old unmarried woman is pregnant for the second time with a Caesarian section already scheduled. Well on in her second trimester, she requests that, at the time of the delivery, the obstetrician 'tie her tubes'. This he refuses to do, citing her young age and unmarried status. 'How do I know you won't change your mind in a few years?'

Is the obstetrician acting properly here?

DISCUSSION OF CASE 2.3

This is an all too common doctor-knows-best scenario. The obstetrician has his reasons, but they are not enough, from the autonomy perspective, to support his refusal to perform a tubal ligation on this patient. If she understands and appreciates the proposed procedure, this should suffice. Of course, he can give her information about it and send her away to think about it, but ultimately the choice is hers to make. Patients may regret any procedure they undergo; the best the clinician can do is hope they truly comprehend the likely outcomes (such as, in this case, the irreversibility of the ligation). Even if the obstetrician had some moral qualms about ligating an unmarried woman, he at a minimum should, from this perspective, refer her to an appropriate colleague.

The problem is that this is an area where the doctor's peers would probably do the same thing. 'Experienced, wise gynecologists', it has been argued, will routinely turn down a woman younger than 25 asking that her tubes be tied.[23] On this view, women have other, very effective and safe, non-surgical methods of birth control. Physicians following a young person's wishes fear litigation from a regretted tubal ligation. But while ligation is a litigation-prone procedure, this is usually on account of an unwanted pregnancy from negligent ligation and not because the gynecologist has coerced the woman into it. Another argument in favour of this view is the reluctance to perform any irreversible procedure on patients if they might be too young to truly appreciate the implications as to what they want: for example, it is prudent to deny a teenager access to purely cosmetic surgery or permanent tattooing. There may be some room here for a limited paternalism. Clinicians need to try as best they can to distinguish a defensible community standard from their own personal distaste for a procedure.

Interestingly, young men would have similar difficulty getting a vasectomy, so the problem isn't one of sexism and isn't discipline-specific. It is not infrequent for women and men to enter a new relationship several years later and want their irreversible steriliza-tion reversed. This professional reluctance to grant a competent patient's request for surgical sterilization may be a holdover from certain religious objections to non-therapeutic sterilization and may be hard to eradicate.

2. The 'bad': the right to foolish choices

Autonomy and the freedom to exercise choice mean, among other things, the freedom to make 'bad choices', ones that may cause harm. Citizens in our society have the liberty to behave in ways that are not always best for themselves (such as drinking alcohol, eating junk food, and smoking), so long as such activ-ities do not harm others. There is an old adage that the right to swing your fist ends where my nose begins. The moral difficulty for clinicians is in knowing how to handle patients' more trying and controversial wishes.

CASE 2.4   DON'T TOUCH MY ARM!

A 64-year-old woman who was about to undergo non-emergency surgery for a prolapsed bladder told the anesthetist before the operation, 'Whatever you do, don't touch my left arm. You'll have nothing but trouble there.' The anesthetist accepted this statement without seeking any clarification of it. Soon after the operation began, he lost intravenous access in her right arm. Ignoring her previous request, he started a new IV in her *left* arm. The operation was completed without incident.

Unfortunately, postoperatively, the IV in the patient's left arm went interstitial and a toxic fluid leaked into the surrounding arm tissue, resulting in a significant injury to the arm. At trial, no evidence was presented of any medical reason for the left arm not to have been touched. However, no evidence was offered supporting the necessity of starting an IV in that arm. The patient successfully sued the doctor for assault (non-consensual touching).[24]

Was this an appropriate judgment?

DISCUSSION OF CASE 2.4

It would seem to be an appropriate judgment, because the doctor ignored the patient's wish. Patients have a right to idiosyncratic beliefs—even if they pose some risk of harm to themselves. In this case, the arm injury was entirely fortuitous—it was not as if the patient had some foreknowledge that harm would ensue if the doctor touched her left arm. Nevertheless, her instructions were explicit and appeared to have been accepted by the anesthetist. He should have sought IV access anywhere else but the left arm.

Of course, it would have been quite appropriate to question her before surgery about her request ('What if I cannot start an IV anywhere but in your left arm?'). If she persisted in her prohibition and he felt this to be unsafe, he could have declined to act as her anesthetist (much as a surgeon would refuse to operate with one hand tied behind his back). *If a patient's request is inherently unsafe and abiding by it skirts negligence or unprofessional conduct, the healthcare professional has no duty to acquiesce to it.* In fact, he or she ought not to comply with it. However, waiting until the patient is asleep under anesthetic is not the best time to question a patient's prior wish.

The principle of autonomy allows patients to define their own ways of living (and dying). While some of these ways will be straightforward, others will seem unusual and perhaps eccentric. Unless these ways are seriously deranged, they should be explored, but not necessarily overruled, by clinicians. Seemingly competent and autonomous patients can choose irrationally by

- thinking about the immediate future and ignoring long-term risks,
- thinking that nothing bad will happen to them,
- acting on unreasonable fears that make them avoid necessary treatment,
- exhibiting extremely eccentric beliefs, or
- adhering to unusual ways of interpreting information.[25]

None of these reasons are sufficient on their own to overrule a patient's wishes. They do suggest that something may be amiss with the patient's cognitive state and act as red flags for the ethical clinician to probe those patient beliefs more thoroughly. Some 'irrational' choices made by patients are true expressions of deeply held patient convictions, whereas others are products of their defence mechanisms, such as denial, in the face of difficult life events.

3. The 'ugly': self-destructive wishes

The autonomy principle can cause some healthcare professionals to feel as if they are handmaidens to less than optimal wishes of their patients, wishes that can border on the self-destructive. This may be something quite different from what they expected when they entered their training program: is their job not to improve and save lives, rather than imperil or end them? Although some patients' wishes are clearly illegitimate and must be resisted, others are less clearly so—especially, where they arise from illness.

CASE 2.5   TRANQUILLIZER TRAP

An 84-year-old woman with a history of coronary disease requests her usual prescription of triazolam, a short-acting benzodiazepine that she has been taking for years for insomnia. Despite repeated efforts on your part to wean her from this drug, she insists on taking it.

Should the drug be prescribed yet again?

DISCUSSION OF CASE 2.5

Elderly people are notoriously overmedicated and this patient runs the risk of falls and confusion secondary to her use of a benzodiazepine, problems that are not infrequent in her age group in any case.[26] Many long-time users of hypnotics and anxiolytics are not readily weaned from them ('But, doctor, I can't sleep a wink without them . . .'). They can hang on to their drugs as tenaciously as to life itself ('You'll pry them from my dead hands . . .').[27]

You must struggle with the task of getting the patient to agree to reduce these risks (which such patients typically downplay) by coming off such medication versus becoming embroiled in a power struggle. You must educate her as to the risks of hypnotics and discuss alternatives with her. In doing so you have satisfied the beneficence principle—and maybe also the autonomy principle if the patient's use of hypnotics compromises her independence.

It could be that this is a battle you are unlikely to win. If you decide to continue prescribing the medication, you should do so prudently: prescribe limited quantities each time, have a discussion about associated risks on a regular basis, document these discussions, making it clear that the patient is making an informed choice, and continue efforts to wean her off this. Of course, it goes without saying that the patient should be carefully and regularly monitored for the development of such adverse effects and a more forceful discussion undertaken if such symptoms do emerge. On a practical level, the patient could well go to another doctor to request the benzodiazepine if you refuse her request. At least you can monitor her use of the medication if you continue to be the one to prescribe it.

The modern allegiance to patient autonomy should not be used as an excuse for not caring and thereby abandoning a patient. It is the clinician's job—his or her fiduciary responsibility—to explore the choices that a patient makes, to invade a patient's privacy (with his or her consent, of course) to make sure the patient is not abandoned in his or her autonomous shell.

Many argue, for example, that allowing mentally compromised patients the 'right' to their self-harming actions says more about our negative attitudes towards mental impairments and the limits of caring than it does about patient autonomy. Similarly, ageist attitudes towards the elderly in many modern Western societies may lead to underinvestigation and undertreatment of various illnesses.

Cases in which autonomous wishes lead to injury to the patient seem to involve the healthcare professional in a more central way.

CASE 2.6   A MAN SHOULD DIE AT HOME!

A spry but frail 94-year-old male patient, long widowed and living alone, has a history of heart disease. At one point he finds himself in a coronary care unit owing to serious heart failure. He begs to be released ('There is no fate worse than this! A man should not die in a hospital!' he cries out to the Home Care nurse who has lately become his de facto primary care provider), but the specialists feel he cannot manage at home and that he will be back in their Emergency Room next week. Although hardly happy, he is not depressed, and he understands the consequences of leaving the hospital. He simply wants to be at home. He is quite prepared to die since he has outlived all possibility of a happy life as well as outliving his family and friends.

Should the health professionals aid him in his wish to die at home?

DISCUSSION OF AND FOLLOW-UP TO CASE 2.6

There seem to be very few options in this case. The patient is quite alone and feels he has come to the end of his days. If incapable, he could be confined to hospital again and treated against his will. This seems an undignified way of treating a very dignified patient. He is thought to be capable of making the decision about where to live and is released to his home despite the risk of death and of re-admission. The community nurse looking after him—who knows him better than anyone else—feels that letting him go is the right thing to do.

In reality, the patient was discharged to his apartment, stopped eating and taking his medications, and died several weeks later. The patient's primary home nurse, who helped get him home, felt some complicity in his death. Had she done 'everything' to help the patient live? Or did she too quickly comply with his wishes because he was an old guy? In the end, although troubled by his death, she felt it was her duty to be the patient's advocate, to ensure that his doctors heard his plea and respected his rights, and that he obtained the supports he needed at home. Her dedication to the patient was remarkable in these days when care can seem callously anonymous.

On the other hand, it could be argued that this patient was in fact depressed. That he stopped eating upon discharge seems to indicate he wanted to kill himself. Was this a rational and competent decision or one influenced by depression? Older patients are notoriously underinvestigated for depression and suicide risk. This patient was at high risk for suicide given his age, sex, ethnicity, and medical problems. Was this patient carefully assessed for the presence of depression? Were all possible residential alternatives explored? It is crucial that allowing him to die was not a lazy way out to get rid of an 'old geezer' and free up a bed for someone younger. Perhaps the nurse was projecting her own feelings of hopelessness onto the patient. The only real way to guard against such personal biases in decision making is to be aware of them and discuss them with others.

Costs to the professional

Sometimes the right thing to do is to allow avoidable harm to come to a patient, especially when that harm is foreseen by the patient and is less impor-tant to him or her than other, more central, wishes and aspirations. This would seem to go against the basic philosophy of the healthcare professions, but it is important to remember that harm and benefit must be defined with patient input. Unfortunately, if helping a patient results in injury or death, the health-care professional can be left with difficult feelings of guilt and regret—this is part of the hidden costs of self-determination.

The careful clinician will make sure a patient's decision to forego care, or to embark on a course that will lead to his or her death, is not influenced by modifiable factors, such as despair or loneliness (see Chapter 11 on End-of-Life Decisions). If such factors are involved, the practitioner should address these as best as possible before going along with a patient who wishes to die or puts him or herself in harm's way. The clinician who has gone that extra mile for his or her patient (as the nurse in Case 2.6 did) need feel no guilt about the patient's outcome. There may be sadness perhaps, if the patient dies too soon, but these emotions are natural when the healer is eclipsed by the fact of irrecoverable illness and the finality of death.

While in North America the patient's right to foolish choices or to make less than optimal medical decisions would be respected by the principle of autonomy, in other jurisdictions the principle of beneficence would no doubt take precedence. Other countries have not yet entirely dealt with the issue of medical paternalism. Indeed, some may never do so. There is no doubt a cultural context in which ethical decisions are made. The wise clinician needs to be aware of these cultural differences and may need to tailor his or her ethical decision making accordingly.

IV. REDUCED AUTONOMY

CASE 2.7   TOO YOUNG FOR AUTONOMY?

A 14-year-old boy, accompanied by his father, visits his doctor for an annual checkup. The father leaves his son in the office while he parks his car. The physician notes the boy is due for a tetanus-polio booster. At this point, the teen refuses the immunization . . . he has a needle phobia. The doctor, thinking the father has left, asks the nurse to hold the patient and give the injection. The teen's father is furious when he discovers what happened in his absence and threatens to make a complaint to the province's regulatory college.

Does this case involve a legitimate violation of the principle of autonomy?

DISCUSSION OF CASE 2.7

The father is right to be angry. Although it may be in the boy's best interests to have the booster and his fear might be irrational, this does not mean his views can or should be ignored. The clinician ought to have assessed this patient's capacity to refuse immunization. Even if the boy was incapable on the grounds of immaturity or lack of appreciation, the clinician should have treated the teen with respect. There would have been ample time to have the patient return for the booster—and perhaps in the interval to have his phobia treated. The physician would rightly receive a reminder from his regulatory college that capable patients of any age have a right to make their own healthcare decisions.

It may be difficult for clinicians to know when to abide by refusals of care by children—especially those on the cusp of adulthood. Young teens can be volatile and hard to mollify. On the other hand, even very young children can be surprisingly capable of understanding and deserve, by the principle of respect due persons, to have their opinions, fears, and wishes taken into account.[28] It can be argued that their assent to treatment should be sought even if the true authority for the decision is not theirs alone. Similarly, patient resistance to and dissent from a procedure ought to be taken into account rather than simply dismissed.

Critical illness, by creating a state of vulnerability in patients, can create roadblocks to the simple exercise of autonomy.[29]

CASE 2.8   A HYPNOTIC REQUEST

The 84-year-old patient in Case 2.5 refuses alternative means of sedation. The following year she suffers a myocardial infarction for which she is hospitalized for three weeks. Her illness is complicated by congestive heart failure and arrhythmias. Upon discharge she once again requests triazolam.

Examination reveals an elderly woman in no acute distress but with subtle changes in her mental processes; she seems more confused than before her myocardial infarction. You discover she has been using higher daily doses of triazolam to cope with feelings of loss over her diminished stamina. Worried that her overuse of triazolam might be contributing to her mental state, you decide to involve, with the patient's reluctant cooperation, a community geriatric team to try to help her cope better with her losses and end her dependence on the drug.

Is this an acceptable encroachment on patient liberty?

DISCUSSION OF CASE 2.8

You have judiciously balanced the patient's wishes with the need to protect her health. Her use of a hypnotic is now excessive and threatening to undermine what autonomy she has left. Her increased physical and mental frailty makes you uncomfortable with simply acceding to her wishes. A physician who does not find the drug use problematic would not be living up to professional standards. One of these is to protect patients from themselves. Does this smack of paternalism? It may, but it is legitimately exercised here because the patient's autonomy is being compromised by her illness and her drug use.

In such circumstances it is difficult to know how far to respect a patient's expressed wishes. Are they authentic expressions of the patient's self, or do they derive from someone who is suffering and under siege by illness or incapacity? Patients can appear competent but be impaired for more subtle reasons having to do with their illnesses (see Case 7.5 'Not like himself').

Ingelfinger argued the patient needs a clinician who will take charge and in whom the patient can believe, if a treatment is to succeed.[30] His views revealed his own personal need for someone to direct his care when he was ill with an incurable cancer. Serious illness does tend to usurp the lives of patients. In such circumstances patients trust that physicians and other health professionals will look after them. Illness has already undermined them; the sick are often less concerned about self-determination than about getting the most beneficial care from a trusted and trustworthy healthcare professional.

Patient waiver revisited

Although some patients wish to maintain control as long as they are able, others are only too happy to have someone look after them in a protective, paternalistic fashion. This hardly seems like an ethically worrisome paternalism because the patient's autonomy is already impaired and the patient has 'waived' (autonomously?) the right to decide. Such wishes should be respected. (If the illness or situation changes, it would also be proper for the physician to discuss with the patient the possibility of resuming control.)

CASE 2.9   A WISH NOT TO HEAR

You are a visiting nurse who is seeing a new patient, a 78-year-old man, for postoperative care at his home. He claims to feel fine, and gives a recent past history of surgery for an 'ulcer'. He says he was told nothing unusual about it but indicates he has a tube to drain bile from his liver. You are perplexed, as a tube is usually only put in to relieve an obstruction, not to treat a simple ulcer. The patient cannot explain this. Later, inspection of his hospital chart and his family doctor's referring note reveals the patient had been told at least twice that he had inoperable pancreatic cancer.

What should you do?

DISCUSSION OF CASE 2.9

You should see the patient again to get a better understanding of his personality. It appears the patient is denying the true nature of his illness. Should you try, once more, to beat down the patient's defenses? If I had satisfied myself that this attempt had been made before, I would not. (A significant number of patients with cancer deny their illness despite clear evidence to the contrary.)[31]

Instead, I would ask him: are you the type of person who likes to know everything about his illness, or would you prefer only your physicians to know? If he answered yes to the latter, I would let him be. Patients have a right to their defences and the right to expect us to look after them. Such needs should not be run over roughshod by a simple-minded allegiance to the principle of autonomy.

CONCLUSION

How patients exercise their autonomy may not be straightforward and may require at one and the same time both respect from and exploration by health-care professionals. The clinician should use his or her skill to decide what he or she thinks is appropriate in the light of the patient's wishes and values. In the proper application of clinical judgment, practitioners should not only know when to respect a patient's wishes and to help them to achieve their goals, but also when not to do so (for example, to protect the vulnerable and the ill from serious harm).

When patient and doctor clash, whose view should prevail? The answer often is that neither view on its own should prevail. Instead, the participants ought to try principled negotiation: common ground should be sought through mutual understanding and respect.[32] By examining the patient's feelings, expectations, worries, and—because of illness—changed functioning in the world, the clinician will be better able to devise a treatment plan that combines the patient's wishes with the physician's obligations. This finding of a common ground tries to avoid unnecessary power struggles and simplistic kow-towing to the patient's expectations.

In Chapters 6 and 7 I will return to the clinician's duty of beneficence and care for non-autonomous patients. The next three chapters will deal with other implications of the principle of autonomy for the practice of medicine.

No Man an Island: Confidentiality and Trust

Thou art the only one to whom I dare confide my Folly.

George Lyttelton, 1744[1]

Achilles: Of this my privacy, I have strong reasons.
Ulysses: But against your privacy, the reasons are more potent and heroic.

William Shakespeare, c. 1602[2]

Deciding on the right thing to do in medicine can be a complicated task, rarely accomplished by simply adhering to one particular moral principle or duty. Nowhere is this more obvious than in the conflicting professional responsibilities concerning the management of patients' private information. Healthcare professionals are expected to respect the confidential nature of patient information and protect it from inappropriate disclosure. In certain circumstances, however, privacy expectations cannot be met for reasons of public safety and private welfare.

I. Confidentiality

CASE 3.1 | DON'T MENTION IT

You are a family physician visited by a 35-year-old married woman who has developed acute anxiety and panic attacks. She reveals

there have been marital problems for some time and her husband is now threatening to leave her. After some discussion, she accepts a prescription for an anxiolytic and the name of a marital therapist. You also recommend she take some time off work. Two weeks later, the patient returns, reporting she is feeling better and ready to return to work. She requests a note for her employer. 'Doctor, please don't say anything in there about my anxiety attacks. I don't want my boss to know anything about my problems.'

Medical practice would be impossible if patients felt unable or unwilling to share information about their private lives with healthcare professionals. Such information, often concerning intimate or even secret matters, is disclosed by patients on the assumption that it will be used for their medical benefit alone.

'Certain duties arise from the special relationship of trust and confidence [between doctor and patient]. These include the duties of the doctor to act with utmost good faith and loyalty, to hold information received from or about a patient in confidence, and to make proper disclosure of information to a patient. . . . When a patient releases personal information in the context of the doctor-patient relationship, he or she does so with the legitimate expectation that these duties will be respected.'[3]

DISCUSSION OF CASE 3.1

There is no need for her employer to know the reason for her absence. You should disclose the minimal amount necessary to allow the appropriate time off work. You write a note to the employer indicating your patient has been absent 'for medical reasons' and is fit to return to work. Your primary duty in this case is to your patient. You must respect her request for her medical information to remain confidential.

Private disclosures, private examinations

Healthcare professionals cannot do an adequate job if they fail to appropriately 'invade' a patient's physical and mental privacy. This is, at one and the same time, a great privilege and a hefty responsibility. In the very first meeting, patients come prepared to confide tremendously personal aspects of themselves—their 'follies', perhaps. Trusting that their clinicians will not disclose their healthcare information to others provides a safe harbour for patients to disclose information they might otherwise keep secret.

Medical communications not privileged

Although medical confidentiality is protected by professional regulations and standards, doctor–patient communications are not 'privileged' per se in Canada. (Privilege means the right to withhold information gained within the context of a 'special relationship' such as that between doctor–patient or attorney–client.) This means doctors must disclose information about a patient if properly requested to do so by the courts. Legal advice around just what is required to be disclosed in court should be sought. For example, a subpoena is not in itself a licence to breach patient confidentiality by releasing any and all private information to lawyers and others but simply a command to attend court.[4] However, one commentator has observed, despite 'lofty' court language espousing medical confidentiality, none of the most important precedent cases before the Supreme Court of Canada actually find in favour of confidentiality.[5]

Charges of sexual assault

One area where medical information is privileged is in the case of sexual assault charges. The fear of having one's personal, psychiatric, and medical information laid bare in a courtroom has made many victims of sexual assault wary of laying charges. Bill C-46 of the Canadian *Criminal Code* is aimed at encouraging the reporting of such crimes by restricting access to medical, counselling, therapeutic, and other personal records of complainants in sexual offence prosecutions. Psychiatrists and other healthcare professionals are protected from having to release information from an alleged victim's medical records *unless* the accused can come up with compelling reasons for this. This prevents 'fishing expeditions' by defence lawyers looking for some reason to cast aspersions on the plaintiff.

All applications by an accused for access to such records must go through two stages: (1) the accused must establish that the records contain information likely to be relevant to an issue at trial or to the competence of a witness to testify, and (2) the trial judge must deem this a legitimate request and only then will review the records in private and decide if they are indeed relevant.[6]

II. CONTROL OF HEALTH INFORMATION

The right to privacy is a fundamental tenet of liberal democracies, closely linked with the notions of confidentiality and patient autonomy. The values of autonomy, liberty, and dignity—all versions of the 'respect for persons' principle—underpin the concept of privacy.[7] At the end of the nineteenth century, for example, two American Supreme Court justices defined privacy as 'the right to be left alone'.[8] In other words, privacy is the right to be free from intrusion or interference. Individuals should be able to define how far others may access their private space—both physical and informational. In the context of health information, privacy means the 'capacity to control when, how, and to what degree information about oneself is communicated to others'.[9] 'The confiding of the information to the physician for medical purposes gives rise to an expectation that the patient's interest in and control of the information will continue.'[10]

Confidentiality is the duty of healthcare professionals to respect patient wishes regarding their private information. It may be defined as 'the obligations of individuals and institutions to use information under their control appropriately once it has been disclosed to them. One observes rules of confidentiality out of respect for, and to protect and preserve, the privacy of others.'[11] This is a standing obligation, not just for physicians, but for nurses and other health professionals as well.[12]

CASE 3.2	WHOSE RECORD IS IT ANYWAY?

A patient is transferring her care to a new physician. A request is made to her former doctor's office to send a copy of her file to the new physician. The receptionist releases the patient's entire file except for the consult letters. To do so, she says, would be unethical because the letters were the property of the other physicians. Some of the consultants' letters are stamped 'Confidential. Not to be released without permission.'

Is the receptionist correct in holding back part of the patient's chart?

DISCUSSION OF CASE 3.2

All the information in the patient's chart belongs to her. Since she has given permission for a copy of the file to be sent to her new physician, the 'confidential' consult letters should be included. If she wishes, she can also read whatever is contained in her chart. (Of course, her healthcare practitioner or his/her institution has to comply in a reasonable period of time and may charge an appropriate fee for copying the chart.)

The medical record

Patients may permit their personal health information to be released, such as to a lawyer for a medico-legal report or an insurance company or to other physicians. It is ultimately the patient who controls what information may be disclosed and to whom it may be disclosed. Although the physical record belongs to the recording professional or his or her institution, the contents of the record belong to the patient. Patients can access their record (see Box 3.1); they can ask to 'correct' it; they can even in some circumstances close part of it off from scrutiny (put it in a 'black box'). Unlimited access to their records is not absolute, however. If concerned that the information in the chart might negatively affect the welfare of the patient or of another person, physicians can sometimes deny patients access to their record or the right to alter it. This denial may, in turn, be subject to court challenge.

> ## BOX 3.1
> Patients may have access to their records in all but a small number of cases.

Psychiatric protection

More protection has traditionally been given to psychiatrist–patient communications, on account of the more private matters that are discussed and the ill consequences that can accrue to patients if their psychiatric history is revealed (see Box 3.2).[13]

> ## BOX 3.2
> Psychiatrists may be '. . . a special breed of physician who require the certainty of confidentiality even if their brethren can exist without it'.

Nonetheless, psychiatrists and other mental health professionals can be compelled to give evidence in court anywhere in Canada. Presumably, the interests of justice may outweigh the benefits of privacy despite the therapeutic relationship.

Not an arm of the law

The duty of confidentiality prevents doctors and other healthcare professionals from becoming part of the administration of justice—a reminder once again that your main allegiance is usually to the patient, not to third parties. The police, for example, may ask a physician to perform a blood test on or release the toxicology report of a patient suspected of impaired driving. Unless the patient has given consent or the police have a valid warrant, the physician should not breach confidentiality and comply with such requests.[14] (There is now an exception to this rule in several Canadian provinces requiring mandatory reporting of gunshot wounds.)

III. Trade Secrets

Patients who find truths about themselves and others hard to handle may ask for help from the healthcare provider to either continue the deception or to look for 'therapeutic' use of secret information. Openness is a two-way street, however.

Secrets revealed by patients

In their day-to-day practices, healthcare providers may be put in the difficult position of having to weigh patients' requests for privacy against their other professional responsibilities.

CASE 3.3

ASSAULT AND BATTERY

You are the family doctor of a 45-year-old woman admitted with syncope and a possible seizure disorder. This is her second such admission. During her hospitalization three months ago, a complete neurological work-up, including a brain scan, failed to reveal a cause for these symptoms. The attending physician on this admission orders the same tests to be repeated.

Informed of the admission, you come to visit her in the hospital. You are extremely worried: two days previously, the patient had come to see you and had confided the real cause of her last admission was a beating, one of many she had suffered at the hands of her husband. She had never disclosed this to anyone before and asked you to keep the matter a secret. You are sure this is the cause for her present admission. After reviewing the admission notes, you realize this has not been considered by the attending physician.

Should you reveal the patient's secret to her admitting doctor?

DISCUSSION OF AND FOLLOW-UP TO CASE 3.3

Spousal abuse is much underreported and often not suspected by healthcare professionals.[15] However, unless the patient is in imminent danger, you cannot invade her privacy by revealing her secret to others until she is ready to do so. Premature disclosure could undermine the patient's confidence in you and make it harder for her to ask for the help she needs. Although the patient may be given unnecessary medical tests if you do not reveal her secret, this is not a strong enough reason to overrule confidentiality. The greater worry would be about allowing the woman to return to her abusive husband. You must ensure that the woman's physical safety is protected by referring her to the local services and shelters.

This patient was in fact persuaded by her family doctor to disclose the true cause of her injuries to the admitting medical team. Many unnecessary tests were cancelled, and the patient received help to deal with her abusive relationship.

In such cases, where the patient's secret concerns only himself or herself, the patient is generally owed the duty of confidentiality. If the healthcare professional feels the patient is wrong to keep a matter secret, he or she should try to persuade the patient to change his or her mind. Unless the patient is in imminent danger of serious harm to life or limb—a true medical emergency—and suffering from some mental malady that prevents recognition of this, the clinician should abide by the patient's wishes, even if they seem ill-advised.

Secrets revealed by others

Secrets about a patient revealed to the clinician by someone else can also be difficult to handle. Such secrets almost always put the healthcare practitioner in a difficult situation because they threaten to compromise the professional's commitment to the patient and his or her autonomy.

CASE 3.4   A CHANGE OF PERSONALITY

A 66-year-old widow comes to see you for a general checkup, having been seen intermittently in the family practice outpatient clinic for a number of years. Her last annual physical revealed little of note, other than she seemed a little odd. On being questioned about her children's health, it becomes apparent that she is estranged from them. Surprisingly, she is not distressed by this and declines your offer of help.

Several weeks later you receive a call from the patient's two children: did you know that she was a virtual recluse, that she had totally cut herself off from them and their children for seemingly trivial reasons, and that she had sent them long letters full of absurd charges? What, they wonder, is happening to her? They ask you not to tell their mother about their call. They fax you one of her letters. It is rife with elaborate religious and paranoid ideas.

What, if anything, should you do about this new information?

The question is often not whether, but how, secret information should be taken into account while protecting and promoting a patient's autonomy (see Box 3.3).[16] The extent of the responsibility to respect a patient's privacy is unclear, especially where a patient's privacy has already been breached by others. If the clinician uses secret information, is he or she not then party to a deception? If he or she does not, might not the patient's health suffer?

BOX 3.3

'We cannot avoid secrets, disconcerting or otherwise. They come to us unsolicited and by surprise, and, once heard, they change forever the way we feel about a patient.'

DISCUSSION OF AND FOLLOW-UP TO CASE 3.4

The children's secret about their mother suggests she might be psychotic, as opposed to merely eccentric. You should use this information to protect the patient's well-being. In this case the motive for the secret seems well-intentioned: what is the mother's disorder, and can it be treated? It would be quite reasonable to encourage the mother's early return to the clinic so that a fuller psychiatric assessment can be done and the possibility of treatment discussed with her.

Should the mother be told the source of your suspicions? While not telling her might fuel her paranoia should she ever find out about her children's call, telling her now might end whatever hope there is of reconciliation with her children. It would seem prudent not to tell her now, pending the fuller psychiatric assessment, but to devise a plan whereby she could be told when the children are with her at the clinic. (This is an exception to the truthtelling rule—see Chapter 4.)

The patient did return to the clinic, where her delusions and confusion were evident. She agreed to go with her children for a psychiatric assessment, where she was diagnosed with late-onset schizophrenia. Unfortunately, she declined all medications and any other professional assistance to treat her illness. As she posed no danger to herself or others, no treatment or confinement could be forced on her. She did not return for follow-up. This may indicate the physician, emboldened by the children's disclosure of private information about their mother, had acted too quickly on this and undermined the mother's confidence in her relationship with him.

Secrets helpful

Information supplied by others can help the healthcare professional better address a patient's best interests and/or compromised autonomy. A relative may let a clinician know, for example, that a patient with a history of alcohol abuse has again fallen off the wagon, or that a diabetic patient's poor glycemic control is because of failure to follow his or her diet, or that a seemingly well elderly patient is not looking after himself properly at home because of a failing mind. Before acting on such secrets, healthcare professionals need to independently ascertain whether they are true.[17]

Secrets unworthy of protection

Must all of a patient's secrets be protected by the practitioner? The short answer is no. It depends on the nature of the secret and the nature of the patient's relationship with the person who divulges the secret. In other words, some secrets are more worthy of respect because they derive from an altruistic impulse (as in the previous case). By contrast, secrets that are self-serving are often not morally acceptable.

CASE 3.5   AN AFFAIR NOT TO REMEMBER

You are treating a 50-year-old businessman empirically for a presumed sexually transmitted disease contracted during a one-night stand on a sales trip two weeks previously. Since then, he has had unprotected intercourse with his wife. You are also his wife's doctor, and he asks you to put her on antibiotics, in case she too is infected. He does not want the real reason disclosed to her.

'Make up some reason, Doc,' he pleads, 'If you tell her what I've done, my marriage will be over.'

Should you agree?

DISCUSSION OF CASE 3.5

In this case the divulger of the secret is your patient, but his secret concerns the welfare of another of your patients. The real question is whether you can treat the wife without her informed consent. This case does not fall under one of recognized exceptions to truthtelling and consent (see Chapters 4 and 5), and so the wife cannot be given antibiotics without some sort of disclosure.

You could encourage the husband to be open with his wife and use it as an opportunity to discuss their marriage. The real problem is that the husband was treated 'empirically', that is, on the presumption he picked up an infection while travelling, so there is no actual evidence as to what the infection is or was. This was not appropriate as there is now no way of cautioning the wife that she may have contracted a contagious disease requiring medical attention. Despite having no laboratory evidence as to the exact nature of the infection, if you think, in your best clinical judgment, that the husband had harboured an agent of infectious disease, you could call Public Health—at least in some jurisdictions—who might in turn alert the wife.[18] I would also want to be reassured that the husband's actions do not represent some wider impulse disorder, such as mania, that puts him or others at risk.

Secrets affecting others

The new genetic-oriented medicine, having had its biggest impact on testing for diseases or for inherited susceptibilities to diseases in oneself or one's offspring, produces novel ethical challenges as well.

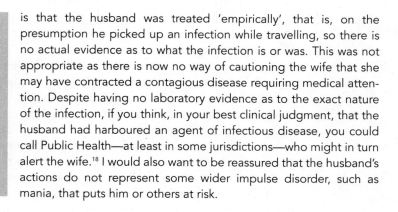

CASE 3.6   ALL IN THE FAMILY?

You are looking after a 24-year-old man who develops ataxia and paranoid ideation. Noticing unusual copper-tinged rings in his pupils, you make a diagnosis of Wilson's disease. (Wilson's disease is a serious illness with protean manifestations that has genetic markers and is amenable to treatment.)[19] Further serological and genetic testing confirms the diagnosis and the patient is started on effective treatment.

The patient has two siblings also in your practice. You advise the patient to disclose his diagnosis to his siblings, recognizing they each have a one in four risk of also having the disease. This, the patient refuses to do, saying he has never gotten along with his siblings and they can 'rot in hell' as far as he's concerned.[20]

What would you do in this case?

DISCUSSION OF CASE 3.6

There is, it seems, a bit of an impasse in this case between confidentiality and beneficence—the patient's wishes are clear and the possible harms to his siblings are also evident. In general, in a conflict between the prevention of serious harm to others and the preservation of privacy, beneficence should prevail. It is unconscionable to allow serious, preventable harm to another person take

place simply on the basis of a blanket principle to protect a 'right to privacy'.

A good clinician—genetics advisor, nurse, social worker, or doctor—would spend time with the patient in an attempt to understand his decision in context. Is his desire to allow potential harm to befall his siblings a manifestation of his paranoid illness? Or is it an extension of bad feelings he has harboured for years?

The right thing is for *someone* to tell the patient's siblings—it would be best if this took place with the patient's consent and indeed if he told them himself. You would certainly be within your professional duty to bring the siblings in for a routine examination and look for evidence of Wilson's disease. Their sensitivity to the disease could be heightened by careful questioning as regards symptoms and signs of the illness.

This ethical dilemma could have been avoided if informed consent to disease testing were more assiduous: the patient could have been warned in advance that, if testing revealed a serious inherited disease, those also potentially affected must, ethically, be informed.

A breach of confidentiality

Long before modern law, Hippocrates said that whatever one heard in the course of medical practice must never be 'spread abroad'.[21] Most modern medical codes of ethics incorporate some such absolutisms about confidentiality but allow breaches wide enough for an army truck to be driven through.

Informal breaches of confidentiality happen all the time: patients are discussed in the halls and even in hospital elevators within earshot of visitors, filing cabinets are left unlocked overnight, patient information is faxed to a wrong number, a hospital healthcare team doing ward rounds talks to a patient about his medical issues in full hearing range of the roommate on the other side of the curtain.[22] More serious breaches of confidentiality occur frequently as well. For example, an inquiry in the late 1970s into the confidentiality of health records in Canada revealed that confidential medical information was revealed frequently and casually by doctors and hospital employees to the police without the patient's consent.[23]

The large number of people—from residents, healthcare trainees, and other healthcare professionals to data clerks and hospital administration employees—with access to the confidential information contained in the hospital chart increases the risk that such information may be inappropriately accessed or misused. Celebrity medical files may be particularly vulnerable to prying eyes.

CASE 3.7   A CASUALTY OF WAR

A Canadian internist-novelist has recently finished a tour of duty as a physician in Afghanistan and decides to write an article about a Canadian soldier he treated. This young man died of wounds suffered in friendly fire. The article, describing in explicit detail the soldier's final hours, is published in a widely circulated American magazine. The soldier is identified by name but permission had not been obtained from his family to make the details of his death public.

Did the physician breach confidentiality in publishing this article?

DISCUSSION OF CASE 3.7

As of this writing, the physician's regulatory college is in the midst of investigating whether he should be subject to disciplinary action. To my mind, there is no question that a breach of confidentiality has occurred. This case raises two questions: (1) If some details of a patient come into public domain, does a duty of confidentiality still exist? (2) Does confidentiality continue after a patient's death?

Answers to both these questions must be 'yes'. Just because someone has been identified in the public domain does not mean he or she has no interest in preserving what privacy remains. A wise judge in 1814 stated, 'Though the defendant might not object to a small window looking into his yard, a larger one might be very inconvenient to him, disturbing his privacy and enabling people to come through to trespass upon his property.'[24]

As for the second question, the respect due persons does not end with death of the person. Just as we treat his or her physical remains in a respectful and dignified way, so should we treat his or her 'informational remains'. This is just common decency.

Professional regulations

It is possible, but rare, for patients to recover damages from a medical professional for breach of confidentiality.[25] This is probably because successful prosecutions would require showing intent on the professional's part to willfully and improperly breach the duty of confidentiality. However, professionals must also live up to regulations set by their licensing bodies which have a lower bar for discipline. Professional regulations bind professionals, as a matter of professional responsibility, to protect their patients' information from others. For example, the code for health professionals in Ontario states that professional misconduct includes 'giving information concerning a patient's condition or any professional services performed for a patient to any person other than the patient without the consent of the patient unless required to do so by law'.[26]

Regulated health professionals may be found guilty of professional misconduct, with resultant disciplinary proceedings, should they, without appropriate rationale (without the patient's permission or unless required by law), disclose private information about a patient. In 1980 a well-known physician and newspaper columnist was found guilty of professional misconduct after disclosing information about a woman (who was named in the article!) in his column. This confidential material, which was obtained from her record, contained information of which even she was unaware. Because she was not his patient, the doctor claimed he owed her no duty of confidentiality. Not surprisingly, the court was unimpressed by this argument.[27]

Privacy laws

Privacy laws are to be had by the legion these days. Federal governments have them, provincial and state legislatures have theirs, too. In medicine, privacy laws remind health professionals of the seriousness of protecting the private health information entrusted in them by patients. In the phrase used in Ontario law, health professionals and their institutions are 'health information custodians'. Information that is scrupulously collected for clinical purposes may be used and disclosed but only with meticulous care.

Many fear an overemphasis on privacy will be bad for patients and bad for research. They argue that this might inhibit healthcare professionals from disclosing needed information to other clinicians in the patient's 'circle of care' and that it might make research too unwieldy. These arguments are not without merit but it should be remembered that when it comes to serious illness, few people will stay at home fretting about gaps in data protection. It is also quite possible for laws to be crafted that allow for reasonable access to patient information and that do not impair high quality research.[28]

Medical practitioners should (1) be aware of pertinent laws or regulations in the jurisdictions in which they practise and (2) avoid the egregious and thoughtless ways in which sensitive patient information can be disclosed. The very good practitioners will look for the gaps where personal information might leak out at their places of study or work and seek ways to fill these in.

CASE 3.8   A VULNERABLE TECHNOLOGY

A medical researcher is running a research study looking at the possible benefits of a new type of medication for diabetes. Because his wife and young children have repeatedly expressed resentment of his staying at the hospital after hours to analyze this data, he has agreed he will work on this at home after the children have been put to bed. The information from the study is put onto his laptop. The data includes patient names, their dates of birth, diagnoses, and test results. One day, he stops off at the grocery store on the way home to buy some bread and milk. When he returns to the car, he discovers to his great horror that his laptop has been stolen from the back seat.

What should the physician do?

DISCUSSION OF CASE 3.8

The right thing to do in this case is for the researcher to inform the appropriate authorities in his hospital about the loss of patient data. Depending on the particular jurisdiction, there may also be an obligation to inform the research subjects of this incident. Although privacy offices in many jurisdictions encourage this, it is only in Ontario, as of the present time, that such notification is mandatory.

While the law aims to strengthen privacy and confidentiality, it must at the same time specify when they may legitimately be breached. This is because the public welfare is often seen to eclipse individual privacy rights.[29]

IV. Limits to Confidentiality

Respecting privacy and maintaining confidentiality are important responsibilities of a healthcare professional—but not the sole responsibilities. The practitioner must constantly weigh their importance against the sometimes countervailing principles of beneficence and justice: '[For example] there may be cases in which reasons connected with the safety of individuals or of the public, physical or moral, would be sufficiently cogent to supersede or qualify the obligations prima facie imposed by the confidential relation.'[30] There are circumstances that permit and others that require that confidentiality be breached.

Mandatory disclosure

In most jurisdictions today, there are a number of circumstances in which it is mandatory to divulge a patient's private medical information:

1. communicable disease
2. child abuse and neglect
3. vulnerable adults
4. driving safety
5. flying safety
6. fitness to work
7. gunshot wounds

1. Public health law
All North American jurisdictions require notification in cases of contagious, communicable, and virulent diseases. For example, in Ontario, healthcare practitioners need only form an '*opinion* that the person is or may be infected with an agent of a reportable disease [and] shall as soon as possible . . . report thereof to the medical officer of health'. This kind of phrasing is found in most public health regulations.[31]

2. Child abuse reporting
In almost all jurisdictions, medical practitioners are required to report any information about the *possible* mistreatment of children. Again, the threshold for reporting is having an *opinion*, based on some reasonable grounds, that the abuse is taking place. Children may be in need of protection because of neglect, failure to provide proper medical treatment, physical or sexual abuse, and so on. Reporting suspected child abuse does not require the consent of the suspected abuser.[32]

3. Vulnerable elderly
Laws to protect vulnerable elderly are not as consistent or available as for children.[33] At the present time, there are few mandates for healthcare professionals to report elder abuse and neglect. In some provinces, there is mandatory reporting of abuse of the elderly or 'serious incidents' in long-term care institutions.[34] For community-dwelling elderly, there is little mandate in cases of suspected neglect, physical, financial, or emotional abuse. Practitioners need to be aware that this too is an area in flux and should familiarize themselves with the laws and regulations in their jurisdictions.

4. Driving safety
In Ontario in 1983 a car driven by a 73-year-old man struck a motorcycle, seriously injuring the two riders. Before the accident, despite knowing for two years that because of cervical spondylosis the man was suffering from weakness of the legs and diminished agility that could affect his ability to drive safely, his family doctor and neurologist failed to report this to the Registrar of Motor

Vehicles. An Ontario court found that their failure to report the patient constituted partial liability for the accident.[35] Although the physicians argued that
reporting was a matter of discretion, the court concluded that the provincial
statute allowed no such exceptions to the duty to report. In this case, the plaintiff was awarded $616,000 with 20 per cent liability assessed against the GP, and
10 per cent liability against the neurologist. Both physicians appealed but lost.

Under highway traffic legislation, physicians in most Canadian provinces and
many US states are required to report the names of patients who, by virtue of
disease, disability, or drugs, may be a danger to others if they drive. (In many
jurisdictions in the world, such reporting is left up to the driver.)[36] Physicians
typically do not relish this responsibility and frequently shirk it.[37] Reporting
such patients can create much distress because driving may appear to be their
last vestige of independence. Nonetheless, the principle of autonomy does not
involve the right to run over others! Consultants as well as family physicians
will be held in breach of such legislation if any of their patients with a known
condition that affects their driving causes a motor vehicle accident and injures
another person.

How weak must someone's legs be, how tardy their reflexes, to impair their
driving? Despite the court's view in the *Toms v. Foster* case earlier in this chapter
that reporting is not a matter of discretion, physicians must use discretion every
day in reporting—is three drinks a day sufficient to impair driving? Five? What
about the use of sedatives? Antidepressants? Is driving safe in very early
dementia? When to report and when not to report can be difficult to determine. Guidelines have been provided and should be known to all doctors.[38]
However, even such guidelines can be vague in certain conditions. When in
doubt, physicians should not hesitate to consult appropriate officials such as
their motor vehicle registrar.

5. Trains and boats and planes

Physicians are similarly required by the federal *Aeronautics Act* to report pilots
and air traffic controllers if they have conditions that might affect flight safety.[39]
Similarly, the *Railway Safety Act* requires physicians to report individuals in
positions critical to railway safety who may be unable to perform their duties.
Merchant seamen may also be required to undergo medical examinations and a
report must be submitted by the examining physician.

6. Fitness to work

Physicians do not have consistent statutory duties to report work-related
medical conditions of their patients. In Canada the Canadian Medical Protective Association has recommended that employees who undergo 'fitness-to-
work' assessments are owed a duty of confidentiality even if the assessment

reveals that the employee has impaired functional capacities.[40] Because such an assessment may have important implications for the patient, a physician doing such assessments must ensure the patient knows who is requesting the assessment and why. Before doing this assessment, the physician should obtain the patient's informed consent to release the results to those requesting it (such as an employer or insurance company).

It is not always clear what to do with a patient who refuses to permit disclosure to the employer of a condition that might constitute a grave danger to others at work. In cases of serious and foreseeable harm to others, especially if imminent, a patient's refusal to consent to the release of pertinent information should not prevent appropriate disclosure by the physician.

7. Other legally required disclosures

Ontario's *Mandatory Gunshot Wound Reporting Act* of 2005 requires public hospitals to report gunshot wounds of patients who present at their facilities. This allows police to act as soon as possible to prevent further violence, injury, or death. Any facility identified by the Act must: (1) make a verbal report to local police authorities if someone is being treated for a gunshot wound; (2) provide that person's name, if known; and (3) give the name and location of the facility. The report must be made as soon as practically possible without interfering with the person's treatment or disrupting the regular activities of the facility.[41]

There is no obligation to keep the patient at the facility until the police come. Releasing to the police any information other than that mandated by the Act would be considered a breach of confidentiality. For example, it is not required to disclose what the patient said about how the gunshot wound occurred. The Act does not mandate all physicians to report gunshot wounds, only the facilities themselves which can then designate the most responsible person to make this report. Therefore, the Act does not apply to medical clinics, doctors' offices, or any other kind of organization providing health services other than those facilities identified by the Act. It makes no distinction between gunshot wounds which are accidental, self-inflicted, or inflicted by another person. All must be reported. To optimize communication, it is recommended the obligation to report be discussed with the patient, as long as this discussion does not put anyone else at risk. Similar legislation has now been enacted in several other provinces.

Physicians must also disclose births, stillbirths, and deaths they attend or of which they are aware. Certain deaths require prompt reports to medico-legal death investigators, such as the coroner or the local medical examiner (see Box 3.4).[42]

> ## BOX 3.3
>
> Medico-Legal Death Investigators' Cases are deaths
>
> 1. resulting from violence, negligence, malpractice;
>
> 2. by unfair means;
>
> 3. related to parturition and childbirth;
>
> 4. which are sudden and unexpected;
>
> 5. from illness not treated by a legally qualified medical practitioner;
>
> 6. from any cause other than disease; and
>
> 7. under circumstances that may require investigation.

Permitted disclosures

In cases of patients who are a danger to others there is a now recognized 'duty to warn'. The US has a fairly clear judicial precedent set by the *Tarasoff* case. In 1969, a university psychologist was told by his patient, Mr Poddar, that he intended to kill a former girlfriend, Tatiana Tarasoff. Concerned, the psychologist and supervising psychiatrist asked the campus police to detain Mr Poddar, but he was released when he appeared rational and promised to stay away from Ms Tarasoff. Two months later, Mr Poddar, who did not return for therapy, murdered Ms Tarasoff. Because no one had warned the victim of her peril, the psychologist and university were later sued for failing to take due care. The California Supreme Court agreed they were negligent in failing to warn Ms Tarasoff.[43]

Although Ms Tarasoff was not the therapists' patient, the court felt she was owed a duty of care because of their relationship with Mr Poddar. The special relationship between patient and therapist engenders *an affirmative duty for the benefit of third parties who might be harmed if the patient is not properly treated.* (Similarly, hospitals or physicians are liable if, because they do not take proper measures, a dangerous patient escapes or harms another patient.) Thus, where a mentally ill patient poses a 'serious and foreseeable risk' to a third party, physicians are obliged to do what is necessary to protect those third persons. If providing 'reasonable care' in such circumstances involves giving a warning, the physician must do so.

The court weighed the importance of protecting the patient's privacy but concluded that this must take second place to 'the public interest in safety from violent assault. . . . The protective privilege ends where the public peril begins.' According to this ruling, where there is a real hazard to an individual or the community and no other way of relieving this hazard, the patient–therapist confidentiality rule must yield to the interests of safety.

A similar precedent was set in Canada in a case which went to the Supreme Court: a psychiatrist was retained by a defence lawyer to examine his client who had been charged with aggravated assault on a prostitute.[44] The lawyer indicated to the accused that what he said during the consultation would be privileged. During the interview, the accused described in some detail his plan to kidnap, rape, and kill prostitutes. The psychiatrist informed the defence lawyer that he thought the accused was dangerous and likely to commit future offences unless he received sufficient treatment. The accused subsequently entered a plea of guilty. When the psychiatrist found out his concerns about the client's dangerousness would not be addressed in the sentencing hearing, he commenced action for declaration that he could disclose his concerns in the interests of public safety. The trial judge ruled the psychiatrist should be mandated to breach confidentiality; when the case was subsequently brought up to the Court of Appeal, it was agreed disclosure was warranted in this case because the threat was clear, serious, imminent, and directed against an identifiable group of persons.

In a later US ruling on *Tarasoff* ('*Tarasoff II*'), the court reaffirmed its view that medical professionals ought to err on the side of public safety when it comes to dangerous patients, despite the possible negative implications for privacy: 'The risk that unnecessary warnings may be given is a reasonable price to pay for the lives of possible victims that may be saved' (see Chapter 7 on Beneficence).[45]

Give warnings to protect others

The argument against these rulings is that, without guarantees of confidentiality, confidence in healthcare professionals will be undermined. Dangerously ill patients will not be identified because they will avoid seeking treatment and so, in the long run, public safety will suffer. Other legal limitations on confidentiality, however, have evidently not undermined the public's trust in medicine. Since the *Tarasoff* case, virtually every US jurisdiction that has ruled on the issue has found a Tarasoff-like duty to warn and/or protect.[46]

As there is no Canadian law requiring citizens to report persons they believe may be dangerous, it used to be thought that doctors are similarly prohibited from reporting such matters. This advice is now recognized as mistaken. Forty years ago a jurist sagely observed: 'No patient has the moral right to convince his psychiatrist that he is going to commit a crime and then expect him to do nothing because of the principle of confidentiality.'[47] The duty to warn is now acknowledged in Canada.

This sea change in opinion came about at least in part due to the conviction in 1993 of Colin McGregor for the first-degree murder of his estranged wife,

Patricia Allen, an Ottawa lawyer. Six weeks earlier, Mr McGregor had informed his physician he planned to murder his wife. His doctor took no action to warn Ms Allen, following codes of confidentiality of the Canadian Medical Association at that time.

A consensus panel, in part funded by the Estate of Ms Allen, made recommendations in 1998 regarding the duty to warn for the medical profession.

> There should be a duty to inform when a patient reveals that he or she intends to do serious harm to another person or persons and it is more likely than not that the threat will be carried out. . . . Taking all the circumstances into account, physicians will want to consider very carefully whether they should report threats and will, if there is any doubt, err on the side of informing the police because of the potential seriousness of the consequences in the event that they decide not to inform.[48]

What remains uncertain is how grave the threat must be to the administration of justice or public safety in order to trigger disclosure.

Professional reporting

Until now, I have focused on the different circumstances under which health professionals are obliged to breach a patient's privacy. Health professionals are also expected to disclose information about the risks that physicians and other health professionals may pose to the public. This is of concern to many as it is not yet clear how far this duty will extend and how vigilant physicians must be regarding their colleagues.

Fitness to practise

Healthcare professionals are not obliged to disclose their own health status to their patients. Nonetheless, it behooves individuals who have a condition that might worsen over time to be knowledgeable about it, to be vigilant in monitoring it, to seek care from appropriate medical practitioners, and to accept professional recommendations regarding care and treatment. Professionals who carry diseases like Hepatitis B or HIV—ones that are transmissible, serious, and might impair the ability to practise safely—are required in some jurisdictions to inform their regulatory organizations, which may then require third-party monitoring and set limits on their practice.

Physicians in Canada are permitted to report their colleagues whom they suspect to be unfit to practise because of illness or addiction. After several rather horrendous cases, the United Kingdom has enacted far-reaching legislation that makes it mandatory to report unfit healthcare professionals and protects whistle-blowers.[49] Whatever the legal status of such reporting, there would seem to be strong moral reasons to report colleagues who are a danger to others.

Traditionally, healthcare professionals have been reluctant to 'blow the whistle' on an incapacitated colleague. This may be out of misguided loyalty or fear of repercussions for themselves.[50] Even when a colleague's infractions are serious, reporting such behaviour will not necessarily find peer support. A profession can close ranks against a member who makes waves. Though whistle-blowing can protect the public from harm, many whistle-blowers have done so at considerable personal risk (see Box 3.5).[51]

BOX 3.5

Guidelines for whistle-blowing:

- Ensure the wrongdoing is grave.
- Document all information well.
- Look for peer support.
- Follow institutional channels of complaint but do not necessarily expect institutional support.
- Make disclosures in good faith.
- Always assume one's disclosure will be made public.

Some jurisdictions besides the UK have legislation in place to protect whistle-blowers. Whether this makes the job of would-be whistle-blowers any easier is another story.

CASE 3.9   TRAINEE TROUBLE

A senior medical trainee finally gets to look after his own patients. He enjoys the responsibilities and is often at the hospital late looking up lab reports and studying the intricacies of his patients' illnesses. A close friend asks if he wouldn't mind looking in on his sister who was admitted recently. The student vaguely knows her and readily offers to help out. He pulls up her chart on the ward computer. To his surprise he finds out she has been admitted following a suicidal drug overdose. The admitting history documents previous attempts at suicide and an impulsive, histrionic personality disorder. The student logs off the computer and wonders what he should do with his newfound knowledge.

What should the medical trainee do?

DISCUSSION OF CASE 3.9

The student is now in a bit of a sticky wicket. He will feel pressured by his friend to disclose this information about his sister. On the other hand he will know such information is intensely personal and not to be shared with others. The student has, without the patient's consent, invaded her privacy and, no doubt, violated the hospital's code of privacy by accessing the chart of a patient not under his care. To make amends he should seek out the appropriate staff person—or perhaps the hospital's privacy officer—and admit the error of his ways. Although done with good intentions, his actions, if discovered by others, could result in disciplinary actions. He ought to have realized that the only persons with authorized access to a patient's chart are the patient, those within the 'circle of care' for the patient, and persons allowed by the patient to do so.

CONCLUSION

Confidentiality is far from a decrepit concept, as some have claimed. It remains a core component of patient autonomy and is defended by the courts and new privacy laws. When confidentiality and privacy are casually breached, patients' autonomy and their trust in medicine are undermined. They can feel as violated as if their dwelling were burglarized. Where they are breached, it must only be for clear and good reasons, such as saving lives and preventing serious harms. In Chapter 4, the subject of another key feature of autonomy—truthtelling—will be considered.

THE POWER TO HEAL: TRUTH, LIES, AND DECEPTION IN CLINICAL PRACTICE

Words which burnt like surgical spirit on an open wound, but which cleansed, as all truth does.

Lawrence Durrell, 1960[1]

Patients have a need for and an interest in medical information independent of issues concerned with consent to medical treatment. This chapter discusses the nature of and complexities associated with such disclosure, that is, truthtelling. Disclosure related specifically to consent will be considered in Chapter 5.

I. TRUTHTELLING AND DECEPTION

CASE 4.1   **A 'WELL WOMAN' WITH A BLURRY PAST**

A 26-year-old accountant, a new patient of your family practice health team, comes in for a 'well woman' examination. She recounts nothing of significance except for a single episode one year ago of weakness in one arm and blurring of vision unaccompanied by headache. These symptoms disappeared within 24 hours. The patient was sent to a neurologist who, after conducting several tests, reassured her that there was no evidence of stroke and advised her not to worry about the episode. She has indeed thought no more about this. Other than chronic fatigue, the patient seems to be currently symptom-free.

When her old medical records arrive, there is a letter from the specialist to the patient's previous doctor stating she almost certainly has multiple sclerosis (MS). The neurologist says it is his custom not to disclose the diagnosis too early as it causes excessive worry. He urges the family physician not to inform the patient.

What should you, as the new family physician, do now?

Physicians and other healthcare professionals regularly make decisions regarding how and how much to tell patients about their medical condition. Although most acknowledge the importance of telling the truth, medicine has been known for its parsimonious approach to truthtelling. Consider the origin of the phrase *doctoring the truth*: 'to treat so as to alter the appearance, flavour, or character of, to disguise, falsify, tamper with, adulterate, sophisticate, cook.'[2] Not very flattering, is it?

Truthtelling is the attitude and practice of being open and forthright with patients. It is not necessarily about telling the 'whole truth', a usually impossible task, but about *intending not to mislead or deceive*. Information necessary for patients to 'make sense' of their medical situation is conveyed. There are so many ways to mislead patients, it takes clinicians some work and thought to decide how best to present patients with information in unbiased ways.[3] Deception, by contrast, turns clinicians away from efforts to help patients gain better insight into their conditions. It involves withholding information from, or actively lying to, patients in order to bring about a certain outcome the healthcare provider desires. Healthcare professionals may deliberately or accidentally engage in deceptive practices with patients for a variety of reasons from the benign (therapeutic) to the malignant (personal gain).

II. Some Reasons Not to Tell the Truth

The eighteenth-century philosopher Kant's view was that lying is *always* wrong—even if necessary, for example, to thwart the efforts of a would-be killer who is seeking out someone you know.[4] Kant reminds us of the importance of principles: one's position, to be justifiable, should be 'universalizable'—able to be made into a rule to be followed by all rational beings. This view seems impractical and counterintuitive. Truthtelling cannot be an absolute—most of us acknowledge that there are times when the full truth must be restrained in proportion to its hazards and pitfalls. This does mean turning one's back on principles if they do not always apply or if they may conflict with other important priorities such as protecting one's friends from harm. There are standards of veracity that may apply in different circumstances.

The standards and expectations for truthtelling in clinical practice may be quite different than those in everyday life.[5] While in the everyday world, tact

may be used to avoid uncomfortable issues, discomfiting truths cannot be
readily or easily avoided in medicine. Historically, the 'truth' in medicine was
used in the service of therapeutics: truthtelling in medicine was done to
encourage 'patient compliance' and not done if it might encourage non-compliance or suffering on the patient's part.

The truth is that the truth *can* hurt patients and this has made doctors wary of
being too forthright. Advanced malignancies, dementia, HIV seropositivity, and
neurological conditions such as MS—serious diseases not amenable to treatment
until recently—have all posed challenges for clinicians to disclose in a
forthright and compassionate way.[6] Patients can likewise avoid unwelcome
truths: for example, many of those at risk for Huntington's chorea decline to be
tested.[7] After all, how many of us would want to know how or when we will die,
supposing such things could be known?

Truthtelling can result in 'labelling' patients, which then can lead to negative
consequences such as excessive worry about the future or the failure to fulfill
role expectations such as work attendance and family obligations. For example,
patients told they had hypertension exhibited decreased emotional well-being
and more frequent absence from work.[8] In another study, more information to
patients with cancer resulted in higher anxiety levels than those not so
informed.[9] Labelling can also result in shunning, discrimination, and exile.
(Think of how patients diagnosed with leprosy, AIDS, or schizophrenia were and
are treated.) Concerns regarding the other very bad outcomes of disclosure—
complete loss of hope, premature death, or suicide—are, however, anecdotal
and lack any real empirical foundation.

The news to be told to patients is also rarely black or white.[10] Uncertainty
about the diagnosis, prognosis, and the potential impact of various therapies
makes clinicians wary of a simplistic approach to truthtelling. For this reason,
many practitioners feel that ruling out deceptive and paternalistic practices is to
forbid use of a needed part of the therapeutic armamentarium, the 'therapeutic
(white) lie'. In this view, medicine is seen as inherently deceptive and paternalistic: its success rests as much in art and acting as in science and evidence. Some
patients, it is said, may wish to be 'deceived' or, at least, not be told 'everything'.
If practitioners can never be careful with what they disclose, they may be unable
to maintain patient hope, the belief that they *will* get better, in the face of
terrible news. Indeed, some patients, under the influence of the 'less than the
full truth' disclosure, do get better, against all odds. This, in some people's
minds, justifies deception.

The psychiatrist Michael Balint, in his analysis of general practice in the
1950s and 1960s, wrote one of the most profound books on medicine, *The
Doctor, His Patient and the Illness*. He held that the strongest drug in medicine is
the 'doctor' and his or her 'apostolic role', the ability to convert the patient to

the doctor's ideas about illness and healing.[11] This entails something more than evidence-based medicine. Physicians need to instill in patients a hope and faith in medicine that goes beyond the results of the latest randomized controlled trial. Even modern medicine would require its healers to have a bit of that old-fashioned snake-oil salesman approach. This may in part account for the 'success' of placebos and, perhaps, of unproven therapies, such as some 'alternative medicines'.[12]

Given all this, it is perhaps not surprising to find how deferential law and social custom were to the common practice of 'doctoring the truth'. Until 40 or 50 years ago, even in Western democratic societies with some sort of commitment to 'informed consent', deceptive practices by physicians were commonly sanctioned as acceptable practice.

In a 1954 case concerning a gynecologist who failed to inform a patient of a large needle left accidentally in her perineum following an episiotomy because it might cause her 'excessive worry', the judge opined that this failure to disclose was acceptable because it was done for the patient's own good: 'I cannot admit any abstract duty to tell patients what is the matter with them . . . it all depends on circumstances . . . the patient's character, health, social position . . . etc.'[13]

Courts were even more loath to find fault with professionals withholding information from patients with serious diagnoses such as dementia, multiple sclerosis, or end-stage cancer, at a time when no effective treatments were available. Patients, especially when ill, were presumed to have difficulty handling the unvarnished truth and so it was the doctor's duty to keep the 'whole truth'—or even a 'partial truth'—from them.[14] Some cultures and families still believe truthtelling is cruel because it may cause avoidable worry in the ailing or frail member. This 'protective deception' has some credence, especially at times when, and in those places where, medicine could offer little tangible help to patients.

DISCUSSION OF CASE 4.1

The patient's previous doctors need to be consulted. How certain were they of the diagnosis of MS? Were there special circumstances at that time to justify not telling this patient her possible diagnosis? A policy of not disclosing potential diagnoses is not consistent with good and prudent medical practice. If a serious diagnosis is made with some reasonable probability—the 'working diagnosis', as it were, and not mere speculation—then the patient needs to be told this in a timely way. The patient should be informed that the diagnosis may be uncertain and warned about what might transpire, what symptoms would be of concern, and when to return for medical care. *In general, the more serious the diagnosis (and especially where consent to effective treatment is at stake), the greater the duty to 'tell the truth'.* Of course, such disclosure should be done cautiously and should be driven by the patient's desire to be informed.

If this patient is not told about the possibility of MS and makes a life decision that adversely affects her condition, the physicians could bear some liability—moral or professional—if she can demonstrate that she would not have made that decision had she known her diagnosis. Likewise, if her condition worsens because she fails to seek out new treatments due to this willful shortfall in truthtelling, the physicians could bear responsibility.

Practically speaking, this patient, as with others who are deceived, will eventually find out that she has been deceived. What will this do to her faith in medicine and her care providers? How could she recover from this wound? Due to such downstream ill consequences of deception, decisions to withhold the truth from patients must be taken with extreme caution.

III. SOME REASONS TO TELL THE TRUTH

There are many reasons, philosophical and practical, apart from Kant's, to make truthtelling with patients the default position (see Box 4.1).

BOX 4.1

Good reasons for telling the truth are:

1. It promotes good outcomes.

2. It reduces risks of harm to patients.

3. It furthers the patient's life choices.

4. It shows respect for persons.

5. It promotes trust.

6. It reduces litigation.

1. Promotes good outcomes

Truthtelling increases patient compliance (concordance) with prescribed medications,[15] reduces morbidity such as pain[16] and anxiety[17] associated with medical interventions, and improves patient comprehension of medical decision making.[18] Informed patients report more satisfaction with their care and are less apt to change physicians than those not well informed.[19]

2. Reduces risks of harm to patients

Non-disclosure and deceit can harm patients in many ways. For example, if not informed about their medical condition, they may fail to obtain medical attention when they should. (This aspect of disclosure, which is most intimately associated with consent, will be discussed in greater detail in Chapter 5.) One difficulty is knowing what level of certainty must be achieved to trigger disclosure. There is no simple answer but, if the healthcare professional reasonably suspects a serious diagnosis, there is an onus to caution the patient about this.

Clinical uncertainty can be shared with patients.[20] Informing patients about the uncertainties and the range of available treatment options allows them to appreciate the complexities of medicine, to ask questions, to make informed and realistic decisions, to assume responsibility for those decisions, and to be better prepared in case the dire prognosis turns out to be correct. Doubtless some patients find the uncertainty confusing and will need to rely more on the healthcare provider's helping hand in making decisions.

3. Furthers patients' life choices

CASE 4.2	NOT TO WORRY

In British Columbia in 1986 a woman in the twelfth week of a much-wanted pregnancy contracted chicken pox. Wary of traditional medicine, she had engaged the services of a midwife for the delivery. The patient and her husband, wanting to keep medical interventions to a minimum, had earlier refused an obstetrical ultrasound. Her family doctor told the woman the fetus could suffer some abnormalities of limb and skin as a result of the chicken pox but reassured her that the risk was small and not a reason for an abortion. The child was carried to term but unfortunately was born with congenital varicella syndrome. She has spent much of her life in hospital.

The parents filed a 'wrongful life' suit against the doctor (see Chapter 9 for a more detailed discussion of this topic), alleging they would have aborted had they known all the risks to the fetus from exposure to varicella. The doctor explained she had not disclosed the serious but unlikely risks (such as cortical atrophy) because she had not wished to worry an expectant mother, especially with reasons that did not in her mind justify abortion.

Was the physician right in failing to disclose all the risks?

Failure to provide information that is of central importance to a patient's future means depriving that person of one means by which he or she can live as he or she sees fit. Rather than asking, 'Can the patient stand being told?' one should ask: 'Can the patient stand not being told?'[21] Certainly, patients should be offered the opportunity to know of medical evils that threaten them. Providing accurate information about an illness that will affect how they will lead their lives in the future allows patients to plan for that future.

Not telling patients some important information about their lives—such as their prognosis—suggests that the healthcare professional knows better than they what should be done with this information. Consider how unlikely this is: for this to be so, the professional would have to be familiar with intimate facts concerning the lives of their patients as well as knowing their values and beliefs and how they would apply them.

DISCUSSION OF CASE 4.2

In this case the suit was unsuccessful because the judge was not convinced this couple would have in fact aborted, given the small risk of serious abnormalities and their reluctance to accept conventional medicine. However, the court did find the doctor's explanation negligent as, 'without complete candour', she could not 'properly assist her patients with such a deep and disturbing decision'.[22] It is actually surprising the doctor won this case—the judge used as the standard for disclosure what *this* patient would have wanted to know. The more common standard is what a 'reasonable person' would want to know: a reasonable person, surely, would want to know about potential defects in order to be better prepared for them, not necessarily just to be able to make a decision to abort the fetus.

Keeping information from patients may be done with good intentions. Generally, however, it is wrong if this results in doctors making particularly intimate decisions for patients, such as ones regarding abortion, that should be the patients' to make. This case is also about shared decision making, which will be discussed in Chapter 5.

4. Shows respect for persons

CASE 4.3   A DARK SECRET

A 20-year-old female student has recently become a patient in your primary care practice. She has been well other than undergoing surgery as a young teen for what she was told were 'diseased reproductive organs'. She knows little else about that surgery.

When her medical records are received, there is a letter from her pediatrician stating that 'she' is, in fact, genetically a male with Androgen Insensitivity Syndrome. (In this disorder of gonadal dysgenesis, patients usually have an XY karyotype with inguinal testes and a female phenotype. Due to lack of responsiveness to testosterone in utero, male genitalia do not form. The child is often not diagnosed until puberty when such individuals fail to menstruate. The testes are removed during adolescence because of the risk of gonadal cancer.) The patient's family and her physicians had decided not to tell the patient of her 'true sex', feeling it would possibly cause great psychological trauma. The letter urges all future healthcare providers not to tell her.

You pride yourself on being honest with your patients; you think it is extremely important that patients be as well informed as possible.

What, if anything, should you say to this patient?

Patients have an interest in any information that concerns who they are as people—beyond the information needed for decisions about medical treatment. Whether patients do anything with medical or 'personal health information', as it is now called, is a separate issue. For example, a patient's desire to take an active role in making decisions about treatment 'may be less strong than [simply] the need for clear and accurate information'.[23]

Patients should, in this view, be told the truth because of the respect due to them as persons; the truth can empower them and encourage authenticity and autonomy. Empowering patients should be recognized as one of the central goals of modern medicine, as important as the amelioration of suffering and the prevention of premature death. Interviews with patients generally support this perspective. For example, in a study done before any treatment for MS existed, patients with the disease felt they had a right to know what was wrong with them. Some were angry about being asked why they wished to know. One said: 'Do I have to explain why? Just so that I know.'[24]

The principle of respect for persons—encouraging valid choice, promoting patient empowerment, supporting authentic hope—calls for honest disclosure. Doctors who withhold critical information from patients are denying them the opportunity to live and die as they see fit—this practice denies patients an opportunity to cope and hope on their own terms. Hope does not require dishonesty.[25] Very ill patients may want someone to look after and guide them, but this does not necessarily mean a preference for ignorance or deception. Allowing others to make decisions for oneself, to be 'taken care of' in the full sense of this phrase, can be consistent with wishing to remain informed about one's condition.

DISCUSSION OF AND FOLLOW-UP TO CASE 4.3

Testicular feminization syndrome (or Androgen Insensitivity Syndrome as it is better known today) is a dark secret for some.[26] In the past, the diagnosis was commonly not disclosed to those with this condition. It is unfortunate that those who participated in the original treatment of this patient failed to consider how her condition might be revealed to her later in life.

At this point we need to know more about the patient: is she the type of patient who wishes to be as fully informed as possible? Unless she evinces a clear wish not to know, she should be told. It is, after all, her life. You should seek guidance from skilled counsellors unless you have had experience with other cases. Disclosing this syndrome could be devastating to an unsuspecting patient, and the effect may be compounded if you fail to explain correctly what the condition means. Her sense of herself could be deeply shaken. Sensitive counselling as to the nature of sexuality and personal identity will be vital. You need to investigate what kind of resources will be available to help this patient cope in the future.

Interestingly enough, when this patient was told the truth, her longstanding feelings that she was 'different' from other women as regards her sexual identity were confirmed. She was relieved to find a physical basis for her feelings. Indeed, she laughed when told about her condition! So much for the expected devastating effects of telling the truth! She did, however, express anger towards her previous doctors and her parents, who had deceived her for so long.

5. Promotes trust

Cabot's 1903 view that physicians should strive to create a 'true impression' in the mind of the patient about his or her condition and thereby foster the covenant of trust between physician and patient is consistent with this perspective.[27] This view applies to all healthcare professionals, not just physicians. This contrasts with the centuries-old medical tradition cautioning against veracity with patients.

Not to tell patients the full truth about their condition is to deceive them. One lie often involves a network of deception and coverup. Proper disclosure to patients saves healthcare providers from entering this labyrinth of lying. Bok notes *it is easy to tell one lie but hard to tell only one*. Deceit undermines the bond of trust between the healthcare provider and patient and produces 'corrosive worry' in patients who are deceived.[28] Deceit can also undermine the public's faith in medicine. Lies from a health professional, whether done for ill or the best of intentions, can seem particularly shocking when revealed to the public eye.

6. Reduces litigation

Failure to be entirely truthful with patients, even if it leads to good outcomes (such as sickness amelioration, avoidance of anxiety), can lead to physician domination of decision making and this can, in turn, lead to patient disappointment, discontent, and litigation. When things don't go well, good communication skills are even more important as a protective factor against legal actions initiated by patients.[29] (A more detailed discussion of disclosure of medical error is to be found in Chapter 8.)

IV. MODERN LAW AND THE PROFESSION

Despite all this, there is no 'law' requiring healthcare professionals to be honest with patients. There is little case law requiring honesty either. Not surprisingly, existing jurisprudence relevant to truthtelling varies among countries and is largely focused on negligent disclosure for consent purposes.

Canadian courts have long recognized the physician's obligation to provide information that would be required by a reasonable patient in the plaintiff's position (*Reibl v. Hughes* 1980; see Chapter 5). Australian[30] and most American jurisdictions[31] similarly use this so-called modified-subjective standard while British courts seem largely to adhere to a 'profession-based standard' of disclosure (what a reasonable professional would disclose).[32] Although the latter standard would seem to favour physicians who fail to disclose, 'it ain't necessarily so'. If the profession is turning in the direction of open disclosure, then clinicians who fail to do so may find themselves without a defence.

Indeed the profession of medicine, at least in North America, has turned squarely in the direction of openness with patients. The American College of Physicians recommends: 'However uncomfortable for the clinician, information that is essential to, and desired by, the patient must be disclosed. How and when to disclose information, and to whom, are important concerns that must be addressed with respect for patient wishes.'[33] It adds that the professional duty to be honest with patients requires due care: 'Disclosure and the communication of health information should never be a mechanical or perfunctory process. Upsetting news and information should be presented to the patient in a way that minimizes distress.'

The British Medical Association notes that the 'relationship of trust depends upon "reciprocal honesty" between patient and doctor' and also encourages the sensitive delivery of bad news.[34] The Canadian Medical Association's Code of

Ethics recommends that physicians provide patients with whatever information that might, from the patient's perspective, have a bearing on medical decision making and communicate that information in a comprehensible way.[35]

V. THE CHANGING PRACTICE OF MEDICINE

The modern emphasis on truthtelling is reflected in the empirical literature concerning the practice of medicine.

What doctors do

Oken's landmark 1961 survey of 219 physicians in the United States found that 90 per cent would not disclose a diagnosis of cancer to a patient.[36] Attitudes towards disclosure were influenced by personal and emotional factors. Many expressed pessimism and futility about cancer treatment. Others feared their patients would become more depressed or commit suicide, although such fears were based on no actual evidence. Oken's study dates from before the advent of informed consent; its findings reflect the era of 'medical paternalism', not so long ago, when doctors made decisions for competent patients.

More typical of the attitudes of physicians today were findings published almost 20 years later. A survey of 264 American physicians in 1979 showed that 97 per cent of them would disclose a diagnosis of cancer.[37] This indicates a complete reversal in the practice of telling patients the truth, at least as far as the diagnosis of cancer goes.

Other studies suggest a less than complete conversion to medical candour. In one US study, physicians who reported that they commonly tell cancer patients the truth said they did so in a way intended to preserve 'hope' and 'the will to live', both valued notions in US society.[38] Compared to their North American counterparts, gastroenterologists from southern and eastern Europe are less likely to be candid with patients about serious disease, believing this to be the best way to preserve 'hope'.[39] Of course, hope and truth are not as mutually exclusive as these practices might suggest.

What patients want

The majority of empirical studies have indicated that patients do want to know the truth. Studies as far back as 1950, reviewed in Oken's 1961 paper, revealed that 80 to 90 per cent of patients wanted to be told if the examination revealed a diagnosis of cancer. Typical of the studies Oken examined was one conducted in 1957 by Samp and Curreri in which 87 per cent of a group of 560 cancer patients and their families felt a patient should be told the truth.[40]

An American survey in 1982 by the President's Commission on Ethical Problems in Medicine revealed that 94 per cent of patients want 'to know everything' about their condition, 96 per cent want to know a diagnosis of cancer, and 85 per cent want to know a realistic estimate of their time to live, even if this was less than one year.[41] More recent reports have indicated that over 90 per cent of patients want to be told a diagnosis of Alzheimer's disease[42] and over 80 per cent of patients with amyotrophic lateral sclerosis want as much information as possible.[43] Studies of older patients, sometimes thought to be less interested in the truth, have shown that almost 90 per cent want to be told the diagnosis of cancer.[44]

Other studies, not surprisingly, suggest cultural influences upon truthtelling preferences. For example, one study found a greater percentage of Korean-born patients preferred to be given less information than did US-born patients.[45] In Italy, lack of candour about the diagnosis of Alzheimer's disease is common.[46] A greater percentage of patients in Japan as compared with the US (65 per cent versus 22 per cent) would want their families to be told a diagnosis of cancer before being informed themselves, and many more Japanese than US doctors agreed with this (80 per cent versus 6 per cent).[47] As a result, patients with advanced cancer in Japan are told their prognosis only if their families consent.[48]

Cultural attitudes are hardly fixed. Recent trends suggest a global interest in obtaining information and a decline in 'professional discretion' to withhold it.[49] North American culture has changed drastically in the past 50 years in the direction of openness, a trend that continues today as more information becomes available on-line. The influence of the World Wide Web on undemocratic and closed systems has been, and will continue to be, profound.

VI. SOME EXCEPTIONS TO TRUTHTELLING

Healthcare professionals need to be clear about when and how they can legitimately conceal important information from their patients. (Similar exceptions to disclosure apply to informed choice and these will also be discussed in Chapter 5.) The four exceptions to truthtelling are:

- patient's waiver
- incapacity of patient
- medical emergencies
- 'therapeutic privilege'

1. Patient's waiver

CASE 4.4   WHO TO TELL?

You are a surgeon who performs an elective laparoscopic cholecys-tectomy on a 32-year-old mother of two. Unfortunately, what appeared to be a gallbladder cyst on CT turns out to be a solid mass. The surgery is converted to an open procedure. An intra-operative frozen section demonstrates adenocarcinoma of the gallbladder, a disease with a poor prognosis. Her estimated survival is six months to a year.

After the procedure, you inform her husband in the recovery room of the intra-operative findings. Devastated, he asks that his wife not be informed of the findings and the prognosis. According to the couple's culture, the husband speaks for the family; he prefers to have her enjoy the remaining months of her life without sadness and stress.

How should this situation be handled?

Studies suggest that 10 to 20 per cent of all patients do not want to know the details of their condition. The right to know is waived when patients tell their healthcare providers they do not wish to know some particular piece of infor-mation that most patients would want and need to know. This waiver may be a legitimate preference on the part of patients and is, in general, their 'right not to know'.

For example, some patients with terminal illnesses may indicate explicitly or implicitly that they do not want to know the full truth. Healthcare professionals should be sensitive to such waivers and carefully ensure that the patient is competent and understands the possible consequences of not knowing. An attempt should be made to canvas the patient's views on disclosure by 'offering the truth' to the patient.[50] Prudent practitioners will document such a waiver and will try to bring the issue up again if the patient's condition changes or if new treatments become available. When such desires are authentic and realistic they should be respected.

In some cultures, patients with terminal illnesses such as cancer may prefer that their families, not they themselves, be informed.[51] It is important to ensure this is an authentic patient waiver rather than a reflection of family members wishing to protect their loved one from bad news. Families who resist disclo-sure to the patient should be counselled about the importance of truthtelling, much as they might be counselled about the appropriate management of any medical problem. Ongoing and respectful communication often, but not always, can overcome family and cultural barriers to disclosure.[52]

DISCUSSION OF CASE 4.4

Of course, the patient must be told at some point of her diagnosis—that is, if she truly wants to know. An interpreter who is not a family member should be sought and the patient offered the chance to say in her own words whether she truly wants to forego knowing. As your obligations are to the patient rather than the family, efforts should be made to speak to the patient on her own, without the family as the intermediary, in order to ascertain her preferences. Certain ethnic and cultural differences vis-à-vis honesty in medical care are best handled with skilled facilitators (such as specially trained social workers or patient representatives); physicians should seek their help if they are uncomfortable with a family's requests for a patient.

The need of others to know

Special ethical difficulties can occur when a patient's wish for ignorance may interfere with someone else's need to know. For example, if a patient refuses to undergo predictive screening for a disease with a genetic component (such as Huntington's or hereditary Alzheimer's disease) others who may be affected if the patient is a carrier of genes for the disease may not know until years later that they too are at risk. Some patients would prefer to know sooner than later that they may be affected by such diseases.

How can physicians balance a person's right not to know with someone else's interest in that information? This difficulty is likely to become more of an issue in the future as the human genome project provides comprehensive information about genetic disorders. We do not have a generally accepted answer to this dilemma for genetic disorders but, nevertheless, there are some (evolving) standards and guidelines that can help us: 'If patients refuse to have information [regarding genetic information] disclosed, nonconsensual disclosure is not legally compelled. . . . [It may be justified] on ethical grounds . . . if the [genetic] risks are . . . serious . . . imminent . . . preventable . . . or treatable.'[53]

2. Incapacity

CASE 4.5   'I'M SO STUPID'

You are a family physician seeing an 88-year-old woman brought by her daughter because of concerns she has become increasingly forgetful and is not looking after herself properly. Not having seen her for two years, you are shocked at how impaired mentally she seems. She scores poorly on simple testing for cognitive impairment—at one point she begins to cry and says, 'What's wrong with me? I'm so stupid!' You stop your interview to console your patient who quickly settles down, laughing, 'Oh, I suppose I'm just getting older. You know, my sister and my mother were just like this.'

You feel she almost certainly suffers from either Alzheimer's disease or vascular dementia. Must you tell her this?

DISCUSSION OF CASE 4.5

Here is where having a longitudinal relationship with the patient helps—there will be ample opportunities in the future to disclose the likely diagnosis if this is what the patient wants to know and can appreciate. At this time, you may be unsure about what the patient is prepared to hear. It seems appropriate to reserve the 'full truth' for another day when you can explore with the patient what she understands about 'getting older' and what would best help her cope with her cognitive losses.

If a patient is mentally unable to understand information that would under ordinary circumstances be disclosed, this is an acceptable reason not to disclose information to that patient. Incompetence is not 'all or nothing', however. Respect for the incapable patient can be shown by tailoring information to the degree that this patient is able to understand and appreciate it.

Children

Special precautions apply to children. Although very young children may be unable to understand their medical condition, their capacity to grasp complex information and make decisions increases as they mature.[54] Parents may request that children not be informed of their condition—such as their genetic heritage—but their requests cannot be absolute. Conditions justifying non-disclosure to a child, such as Androgen Insensitivity Syndrome, may no longer hold as the child matures. Decisions to withhold important information from a child should therefore incorporate a plan for disclosing the information as the child grows older (see Box 4.2).

Failing to be honest with children can have lasting negative psychological consequences for them—such as depression and loss of self-esteem.[55] Lack of candour with children can also negatively impact their parents as well. In one study, parents able to be forthright about death with their dying child felt such

> ## BOX 4.2
>
> Decisions to withhold important information from a child should incorporate a plan for disclosure as the child grows older.

open discussion helped them and their child. Parents unable to be so forthright later regretted their reticence and experienced guilt and lasting unhappiness.[56]

3. Medical emergencies

When a patient's medical condition is so unstable that disclosure is considered unsafe or too time-consuming, it is acceptable to withhold certain information (see Box 4.3). To be justified, the emergency exception to the disclosure rule must meet several conditions:

- The emotional or physical condition of the patient must be so severely affected at that time so as not to permit safe communication of information that would ordinarily be disclosed.
- The physician should attempt to revisit the issue of consent and disclosure when the patient appears more stable, that is, when the emergency abates.
- The physician's notes should record his or her thinking in this regard and provide some evidence justifying the use of the emergency exception to disclosure rule.

> ## BOX 4.3
>
> Emergency exception to disclosure
>
> If the unstable condition of a patient may be made worse by disclosure, re-visit the issue when the patient is more stable and be prepared to justify non-disclosure.

4. Therapeutic privilege

'Therapeutic privilege' is invoked when a health professional decides for a seemingly capable patient that it is in the patient's best interests not to know certain information. Doctors (and families) can worry that disclosure might take away hope from patients. This may say more about physicians' and families' ability to cope with telling the difficult news than patients' wishes for deception.

Courts in the US, Canada, and the UK have granted that there may be an exception to truthtelling when the patient's emotional condition is such that the disclosure of bad news could itself cause harm.[57] The most relevant test for non-disclosure is 'whether the disclosure would in itself cause physical and mental harm to this patient'.[58] Strictly speaking, practitioners should understand that *therapeutic privilege is a variant of the emergency exception (or perhaps the incompetence exception) to the rule of disclosure.*

In one case, for example, a physician was found negligent for failing to tell a patient of his risk of having (possibly) acquired HIV infection from a transfusion. Although the doctor argued he had done so to protect the patient from information that would only cause him psychological harm, the court held that *this* patient would have wanted to know this information, even though there was little that could be done at the time for HIV.[59] One key issue in this case was the prevention of harm to others, so this was a case not just about the duty of truthtelling owed to the patient.

Lies
What about the 'therapeutic white lie' mentioned earlier in this chapter? Must one be brutally honest, even in the most dire of circumstances?

| CASE 4.6 | 'AM I GOING TO MAKE IT?' |

A young woman is brought to the emergency room in circulatory collapse. She is hemorrhaging from a lacerated liver. You are an experienced ER nurse who thinks her chances for survival are quite slim to none. The patient is still conscious and alert as she is being wheeled down the hall to the operating room. Just as the cart is about to roll through the swinging doors she asks you, 'What's going on? I'm not going to die, am I?' Stunned for a moment, you wonder how to respond. Your immediate reaction is to reassure the patient—'Of course not, you'll make it.'

Is this the right response?

DISCUSSION OF CASE 4.6

This is clearly an emergency situation. Your reassuring immediate reaction may lessen the patient's anxiety and, so it is argued, could improve the chances of a successful outcome. This response, no doubt what anyone would want to hear, gives the patient no opportunity to express any last wishes she might have . . . along the lines of, 'If I don't make it, make sure . . .'' A more measured reply, then, would be to tell the patient that she is seriously ill but everything

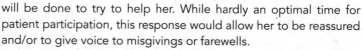

will be done to try to help her. While hardly an optimal time for patient participation, this response would allow her to be reassured and/or to give voice to misgivings or farewells.

If you were the patient, what would you want to be told? That you might die? Or would you want to be 'reassured' that everything will be fine? There are no right or wrong answers *per se* here, but some mix of truthfulness measured with compassion would seem to be most appropriate.

Deceptive practices

Is more direct deception with patients ever acceptable? Is it, for example, ever justified to engage in deceptive practices concerning a patient's medications?

CASE 4.7   BY ANY MEANS POSSIBLE

An 88-year-old man with Alzheimer's disease, a resident of chronic care for five years, has become increasingly resistant to most aspects of care. He particularly enjoys spitting out his pills with great gusto. Recently, he has become more aggressive and seems bothered by paranoid delusions. You, as his primary nurse, are instructed by the attending physician to give him antipsychotic medication by 'any means possible.' You decide to do so by crushing the pill and hiding it in the patient's ice cream.

Is this an acceptable practice?

DISCUSSION OF CASE 4.7

Antipsychotics used in the elderly are not innocuous but can sometimes have a beneficial impact on dementia-associated behavioural difficulties. Such behavioural disturbances can be hazardous, not only to others, but to the individual. The argument may be made that deception is justified under these circumstances when there is no other way of achieving the desired goal of behavioural control. In addition, the hazards of the surreptitiously administered medication must be less than its anticipated benefits.

One could also argue that respecting such patients is achieved by ensuring they get medications that can help restore what autonomy they have left. One could imagine a patient, when well, saying: 'If I am ever demented, please treat me in a way that is appropriate and dignified.' This is not a rationale for doing anything at all with such a patient but would justify some measure of deception if necessary.

Out of considerations of prudence and proper nursing practice, you must ensure the whole team and patient's family/substitute decision maker are on side with this course of action.

Placebos

Another form of active deception is the use of placebos in clinical care. Clinicians have commonly used the deceptive practice of placebo medicine to protect a patient from harm, for example, giving a placebo pain medication to a patient who endangers himself with excessive drug use. Placebos may be rationalized by some variant of therapeutic privilege ('the patient can't handle the truth') or the incapacity exception to disclosure.

Placebos trade on medicine's prestige and power to achieve their desired effect. They are akin to the smoke and curtains used by the Wizard of Oz. Once revealed as what they really are, though, they cannot be used again. As a result, they are rarely justifiable because they can cause patients harm, undermine trust in the medical profession, and destroy any possibility of a therapeutic alliance. They are also usually, medically speaking, poor ways of managing problem patients.

Placebos are best reserved for use in clinical research trials where participants know they may get a placebo instead of the active test substance. In this case the placebo arm stands for the natural course of the studied condition and is justified by the patient's informed consent. (In research some participants may be randomized to receiving a placebo to evaluate whether the test substance is better than doing nothing. Participants in such research must be told about the placebo arm and its implications in consenting to the study.)[60]

Lying to help the patient

If lying to patients is usually morally wrong, what about lying to others to promote a patient's best interests? For example, a patient needs an MRI. Suppose his physician is aware there is a considerable wait time for such imaging but also knows the booking clerk well. Would it be ethically acceptable to 'play up' his patient's symptoms and use his personal relationship with the booking agent to move his patient up in the queue? There is evidence healthcare providers would be inclined to deceive third parties, such as hospital staff or insurance companies, to further their patients' interests.[61]

This practice seemingly pits beneficence against justice, so we will examine this conflict in greater detail in Chapter 9 on Justice. Most people would probably favour physicians acting in mildly deceptive ways ('white lies') if needed to benefit the patient. The concern is that gaming the system works only if everyone does not do so. Clinicians should treat these tactics as precious short-cuts through the system that are to be used but rarely—in true emergencies and not simply for patients who think they are entitled to bypass the unwashed masses, the 'hoi polloi'. Part of the bad news that sometimes must be disclosed to patients is that, not only do they have a problem, but they also have to join the queue and wait, along with others, for definitive testing or treatment.

Breaking bad news
It can be difficult to predict what information a patient will find upsetting or how upsetting that information will be. Poor disclosure practices, even if the information conveyed is accurate, can have devastating consequences for patients.[62] Such disclosure is typically done too hurriedly, in the wrong setting, without appreciation of the patient's circumstances, and without addressing the patient's real needs and fears. Patients need to know, for example, not only a diagnosis, but what it may mean for them, and their family, now and in the future.

Studies show that the way in which the information is given may be just as important as the information itself.[63] Care must be taken that information is given at the right time and in the right place, a 'compassionate milieu'.[64] Even if telling the truth does have some negative consequences, this does not in itself warrant non-disclosure. It is important to break bad news carefully and considerately. The news may be brutal for a patient; the telling of it need not be (see Box 4.4).[65]

BOX 4.4

The hurried telling of bad news in a busy clinic with little explanation and no opportunity for the patient to ask questions can result in unnecessary psychological and emotional pain.

Good communication skills are essential to truthtelling. Done well, information sharing—which includes conveying 'bad news'—will generally improve patient satisfaction and the quality of medical care.[66] In all cases of such sharing, just how and when to discuss the patient's situation, and how much to say at any one time, will vary from one patient to the next.[67] This is the art of truthtelling, relying on the skills and attitudes of the doctor to 'take the patient into his (or her) confidence' and give him (or her) a 'true impression' of his (her) illness.[68]

Suggestions for sharing information
- Be well prepared for the session by having a plan for disclosure before the interview. You need to be as informed as possible about the patient's situation, and know how to get answers for the patient if unable to answer his or her questions. You need to know what the patient needs to do next.

- You may best prepare patients for 'bad news' by warning them that what you are about to tell them is something very difficult.
- Straightforwardness in language and lack of prevarication are essential. You ought to keep medical terms simple, but this may be hard to do; you must make reasonable efforts to help patients understand the news in their own terms.
- Patients must have time to express their fears and worries and will need to understand how the illness is likely to affect their future. You should be available to schedule follow-up sessions as needed, especially if the information is serious or uncertain.
- The sharing of information, whether good or bad, is best done when you and the patient have time for each other. Both parties should be reasonably comfortable; you should sit, not stand. Privacy and a pleasant room are extremely helpful.
- Patients and professionals give non-verbal cues as to how well each is listening to the other. Patients may express strong emotions; this is to be expected and acknowledged. You must be sensitive to the cues from the patient as the bad news is disclosed.

CASE 4.8 'WHAT'S UP, DOC?'

You are a clinical clerk in your final year of medical school, looking after a 60-year-old businessman dying of metastatic adenocarcinoma of uncertain origin. The internist responsible for this patient tells you that the patient is unaware he is dying of cancer. 'It was the family's wish and I went along with it,' she says, 'He thinks he has a bad virus, so don't say anything.'[69]

One day the patient tells you he has blurred vision in the morning that clears as the day goes on. You realize this is an ominous symptom in someone with cancer; it usually means there is papilloedema from brain metastases. Indeed, when you look at his eyes, there is classic retinal papilloedema, just as the textbooks show.

'Well, Doc, is it from the virus?' he asks.

How should you respond?

DISCUSSION OF CASE 4.8

Clinical clerks are often put in a difficult position by the attending staff if the decision has been made to deceive a patient. Trying to be a good 'team player' and not rock the boat may compromise the student's moral integrity.[70] There is no easy way of resolving this particular case. You could seek advice from a senior resident or,

better still, the attending staff person herself. A reasonable answer—one that reflects your humble role—is to say to the patient, truthfully, that you are uncertain of your findings and need first to discuss them with a senior physician. In so gaining time, you and your senior staff may be able to find a way of breaking the bad news, finally, to the patient. By that time, the patient will likely have long suspected the worst. You will then have to figure out how to answer the inevitable question from the patient, 'Why didn't you tell me earlier?'

Conclusion

Modern healthcare professionals have a standing professional obligation to disclose important information to their patients. Some circumstances justify non-disclosure, but these need to be examined thoughtfully and then documented. Although it can be upsetting to give bad news, you should not feel you have to protect your patients from such news. There are ways of delivering it that can soften the blow.[71] The task for healthcare professionals is to combine honesty and respect for patient autonomy with caring and compassion.

In Chapter 5 I will look at healthcare professionals' responsibilities regarding disclosure for the purposes of informed consent.

CHAPTER 5

THE POWER TO CHOOSE: DUE CARE AND INFORMED CONSENT

Over himself, over his own body and mind, the individual is sovereign.

John Stuart Mill, 1859[1]

Respect for the patient's right of self-determination on particular therapy demands a standard [of disclosure] set by law for physicians rather than one which physicians may or may not impose upon themselves.

Canterbury v. Spence, 1972[2]

Informed consent has been called a 'sword and shield', a doctrine and a practice by which patients may protect themselves from unwanted interventions and take responsibility for shaping their lives as they see fit.[3] This can also be a shield for the physician, a protection from litigation. The best defence—and best prevention—against suits alleging failure to obtain consent is to communicate faithfully in a timely and honest way with patients and help them make decisions that best express their genuine wishes. In this chapter I will examine the requirements for consent in greater detail.

The rationale for consent is not primarily a legal one, of course. Consent is fundamental to the modern liberal idea of democracy. As the nineteenth-century British philosopher John Stuart Mill wrote in his wonderful essay *On Liberty*: 'the only purpose for which power can be rightfully exercised over any member of a civilized society, against his will, is to prevent harm to others. His own good, either physical or moral, is not a sufficient warrant.'[4] Consent in healthcare is about realizing this philosophical idea in a traditionally hierarchical and paternalistic profession.

CASE 5.1   A SIMPLE PROCESS

A 78-year-old man with a long history of 'wear and tear' arthritis presents with a disabling exacerbation in both knees. He is well other than having a remote history of stomach ulcers and is on no medications. As his primary care physician, you feel he should have certain tests done (knee X-rays and some bloodwork) and you believe he would probably benefit from an anti-inflammatory pill. You inform him of your diagnosis and explain what he needs done and why you think he may be helped by that particular medication. You also explain the potential risks of the medication (high blood pressure, kidney impairment, bleeding ulcers, rarely death). The patient accepts your recommendations.

Consent is a simple process, right?

I. THE ESSENCE OF INFORMED CONSENT

No medical intervention done for any purpose—whether diagnostic, investigational, cosmetic, palliative, or therapeutic—*should take place unless the patient has consented to it.* For this to be an informed choice, the healthcare professional must have a discussion with the patient about his or her condition and the proposed treatment, and then elicit the patient's preferences regarding that treatment.

DISCUSSION OF CASE 5.1

To the best of your ability, you should ensure that the patient fully comprehends your explanation of his illness, the proposed tests, and the various treatment options plus the potential hazards of recommended therapy. If you are satisfied he understands these matters, you can offer him a prescription. You may wish to ask the patient to explain in his own words what you have told him and enquire if he has any other questions or concerns. You may also briefly document the nature and substance of such a discussion in the patient's chart. If the patient later develops a complication from the anti-inflammatory medication, you can be reassured you have acted properly by having previously disclosed this risk to him and allowing him to choose that risk. In so accepting this risk, the patient *usually* assumes responsibility for the adverse event if it should occur.

> ## BOX 5.1
>
> Consent must be
>
> 1. *specific* as to the proposed intervention,
>
> 2. *informed*, and
>
> 3. *freely made* without fraud or duress.

Consent is not always as simple a process as in this particular vignette; patients vary in how much they want to know and are able to know, clinicians will tailor their disclosure to patients depending on circumstances such as urgency, time constraints, patient capacity, and so on. The complexities here can be addressed by remembering what is important when it comes to consent.

II. ETHICAL CONSENT

Although there is much legal material relating to consent, which we will soon examine, it is vital to remember its ethical underpinnings. The notion of informed consent is derived from the principle of autonomy which holds that health professionals ought not to act autocratically. They should respect and promote the freely held views and choices of their patients (at least, as far as health matters go). The legal requirements for consent often inform healthcare professionals of the minimum they are required to do, stressing the importance of documentation (which, by the way, is important) and legal protection for the healthcare practitioner (important, too). Informed choice can therefore seem to be an onerous matter if the clinician thinks he or she is duty-bound to explain every risk and complication for every procedure or intervention and ensure all this is captured in the patient's chart. But good information sharing with patients will, in many cases, take care of the clinician's legal concerns (see Chapter 4 on Truthtelling).

Merely reciting to patients a litany of side-effects or possible complications and having them sign a consent form so as to avoid being sued is not the first foundation for appropriate patient choice. Patients frequently lack the critical skills required to make accurate risk-to-benefit calculations of medical interventions.[5] They also can have a poor understanding of written consent, believing its primary function to be, as it often is, simply to protect hospitals and doctors.[6]

Healthcare practitioners, too, may have a poor understanding of shared decision making and frequently make decisions for capable patients. One study showed that discussions with patients about risks are often truncated, especially with complex interventions, and assessment of patients' understanding of what is being asked of them infrequent.[7] True shared decision making needs new models of sharing complex information and better training of healthcare professionals.[8]

The ethical foundation for consent often calls for clinicians to do something more than what they are legally bound to do. A few unscripted extra minutes with patients, asking them some questions about their lives, can lead to a better understanding of them as individuals. By so doing, clinicians can support their patients in making the decisions that are right for *them*, as opposed to decisions that simply reflect the professional's recommendations. This conversation can also minimize the risk of unrecognized patient expectations.[9]

BOX 5.2

'The following is an act of professional misconduct: performing a professional service by which consent is required by law without consent.'

It should go without saying that any medical intervention requires patient involvement. However, patients vary in their interest in and current capability for such involvement. The clinician may be tempted to cut corners around the requirements for informed choice if the patient seems uninterested in being involved in the decision. However, some decisions are weightier than others and require scrupulous attention to how they are made. Decisions especially calling for the involvement of the patient include those in which

- there are major differences in the possible outcomes (for example, death or disability) of different treatments;
- the likelihood of complications is much greater for one treatment than for another;
- the choice of treatment involves trade-offs between near and distant benefits;
- the apparent choice between outcomes seems marginal, but the treatment options are quite distinct;
- a patient is particularly averse to certain risks; and
- a patient attaches special importance to certain outcomes.[10]

An ethical consent, as opposed to a purely legal one, gives patients the opportunity to participate in medical decisions as much as they are able and willing to do.

Failing to provide adequate information to patients so they may make informed choices can place physicians (and other healthcare professionals) at legal risk. *Reibl v. Hughes* was the landmark Canadian case illustrating this.[11]

III. THE DOCTOR WHO DIDN'T: THE CASE OF MR REIBL VERSUS DR HUGHES

Mr Reibl was a 44-year-old patient with a history of severe migraines who was operated on by Dr Hughes in the early 1970s to remove a blockage in his left internal carotid artery. The lesion was not causing any neurological problems and so the surgery was performed on an elective, not emergency, basis. (This blockage was not even responsible for the patient's migraines, although it might have caused him trouble, such as stroke, later.) Unfortunately, Mr Reibl suffered a stroke as a result of the procedure (a recognized surgical risk) that left him impotent and profoundly paralyzed on his right side. Dr Hughes had not specifically warned the patient of this risk or of the 1 in 7 likelihood of its occurring due to the procedure. The doctor later explained his rule was 'never to tell such things' to his patients. Instead, he told Mr Reibl that, in a general way, he would 'be better off with the surgery'.

Dr Hughes did not obtain consent in the modern way.

After 10 years of litigation, the Supreme Court of Canada found Dr Hughes guilty of negligence, not because of the bad outcome (that was just ill luck), but for failure to ensure true informed consent when he neglected to provide critical information to Mr Reibl. The court decided a *reasonable person* in Mr Reibl's position would have waited to have the surgery, if information about the risk of stroke had been given. This was especially so since the surgery was elective, that is, optional, at least in terms of timing. In addition, because Mr Reibl would have been eligible for a full disability pension in just 18 months, a reasonable person in his position would have delayed surgery until then, in case such a bad outcome did eventuate. Thus, it was the particular circumstances of this patient that made the doctor's omission in disclosure so erroneous. The court wrote:

> [T]he issue of informed consent to treatment is a concomitant of the physician's duty of care. A surgeon's duty to exercise due skill and care in giving his patient reasonable information and advice with respect to the risks specifically attendant on a proposed procedure arises out of the special relationship between them. It is a particular case of the duty which is cast on professional persons in a fiduciary position called upon . . . to give information or advice to a patient.[12]

To avoid negligence, physicians and surgeons must not only be technically proficient but exhibit certain moral skills as well. Their fiduciary, or trustlike, relationship with their patients means they must try to have their interventions serve their patients' wishes and interests. At a minimum this requires truthful and adequate disclosures to patients (see Box 5.3). Dr Hughes abrogated his ethical responsibility by not ensuring Mr Reibl's choice was an accurate and considered reflection of his own views and interests.

BOX 5.3

The lesson: Securing informed consent to treatment is a necessary part of the physician's duty of care.

The rule: Disclose what a reasonable person in the patient's position would want to know.

Negligent practice

Negligent practice will encompass not just faulty technical skill but also failure to involve patients properly in their own care—for example, failing to inform them of the important side-effects of a drug.

CASE 5.2   THE UNDISCLOSED SIDE-EFFECT

A patient with a five-month history of a sore shoulder was treated by her physician with drugs that included an antipsychotic and an antidepressant. The physician had not disclosed to the patient that these were psychotropic medications nor had he told her about possible side-effects. Only on discussion with a relative who was a nurse did the patient realize that the drowsiness, weakness, and blurred vision she had experienced could be due to the drugs. The physician was found guilty of failing to maintain the standards of the profession because he had not informed the patient of these potential side-effects.[13]

DISCUSSION OF CASE 5.2

It can sometimes be difficult to decide what side-effects to warn patients about. Patients often say they want to be informed about 'all possible side-effects'—an impossible task.[14] In such discussions, the focus should be on the *likely* side-effects and the *serious*, but less common, side-effects. In general, the more serious the possible side-effects, the more vigilant the physician must be in monitoring the patient and the more careful in disclosing such information to the patient. If in doubt, it is better to take extra time and inform the patient.

IV. THE ESSENTIAL ELEMENTS OF CONSENT: WHEN, WHO, WHAT, HOW?

1. When should consent be obtained?

Now to some legal details—details that matter a great deal to physicians and patients.

Whenever anything is done for a medical purpose for or to a patient, consent must be obtained. Prescribing drugs, ordering tests, giving vaccines, proposing surgery for curative, cosmetic, or palliative purposes—all these interventions require consent. Consent may be sought for discrete medical interventions or for a plan of treatment as a whole. The more serious the patient's condition or the proposed intervention, the more careful the clinician should be in obtaining consent from the patient.

While anything that clinicians do to their patients, such as psychotherapy or prescribing and administering drugs, has potentially serious adverse consequences, it is more common for healthcare professionals who physically 'invade' their patients' bodies to be sued for negligent consent. In general, *procedures that involve physical trespass upon a person's body must meet a higher standard of consent.* Such trespass would include not only surgical procedures but also any touching of a patient, including the penetration by hand, device, or drug of any orifice of the patient's body. Rectal and vaginal examinations and treatments are particularly intimate and should call for explicit consent.[15] It is also clearly important, where possible, to obtain consent for procedures done while patients are unconscious (such as intimate examinations done under anesthesia).[16]

Physicians are authorized by their patients only to do the treatment for which the consent was obtained. There is wrong done to a patient who, for example, consents to a hernia repair but has a testicle removed or agrees to a Caesarean section and gets a sterilization as well. If the patient gets something substantially different from what was agreed to, the doctor is liable for charges of trespass or battery. (The doctor who removed the testicle got off in court because the testicle was diseased and its removal was considered an emergency operation necessary to save the patient's life. The doctor who sterilized the woman did not.)[17]

2. From whom should consent be obtained?

In obtaining consent for an intervention, the healthcare professional must decide upon another aspect of the matter: is this patient competent to give informed consent?

Competence presumed

Barring evidence to the contrary, patients are presumed to be competent, that is, *having the mental capacity to give consent*. A medical intervention should take place only if (1) the patient has the appropriate capacity and has given consent or (2) someone else authorized to make decisions on behalf of an incapable patient has consented to it. (See Chapter 6 for a fuller discussion of capacity and substitute decision makers.)

CASE 5.3	A SHOT FOR PREVENTION

You are a medical trainee doing your rotation in a community health centre. An 80-year-old widow is brought by her son for her annual influenza vaccine. In explaining its risks and benefits, you realize the patient is not following your explanation. An inspection of her chart reveals a five-year history of progressive dementia with a decline in many aspects of daily functioning. A brief examination reveals a patient who seems to have difficulty understanding what is being asked of her. She blankly looks at her son and asks, 'Who is that person and what does she want?' The son gives you permission to give his mother the injection, saying she always wanted it in the past.

Whether or not the patient agrees with the proposed intervention, the healthcare professional must assess the patient's mental capacity. This does not have to be a complicated or detailed assessment, unless there are particular reasons to be concerned. Nurse, social worker, occupational therapist, medical trainee, and physician, as well as families or others close to the patient, all have unique roles to play in the assessment of a patient's capacity (is a patient, for example, acting in or out of character?).

Seek a surrogate

If the patient is truly incapable, then consent must be obtained from a 'substitute decision maker'. Until recently in medicine the search for the proxy decision maker was an informal one. However, with the advent of certain legislation, especially concerning advance directives and substitute decision making, this process has become more formal (see Chapters 6 on Capacity and 11 on

End-of-Life Decisions). There are limitations on what surrogates may consent to on behalf of the incapable patients—for example, in many jurisdictions surrogates may not consent to a patient's participation in medical research or consent to the removal of tissue for experimental purposes (but see Chapter 7 on Beneficence).

DISCUSSION OF CASE 5.3

The question in this case is: does the mother understand what is being asked of her, that is, to accept or reject the vaccine? It is clear after a few minutes of observation that this patient cannot do so and accordingly cannot give a valid consent. Another person has to make this decision for her (see Box 5.4). Who is better situated to do so than her closest relative, her son, who knows her previous wishes and can decide what treatment is in his mother's best interests?

BOX 5.4

Practically speaking, if the patient is incapable as regards a particular medical procedure, then that patient can no longer make his or her own choice about that procedure. Someone else must make it for him or her.

Refusal by relatives

What about the situation in which relatives refuse recommended treatment on behalf of a seemingly *capable* patient?

CASE 5.4   AN OBSTRUCTED DELIVERY

You are an obstetrician about to deliver a 26-year-old non–English-speaking patient in her first pregnancy. She was admitted to the labour and delivery ward just hours before in spontaneous labour at close to 41 weeks' gestation. Her antenatal ultrasound was normal. Things have now slowed down. Her cervix is now dilated at 6 cm and the fetal head at spines -2. (This means the pregnancy is full term, the woman is ready to deliver, but the baby is stuck way up in the birth canal.) The fetal monitor shows a complicated pattern suggestive of severe fetal distress. A fetal blood sample obtained 10 minutes ago comes back as pH of 6.90 with a base deficit of -24. (This suggests the baby lacks oxygen.) You have already discussed these findings with the patient with the aid of an interpreter and recommended an emergency Caesarean section due to fetal hypoxia. She had agreed, but wanted her husband to sign the consent form. Her husband is furious when he arrives. 'In our culture,' he says vehemently, 'it is the men who decide these issues for women. In our hospitals back home, the husband's consent is first required.' He refuses consent for the surgery.

What would you do now?

DISCUSSION OF CASE 5.4

While one ought to respect the cultural values of minority groups, this does not require that one abide by all their cultural dictates, especially where preventable serious harm to others might occur. You should respectfully ask the husband why he is refusing— perhaps he is miffed that you spoke to his wife first. He also may not be fully aware how dire the situation is for his wife and the baby. You should make reasonable efforts to inform him and seek his *assent* to proceed—that is, that he will not obstruct the appropriate care for his wife. The central patient in this scenario, the woman, has already given her consent and that is all that is needed to urgently proceed.

3. Who is responsible for obtaining consent?

The patient's treating physician is ultimately responsible for obtaining consent but may delegate it to others (such as nurses or medical trainees). The prudent attending physician should obtain the consent in advance (for example, in his or her private office) and document the subject of the discussion.

If the hospital staff or trainees will be obtaining consent later, the attending physician should make sure that those designated to obtain the actual consent do so in a way with which he or she is comfortable. Expanded roles of various healthcare professionals may involve a component of the 'consent' process (such as a nurse getting a patient to sign a surgical consent form) but the ultimate authority will rest with the most responsible physician. Most jurisdictions disapprove of medical trainees—like clinical clerks—obtaining patient consent for surgical consent as they may ill understand the intricacies of the decision that has to be made.[18] Unless such trainees exceed their authority and seek consent on their own, the responsibility for the adequacy of the consent will, once again, largely rest on the shoulders of the most responsible physician.

Similarly, those designated to obtain consent should ensure that they fully understand the nature of the procedure for which consent is being obtained. If they do not, they should seek guidance from others rather than obtain a faulty or invalid consent. An improperly obtained consent increases the legal jeopardy and ethical problems for all concerned and makes it impossible for the patient to participate properly in the consent process.

4. What should be disclosed?

Information detailing the essential qualities of the proposed intervention must lie at the 'heart' of the conversation between healthcare practitioner and patient.[19]

Patients need information for choice

Patients' needs for and expectation of information have been well established (see Chapter 4 on Truthtelling). In general, studies show that patient standards are generally much higher than what physicians attempt or achieve. (The reason doctors get away with poor disclosure is, quite frankly, that it often fails to cause patients litigable harm.) However, clinicians are mistaken if they think *Reibl v. Hughes* requires them to tell patients 'everything' about a procedure in order to ensure consent is 'informed'. This is not the case. When it comes to proposed interventions, *patients need only the relevant information that will allow them to choose among the alternatives in a fashion consistent with their own values and beliefs.* This is what clinicians must tell patients.

Reasonable-person standard

The modern standard for medical disclosure is not telling patients *'everything'*—nor is it telling patients just what other physicians tell or don't tell. *The standard instead is: what would a reasonable person in the patient's situation wish to know about the intervention before deciding whether to accept it?* It is then up to the patient to decide whether to accept or reject the proposed intervention (and its potential hazards). A duly informed patient not only makes a free choice but also assumes upon himself or herself any of the (non-negligent) risks of the agreed-upon intervention.

It is particularly important to discuss with the patient the various treatment options (including the option of no treatment at all—see Box 5.5)[20] and to explain the likely risks and benefits of the various options. The risk/benefit assessment should take into account the patient's particular circumstances (for example, occupation). Values or beliefs that a patient feels to be especially crucial, such as a refusal of blood products, ought to be discussed, as they may have an effect on which choice is best for a patient. The prudent clinician will not only tell the patient what a reasonable person would want to know, but also what this *particular* patient wants to know and will strive to do so by utilizing informational aids and by encouraging the patient to ask questions and answer these as best he or she can.

BOX 5.5

Whatever alternatives are available to patients, it is helpful to remind patients they always have the 'zero option'—the opportunity to do nothing.

Material risks

Specifically, the clinician ought to tell the patient his or her prognosis with and without treatment, the treatment alternatives (including the 'no treatment' option), the success and failure rates of the various treatments, the 'material risks' of treatment (common and serious risks inherent in a procedure that a reasonable person in the patient's circumstances would want to know), any matters the patient asks about, and the clinician's recommendation regarding treatment (see Box 5.6).

BOX 5.6

Informed consent requires discussion of

- the exact nature of the proposed treatment;
- the alternative(s);
- the prognosis with and without treatment;
- the risks and benefits of the treatment and of alternatives;
- serious risks, even if unlikely; and
- any questions the patient may have.

Serious risks (such as death and permanent disability) should be disclosed even if they are very unlikely to occur. Common and therefore required-to-disclose-risks are those with a >1/200 chance of happening while not-mandatory-to-disclose-risks have a <1/1x10^6 chance of happening. Dr Hughes's non-disclosure of a 'material risk' of the procedure (serious, 1/7 chance of happening) failed to meet this requirement and therefore was, in the court's eyes, negligent.

By contrast, the 'one-in-a-million' chance seems a pretty good cutoff for disclosure of even serious risk. 'Reasonable patients' would not make a medical decision based on such remote risks. Whether this applies to *all* procedures is hard to know, but doctors have not been found negligent, for example, in failing to warn a surgical patient of the remote risk of necrotizing fasciitis.[21] It could well be that the courts might find such remote risk information more germane to less 'medically necessary' procedures like liposuction—less necessary procedures would make reasonable people think twice about them if there are any possible serious adverse outcomes. The important thing here is not so much the precise risk of an adverse event occurring—*it is providing patients with information that will make a difference to their decision making.* Information that patients would use to inform their choices is information that must be provided by healthcare professionals.

While one should not unduly alarm patients with every possibility, one should also not falsely reassure them or 'sell' them on surgical interventions or pharmaceutical products. Patients must be given leeway to experience their sensitivities and exercise their idiosyncratic preferences. Ironically, the unduly anxious patient who frets about potential but rare side-effects of a treatment may well be the one patient who ends up suffering those very side-effects if *not* forewarned by the clinician. Disclosure for consent purposes should be complete and adequate and not designed to prevent a patient's emotional responses to information. Of course, it is quite appropriate to try to understand and address a patient's unusual beliefs or emotional reactions to proposed interventions so that 'non-compliance' or threats to patient welfare can be anticipated and addressed beforehand.

Elective Procedures

It is always right to encourage decisionally reluctant patients to participate in choices that have important implications for them. In fact, certain decisions ought not to be made by healthcare professionals if the patient will not make them. Decisions concerning cosmetic or experimental procedures (neither required at all for the preservation of the patient's well-being) often involve values that only the patient can implement.

Some legal decisions have suggested that one must disclose even minimal risks (the one-in-a-million risk) for elective procedures and all possible risks for cosmetic ones (see Box 5.7).[22] Such requirements go far beyond the requirements for ordinary necessary procedures that require disclosure of the kind of information that a reasonable person would want to know.[23] Physicians may have a financial interest in patients' undergoing such procedures; hence, it is important to ensure that the decisions made by patients are not unduly influenced by the doctor's opinion. One can only hope that cosmetic surgeons are doing an exemplary job of ensuring informed consent.

Physicians who choose not to inform patients properly about the risks of interventions assume extra risks (of negligence) upon themselves should the

---

BOX 5.7

'In the case of elective surgery, there can be no justification for withholding information.'

patients suffer injury or loss due to the unexplained risks. They have also failed in the moral duty owed to patients by not offering them the time and dialogue they deserve as human beings (see Box 5.8).[24]

BOX 5.8

'Treat the patient as though he [or she] were your best friend and you are telling him [or her] all about the proposed treatment.'

Treatment alternatives

Must clinicians tell patients about treatment alternatives? The answer to this question is yes, if the alternatives are truly different and this patient would want to know about these alternatives to make an informed choice.

Important options ought to be disclosed to patients—even if the consultant does not perform them. Because patients may not be sufficiently well informed to know to ask, clinicians should not wait for them to ask before disclosing. Even locally unavailable options ought to be mentioned if they might better meet a patient's interests. Of course, very unusual or unproven therapies—say, homeopathic remedies—do not require disclosure if they do not conform to a reasonable standard of care.

5. How should consent be obtained?

Deciding just what and how patients should be told can be tricky. Professionals should organize their time so that effective communication with patients can take place. 'Effective' means, in this context, communication habits and tactics aimed at targeting patient perspectives and successfully incorporating them into any treatment plan. Doctors, in particular, should strive not to dominate the discussion or interrupt patients '30 seconds or less' into the consultation.[25] Healthcare professionals need to ask their patients: 'What are your concerns? What else would you like to know? Does this make sense to you? Is there someone else that you would like to talk to about this?' These questions take only an extra few minutes per patient visit and patients should then be given all the time they need to make their decisions. Taking time to talk to patients and listen to them helps ensure that they are truly agreeing to a procedure and not simply going along with 'professional opinion'.

Help with complex decisions

While medical care has become more complex, the conversations between healthcare professionals and patients and/or their families have not kept up (see

Box 5.9).[26] The typical 10-minute medical consultation remains unchanged, time that is hardly adequate for any serious discussion of treatment alternatives and their risks. Fully informed of the possible harms and benefits of a treatment, patients tend to opt for the less invasive and the less prescription-drug-dependent course of action.[27]

BOX 5.9

'The goal is changing to become one of informing people enabling them to make their own choices, regardless of whether this reduces risk.'

Consent forms

It is often asked whether prescribed hospital consent forms, signed by patients, would protect healthcare professionals from litigation regarding consent. The short answer to this question is no, but they can be helpful. Consent forms are simply evidence that a discussion of the procedure in question took place. If no such discussion took place, a signed form is worth little. Of course, if such prescribed forms are available, they should be used, even if only for their evidentiary role and to comply with institutional protocol. (They should also always be used in any significant medical research.)

Research reveals that many patients do not recall much about the contents of consent forms—if they read them at all. As well, certain factors, such as advanced age and impaired cognitive functions, can impair the quality of a patient's consent.[28] In such circumstances, physicians have an obligation to help the patient understand, as much as is reasonably feasible, the proposed interventions. Relying on consent forms is a poor substitute for having an open conversation with patients about the proposed treatment (see Box 5.10).

Patients Who Withdraw Consent

CASE 5.5   'STOP THE TEST!'

A 58-year-old woman agrees to undergo a colonoscopy. During the procedure, despite mild sedation, she suddenly experiences severe pain and cries out, 'Stop! I can't take this anymore!'

May the physician continue the examination?

The doctrine of consent gives the patient the definitive right to refuse medical interventions. Such refusal may conflict with other important goals, such as the

BOX 5.10

Help patients understand medical procedures by

- explaining matters simply,
- defining the decision and the options clearly,
- wording patient information materials carefully,
- providing written information or other media decision-aids,
- having patients bring a relative to the discussion,
- encouraging patients to ask questions,
- offering the option of a second opinion,
- ensuring ample time for decision making, and
- asking patients to repeat in their own words what they have understood.

expectation that medical care ought to prevent needless suffering or avoidable death, but it is nonetheless to be respected. What if, however, a patient appears to withdraw consent during a medical procedure? Must such no's always be heeded?

The answer to this question is yes, but special precautions must be taken. In a recent case before the Supreme Court of Canada this question was discussed in some detail.

Giovanna Ciarlariello was an Italian-speaking cleaner diagnosed at age 49 with a sub-arachnoid hemorrhage. To find the source of the bleeding, a cerebral angiogram was done after several explanations to obtain consent were made by radiologists and an intern at two adjoining hospitals. After an explanation with a family member present, the consent was signed by the patient's daughter.

During a second angiogram, the patient seemed to hyperventilate, lost some power and feeling in her limbs and, when calmer, said, 'Enough, no more, stop the test.' Temporarily stopping the test, the physicians noted an improvement in the patient's condition and recommended continuing the test since it was almost complete. The patient agreed. During the final dye injection the patient was unfortunately rendered quadriplegic and later died.

Her estate sued the physicians, arguing, among other things, that it was wrong to continue with the angiogram when the patient had withdrawn her consent.[29]

Halt unless serious harm

At issue in this case was the nature and extent of disclosure owed by a doctor to a patient who withdraws consent for a procedure during its administration. In general, *if consent is withdrawn, the procedure should be halted unless doing so might seriously harm the patient*. In this case, however, the patient appeared to consent to the test's completion. Was her consent valid? The court felt it was because (1) the patient had previously consented to the same procedure, (2) the risks had not seemingly changed, and (3) the patient seemed to understand what was being asked of her in the procedure room. As her consent was valid, the physicians had not erred in completing the test.

The physicians were lucky in this case. First of all, the court agreed that they had done a thorough job of explaining to the patient and her family the nature and risks of the procedure. Second, the court agreed there appeared to be no change in the material risks of the test despite the episode of hyperventilation. Third, the court felt she understood enough of what was happening after that episode, despite not having an interpreter present, to be able to give consent.

Onus borne by doctor

Physicians should be careful about drawing the conclusion from this case that one can ignore a patient who withdraws consent during a test. *If the procedure is continued, the onus is borne by the doctor, who must ensure that the patient has understood what is happening.* In particular the physician may have to demonstrate later that the patient understood the explanation and instructions given to continue the procedure. If this cannot be done, especially if the material risks to the patient have changed, the test should not be started again. While the entire consent does not have to be obtained again during the procedure, new material risks must be divulged, and the patient must have the capacity to understand them. If the patient lacks this capacity, he or she cannot give valid consent to continue the procedure, and it would be wiser to stop it unless the patient would be put in undue danger. (Of course, substitute consent could be obtained so long as it is not used as a vehicle to override that to which the patient would have consented.)

DISCUSSION OF CASE 5.5

The physician would be unwise to continue the examination. He or she should, of course, try to ascertain why the patient felt pain and attempt to relieve it. The patient should have the risks and benefits of continuing the procedure explained. If she is adamant about stopping and understands its implications, despite sedation, her wish should be respected. (Of course even a seemingly less rational wish should be respected if the pain could only be relieved by withdrawing the colonoscope.) A physician was recently found guilty of battery for continuing with a sigmoidoscopy in spite of a patient's cries to stop due to pain. In that case the patient suffered a punctured bowel after the doctor had been asked to stop.[30]

V. Exceptions to Consent

There are circumstances that sometimes allow an exception to the duty to seek informed consent from a patient (see Box 5.11). These circumstances are similar to those that justify an exception to truthtelling, already detailed in Chapter 4.

BOX 5.11

Exceptions to requirement for consent:

- waiver by patient
- incapacity of patient
- emergencies
- 'therapeutic privilege'

---

1. Patient waiver

Patients may waive the normal consent process by, for example, asking the doctor to 'skip the gory details' about a particular intervention. Such a request needs to be examined further by the clinician. Why does the patient not wish to be informed? Are there misconceptions that need to be dispelled? Is the patient truly capable of giving consent? How serious is the proposed intervention and what are its consequences likely to be for the patient? Is the procedure experimental? If not, how well established is it and how well known are its complications? These questions deserve careful exploration. Patients still trust doctors to make decisions in their best interests, and frequently waive information from doctors. As well, while wanting to be informed, patients may sometimes wish not to know the details unless absolutely necessary.

When it comes to a particular medical intervention, a patient waiver may or may not be acceptable. Patients need to know certain information to be properly prepared for a procedure. For example, patients undergoing cardiac surgery need to know that after the operation they will likely wake up on a ventilator in the intensive care unit and so should be informed as to what this experience might be like. They may not need to know that blood will be taken every hour or that their throat will hurt after intubation. For elective or cosmetic interventions, specifically because they are optional, the physician is within his or her rights not to accept as a patient someone who requests to be left in ignorance of the risks faced in undergoing such interventions.

If the physician is prepared to accept the patient's waiver, it would be wise to document the discussion around this in case of some adverse event. However, dangerous or risky procedures, especially if new and bordering on the experimental, are particularly ill-suited to 'waivered' consent. And of course, waivers should not be accepted from incapable patients. (Instead, a substitute decision maker should be sought.)

2. Mental incapacity of patient

Incapacity of a patient is not a true exception to the consent rule except in an emergency (see Box 5.12). Consent must still be sought, but from a proxy decision maker who has been properly informed as the patient would have been if capable. (For a detailed discussion of incapacity, see Chapter 6.) In certain situations where the patient retains some decision-making capacity, the health professional—nurse, physician, trainee—may still choose to inform that patient about an impending medical intervention. This allows the patient to participate as far as he or she is able in the decision. (One may be pleasantly surprised at how much the patient can understand the intervention.) It may also help the patient prepare for whatever consequences, such as pain or disability, that might follow from the procedure.

> ## BOX 5.12
>
> If a patient is incapable, consent is still required, albeit from a substitute decision maker. Except in emergencies, healthcare professionals cannot act as decision makers for their incapable patients.

3. Emergencies

This is the most commonly used exception: consent need not be obtained when the patient is at imminent risk of suffering serious injury (severe suffering, loss of limb, vital organ, or life) and obtaining consent is either not possible—for example, the patient is comatose—or would increase the risk to the patient.[31] It is assumed that in emergencies most patients would want what is necessary to be done to rescue them from serious harm or severe suffering (see Box 5.13).

Trying to obtain consent could jeopardize the patient's safety by wasting time, thus unreasonably delaying life-saving care.

> **BOX 5.13**
>
> The emergency rule is a social insurance rule: it assumes that most people would want to be saved in an emergency.

There is an exception to this exception to the consent rule: where the competent patient had previously refused the emergency treatment normally offered. Under such circumstances treatment may *not* be administered. (See *Malette v. Shulman* in Chapter 2 on Autonomy.)

Suicide notes do not set comparable limits to treatment, as they are presumed to originate from a mind incapable of informed refusal.[32] Many suicidal acts are disguised requests for help and not 'autonomous' refusals of assistance. Often acting impulsively and in a situational crisis, most suicidal patients if saved, do not attempt suicide a second time (see Box 5.14).[33]

> **BOX 5.14**
>
> The exception to the emergency rule does not recognize suicide notes because it is assumed that patients are incapable when they write them.

4. Therapeutic privilege

CASE 5.6   AN UNSTATED RISK

A 45-year-old man is advised to have a radiological test as part of a work-up for haematuria. He is not warned by the radiologist of the possibility of a serious allergic reaction to the contrast dye because it is thought this might cause him undue anxiety. The patient has such a reaction to the dye during the test and nearly dies.

Therapeutic privilege is the failure to involve capable patients in a medical decision on the grounds that it might harm them (by increasing their anxiety); it is an increasingly outmoded and paternalistic exception to consent and disclosure. It is better recast as one of the other three exceptions to consent. Physicians would be well advised to avoid this exception and, instead, learn to deliver bad news in a sensitive way.

DISCUSSION OF CASE 5.6

The patient was wronged in not being informed of a remote but serious risk. No matter how well intentioned and no matter that many physicians would act in this way, the lack of disclosure is a clear abrogation of the disclosure and consent rule. As a result of risk disclosure, patients may, in the healthcare professional's opinion, 'irrationally' choose not to undergo tests that are medically indicated, but that is their right (see Chapter 6 on Capacity).

Patients not always suggestible

It is sometimes thought that giving more information to a suggestible patient about the potential negative outcomes of a treatment may *itself* produce negative results, thus harming the patient's well-being. Anecdotes aside, research does not entirely bear this out. For example, giving patients very detailed information about the risks of hernia surgery did not increase their anxiety.[34] Warning patients about the potential side-effects of certain prescribed drugs (antihypertensives, antibiotics, and anti-inflammatory pills) did not make it more likely they would experience such side-effects.[35] Greater information disclosure to advanced cancer patients did not increase poor patient outcomes and only increased their anxiety levels, in this study, if accompanied by encouraged participation in their own care.[36] (Participation by patients in their own care can be anxiety-provoking especially if the decisions are difficult ones and novel to the patient.)

CONCLUSION

High standards are expected of modern healthcare professionals when it comes to consent for medical care. Patients not receiving important information in a timely way may have grounds for concern and grievance. Informed choice is not just a matter of respecting autonomy; it is also about acting in ways that are helpful to, and experienced as helpful by, patients. Knowing how best to help and how far you must help a patient is part of your professional role as a healthcare professional. Helping and not harming obviously raise questions about the principles of beneficence and non-maleficence that will be examined in Chapter 7.

6 | THE WANING AND WAXING SELF: CAPACITY AND INCAPACITY IN MEDICAL CARE

The policy of the law is that where a person, due to mental illness, lacks the capacity to make a sound and considered decision on treatment, the person should not for that reason be denied access to medical treatment that can improve functioning and alleviate suffering.

Chief Justice McLachlin, 2003[1]

This chapter will examine the healthcare professional's complex responsibilities regarding the care of incapable patients—whether they are elderly, young, or in-between—who may be vulnerable. The healthcare professional's duty to provide effective medical care and protect such vulnerable individuals from harm must be balanced against the right of competent persons to make their own decisions, even if they are considered 'bad' ones. Challenges exist in deciding who needs protection from themselves and what, if any, limits there are as to how far a clinician can go in protecting patients with diminished or impaired capacity.

I. ASSESSING CAPACITY

CASE 6.1	'TALK TO ME, NOT MY DAUGHTER!'

A geriatric psychiatrist, consultant to a local nursing home, is asked to see an 87-year-old woman with advanced Parkinson's disease who is complaining of frightening visual hallucinations. The patient has marked rigidity and is quite unstable when walking. She requires help from staff for many of her activities of daily living. There is no obvious evidence of dementia. It is unclear whether her psychiatric symptoms are secondary to her medications or the illness itself; her medications cannot however be reduced because of the severity of her physical symptoms. The patient has partial insight into her psychotic symptoms; she and the psychiatrist agree these are distressing enough to warrant a trial of an atypical antipsychotic. She is warned about the potential for worsening of her Parkinsonian symptoms with antipsychotics and agrees that the novel antipsychotic least associated with such side-effects will be tried at a low starting dose.

A note is left in her chart recommending this medication. The attending physician at the nursing home accordingly authorizes the order. As is common in many nursing homes, the protocol of routinely obtaining consent from relatives for any medication changes is followed and so this patient's daughter is contacted. She refuses consent for the antipsychotic, downplaying her mother's symptoms but also expressing concern she may become overmedicated. When the psychiatrist returns the next month for his regular visit, he discovers the order for the antipsychotic has been cancelled by the attending physician.

Under the circumstances, was the attending doctor's action appropriate?

DISCUSSION OF CASE 6.1

Told the reason she did not get the medication, the patient responds angrily, 'What's my daughter got to do with it?! I'm the one who's going to be taking it! If I get side-effects, then I'll let you know and we can stop it!' Indeed, she is right to be upset. The patient is quite capable of comprehending and making a decision about antipsychotic medications. She might be old, infirm, and incapable of meeting all her physical needs, but this does not mean she cannot make an informed choice about the treatment of her hallucinations. The daughter is not the person to make the final decision about medications for her capable mother. With the patient's permission, the psychiatrist calls the daughter, as a matter of courtesy, to inform her as to the reasons for the medication and as to her mother's capacity. After some discussion, the daughter agrees a trial of medication seems reasonable. Even if she disagrees, however, the medication can be ordered, because the mother has already made an informed choice for this.

Competencies, not competence

When we speak of competence or capacity (throughout this book, I use capacity and competence interchangeably), we are talking not about a global ability but rather a person's competence or ability to perform some *specific* task or to make a *specific* decision. Different domains of competence include the ability to make a treatment decision, manage one's financial affairs, make a will, appoint a lawyer for personal care, drive a car, stand trial, or decide whether to enter a long-term care facility. Within each domain are specific decisions to be made. Whereas in the past competence was conceptualized as 'all or nothing', we now should talk about domain-specific competence and decision-specific competence. Some patients, such as infants or those in a coma, are globally incompetent. More commonly, however, an individual may be competent in one domain and not another (although in practice incompetence in one domain may signal incompetence in others). Even here, the presumption of global capacity for all decisions within a domain may not be correct; there is often a hierarchy of decisions with each domain, ranging from the simple to the complicated. Competence is better conceptualized, then, as a set of competencies.[2]

In Western medicine (and law), all persons are presumed to be competent unless there are reasonable grounds to suspect otherwise. The onus is on others—such as healthcare professionals—to prove incapacity rather than for an individual patient to prove competency. Capacity assessments may be done under a variety of circumstances, both informally and more formally. Whether a more formal assessment is required depends on the decision to be made. How serious is it? What are the implications of the decision for the patient and others? Frequently, and probably most commonly, informal capacity assessments are done by clinicians every day—more formalized assessments are generally only required for decisions of greater importance. Such decisions, such as requests for risky experimental interventions or refusals of life-sustaining care, give rise to more exacting assessments of capacity. Surveys have shown incapacity to be extremely common in hospitalized patients and frequently unrecognized. (See, for example, Case 11.3, 'No CRAP vs. No CPR'.)[3]

Practitioners need practical ways to accurately assess various types of capacity for situations of importance, but these unfortunately are often lacking or not standardized. The difficult cases are those where a patient's capacity is borderline.

Competence operationally defined

Many operational definitions of competence have been proposed, but none has universal acceptance. The US President's Commission on Ethics in Medicine suggested that competence requires all of the following:

- a set of core personal values and goals,
- the ability to communicate,
- the ability to understand information,
- the ability to reason and deliberate,
- the ability to choose, and
- consistency between one's choices and one's underlying values.[4]

Does lack of one of these elements mean that someone should be considered incompetent? Not necessarily. It would depend on the circumstances, such as how the patient is actually functioning in the decision context and what choice has to be made. Competence is a spectrum that varies with the task and the decision. Moreover, a patient may only be temporarily incapacitated by drugs or illness and retain an underlying ability to perform the requisite task. Other patients, such as the patient in Case 6.1, can look incompetent but still have an ability to make a competent decision. As we have to make judgments concerning someone's capacity (in order to know whether to abide by his or her wishes or not), we cannot avoid establishing thresholds or protocols for specific capabilities. Practically, however, rules around determination of capacity for particular tasks can vary in different jurisdictions. There is often little guidance around the specific means of assessing certain kinds of competence. Although different capacity assessment tools are available, none are universally accepted or consistently used.[5]

> **BOX 6.1**
>
> Competence is not a diagnosis, but an assessment of functional capacity.

Tests of competence

Five tests of competence to consent to medical treatment have been proposed:

1. expressing a choice
2. expressing a 'reasonable' choice
3. expressing a choice based on 'rational reasons'
4. showing an ability to understand the information necessary to make a decision
5. showing an ability to appreciate one's situation and its consequences[6]

Test 1 is the least restrictive and the least helpful in that it would authorize any choice made by a patient. Test 2 is inadequate because it fails to recognize the patient's autonomy and it privileges medically desirable outcomes, the 'best interests' of patients as defined by healthcare professionals. Competence assessments are often done out of concern when patients refuse to consent to something others would see as necessary or beneficial but this does not in itself imply incapacity.

Test 3 is more acceptable as it looks less at outcomes and more at the process by which the patient arrives at a decision. It threatens to collapse into Test 2 if the set of 'rational' reasons is too circumscribed. Society recognizes the right to make decisions on the basis of idiosyncratic or unusual beliefs, especially if they are deeply held. This test would be more acceptable if it simply applied a consistency processing standard: a patient is deemed less than fully competent if his or her goals do not follow consistently from underlying beliefs or values. Yet inconsistency is not necessarily a mark of irrationality. We all are less than consistent in our beliefs and practices—but this does not mean our choices should be ignored or overruled.

Tests 4 and 5, including some variant of Test 3, are the most frequently used criteria for competence.

No one criterion will accurately predict all patients who are incompetent. Gutheil and Appelbaum define the key elements for competence as

- being aware of the nature of one's situation,
- having a factual understanding of the issue(s), and
- being able to manipulate information rationally to make a decision.[7]

Each element represents a different aspect of capacity; that is, appreciation, understanding, and reasoning, and all should be met in some fashion for a person to be considered capable.

Appreciate and understand in the law

In most parts of North America, legislation uses similar language in describing capacity (see Box 6.2).[8] Under the current regulations in Ontario, for example, a person is considered capable of making a treatment decision if: 'able to understand the information that is relevant to making a decision concerning the treatment and able to appreciate the reasonably foreseeable consequences of a decision or lack of decision'.[9] *This compound standard for competence to consent corresponds to the most clinically relevant tests of competence.*[10] For any particular task or decision, one must have certain knowledge ('understanding') and be able to apply this knowledge to oneself ('appreciation'). Applying compound standards for assessing competence will more accurately reveal a person's true decision-making capacity. Studies have shown that patients who do well on the

BOX 6.2

To demonstrate the understanding required to accept or refuse a medical treatment, one must understand

- one's condition,
- the nature of the proposed treatment,
- alternatives to the treatment,
- the consequences of accepting and rejecting the treatment, and
- the risks and benefits of the various options.

understanding criterion of competence ultimately may fail to be competent because they are unable to appreciate their situation or to reason properly.[11]

The ability to understand one's situation is one aspect of competence that can be most readily assessed—for example, by having the patient recite back the potential risks and benefits of treatment or no treatment. Less easy to assess are those patients who are able to recite the facts but whose reasoning is so clouded by strong emotions or delusions that they cannot truly appreciate the meaning of the facts in relation to themselves. Such impairment of mental faculties can be subtle and require careful consideration by clinicians.

For example, certain patients can appear glibly competent but actually be incapable of deciding on their treatment because of denial or hopelessness.[12] Some patients, because of brain injury or inadequate development, may lack the cognitive capacity to make decisions. Other patients may have a thought disorder or suffer hallucinations or delusions that can floridly interfere with their ability to apply their knowledge. If such processes materially affect their mental capacity to perform various tasks or make certain decisions, they should not be considered capable in relation to those specific tasks or decisions (see Box 6.3).

BOX 6.3

To demonstrate the appreciation needed for decision making capacity, a person must

- acknowledge the condition that affects himself or herself;
- be able to assess how the various options would affect him or her;
- be able to reach a decision and adhere to it; and
- make a choice, not based primarily upon delusional belief.

CASE 6.2	BEYOND HELP?

BEYOND HELP?

You are a psychiatrist looking after a 50-year-old woman with a history of recurrent depression who presents with a prolonged exacerbation of her illness. Her only daughter passed away due to breast cancer eight months previously. She is actively suicidal and has stopped performing most of her day-to-day functions, including her self-care. She acknowledges that drugs and ECT are interventions that might help some people—indeed, in the past her own depressions have responded to ECT and antidepressants. She now refuses treatment on the grounds that they 'can't help me'.[13]

What should you do?

DISCUSSION OF CASE 6.2

The patient's competence to refuse treatment needs to be carefully examined. Although she backs up her refusal with a seemingly justifiable grief (who wouldn't be depressed if their only offspring died?), thorough examination may reveal that all aspects of her life are seen in a gloomy way. She may not be able to appreciate what treatment has done for her in the past and might do for her in the future. If so, her refusal of treatment may not be a capable one.

Because of the seriousness of her illness and the lack of alternatives, if she continues to refuse any treatment and the risks to her life remain high, authorization for involuntary treatment should be pursued vigorously under the auspices of appropriate mental health legislation.

Consequences of decisions

You should be particularly vigilant about a patient's mental capacity when he/she puts him/herself in (avoidable) harm's way *and*

- there is evidence of confused and irrational thinking,
- the person cannot retain information,
- the patient's wishes and/or alertness fluctuates,
- the person is suffering so much that understanding is or would likely be impaired, or
- the person is so under the influence of drugs or alcohol that judgment is impaired.

Notice that we have not said such patients *are* incapable. These circumstances are red flags calling for a careful assessment of their choices. How strong must an emotion be or how poor must a person's cognitive faculties be to make his or her judgments unreliable? There is no simple answer. In part, it will depend on how important the decision is. Decisions of enormous import call for a greater capacity than less weighty decisions. In general, decisions that pose greater risks to patients, such as refusing consent to life-saving interventions, will require physicians to be particularly vigilant about capacity and ensuring the right people are involved in the decision making (see Chapter 11 on End-of-Life Decisions).[14]

CASE 6.3   'I'VE SEEN WORSE!'

You are one of the attending physicians at a chronic care facility. One of the residents, an 84-year-old war veteran with no living relatives, unable to look after himself owing to physical frailty and mild cognitive decline, develops gangrene in his foot due to poor circulation; it does not respond to medical treatment. Advised to have the foot amputated, he refuses, saying, 'My foot will get better on its own. I've seen lots worse during the war!'

Should you accept his refusal of treatment?

DISCUSSION OF AND FOLLOW-UP TO CASE 6.3

You should examine the patient's reasons for refusing life-saving therapy (see the discussion of Case 11.3, 'No CRAP vs. No CPR'). If he is able to understand that he has gangrene and will die without surgery, his refusal should stand. If he denies the seriousness of his condition (that he has gangrene and that he will die), his wishes should be overruled. Overruling his wishes would be justified by his inability to apply the knowledge of gangrene to his own condition. *It is not the degree of cognitive impairment which defines competence to make a treatment decision but rather the ability or inability to understand and appreciate.* An appropriate substitute decision maker should be found to make the decision that is in the patient's best interests (assuming he has no capable wishes applicable to this circumstance).

The starkness of the two contrasting options should not obscure the fact that his healthcare team has much work to do. First and foremost, the clinicians involved in his care—hopefully, a multidisciplinary team of doctor, nurse, social worker, occupational therapist, physiotherapist—should make every effort to understand the situation from his perspective. Second of all, they all need to do their assessments not once, but several times over time. Third, they need to ensure that there are no countervailing factors, such as loneliness or abandonment, that would make his choice a less than voluntary one. Fourth, they need to ensure that his capacity has been carefully assessed by the right people. (In most jurisdictions, it would be the clinician proposing treatment who's responsible for the evaluation.)

Finally, they should make a decision as a team about his capacity, in a consensus-driven way. Such multidisciplinary teams may be more likely to make, and be seen to make, appropriate and non-arbitrary judgments regarding a person's capacity than single-profession based judgments. (Here I would suggest that the courts, sometimes asked to make pronouncements on a patient's capacity, are also a single-based profession and so less likely to be accurate in their conclusions—especially as they may never meet the person concerned. See the *Starson v. Swayze* ruling later in this chapter.)

This patient did indeed deny he had gangrene. Despite this, he was able to acknowledge that he would be, in his own words, 'a fool to refuse surgery' *if* he did have gangrene. That was what the team looking after him thought, too, as his quality of life was quite reasonable. The patient was not so foolish that he rejected the healthcare view—he was prepared to admit that the clinicians just might know better than he whether he had gangrene or not. He was, in other words, willing to defer to the professional opinion. As this was thought to be a capable deferral, no substitute decision maker was needed. A team meeting was held, after which, with much encouragement, he agreed to amputation and survived for several more years.

A patient's competence may wax and wane depending on illness and other circumstances. It is well known that patients with cognitive impairment or with various sensory deficits may worsen cognitively with a change of setting or with the time of day. Therefore, to get an accurate picture of a patient's functioning, clinicians may need to visit the patient several times or in different places. Many clinicians only assess patients based on a small window of time. If the patient has a good day, however, he or she may be falsely determined to be competent. Serial assessments over time would be more likely to uncover a reliable and consistent pattern of behaviour that could be assessed as capable or not capable (see Box 6.4).

BOX 6.4

Circumstances that do not on their own warrant a finding of incapacity:

- advanced or very young age;
- poor education;
- physical disability, such as impaired ability to communicate;
- different cultural or religious background;
- idiosyncratic or unusual beliefs;
- psychiatric illness, including disagreement over diagnosis; and
- refusal of treatment.

CASE 6.4   STILL CAPABLE

A 24-year-old man with an active and untreated paranoid disorder presents to the emergency room with a comminuted fractured arm. His injury and the surgical method for correcting it is explained to him. He's willing to have surgery and consents to it. Nonetheless, the surgeon wonders if his mental disorder prevents him from giving valid consent and pages Psychiatry to see the patient.[15]

You are the psychiatrist on call. Must you see him before the surgery can proceed?

DISCUSSION OF AND FOLLOW-UP TO CASE 6.4

In theory, all patients with possible impairments of decision-making capacity should have a capacity assessment done whether or not they consent to treatment. In reality, it is often only those refusing treatment who receive such assessments. The surgeon is right to think about capacity in the case of someone who goes along with treatment. However, the important factor is not the presence of a mental disorder with delusions, but whether the mental disorder significantly affects the specific treatment decision to be made. If the patient can understand and appreciate the decision, then his consent to surgery should be considered valid. As such, a Psychiatry consult is not mandatory before proceeding to surgery. The surgeon's assessment in this case should suffice, unless he is asking for a psychiatric opinion because he is uncertain.

This patient's delusions did not include the surgeons, who he felt were on his side.[16] Despite his disorder, he was able to weigh the risks and benefits of surgery. He was considered competent for the purposes of the consent for surgery.

Substitute decision makers

Competence assessments must be done carefully because their conclusions will have a significant impact. *If a patient is found incapable, he or she loses the authority to make his or her own decisions.* A substitute decision maker must then be found. In most jurisdictions, such substitutes are allowed to make decisions for the incapable patient so long as they follow the patient's prior wishes or, if those are not known, the patient's best interests. Sometimes, as in the UK, a formal court order must be sought in order to be appointed as the substitute decision maker.[17] In other parts of the US and Canada all that is needed is an advance directive from the patient stipulating who is allowed to make decisions if the patient cannot. In these same jurisdictions, an order of proxies is also provided if there is no prior directive from the patient (see Chapter 11 on 'living wills').

Guides for substitute decision makers

CASE 6.5	'I CAN'T LET HIM DIE!'

An 88-year-old veteran is admitted to hospital with community-acquired pneumonia. Initially, he responds to antibiotics, but then rapidly declines. Going into respiratory failure, he experiences an episode of cerebral hypoperfusion, resulting in a persistent vegetative state. He is unable to swallow and is receiving nutrition through a gastrostomy tube. His wife insists that 'everything be done' to keep him alive—including cardiopulmonary resuscitation and return to the ICU should he get sicker.

When asked how her husband would respond if he could see how he was now, the wife replies, 'Oh, he would be appalled. He told me he never wanted to go like this, all these machines and so forth. But I can't abide by his wish—I can't just let him die!'

Substitute decision makers for incapable patients are usually family members but could be anyone with insight into the patient's values and beliefs. When patients are deemed incompetent for medical decision making, what standards should guide those making decisions for the patient? The usual answer is that they ought to abide by

- the unimpaired wishes of the patient, if known, and
- the patient's 'best interests', where the patient's wishes are unknown or not applicable.[18] This includes an assessment of (1) the patient's values and beliefs when he or she was capable if they might pertain to the decision about treatment, and (2) the patient's well-being in relation to the proposed treatment and its alternatives. (Will the proposed treatment reduce the patient's risk of disease or death? What are the alternatives? What are the disadvantages of each option for the patient?)[19]

DISCUSSION OF CASE 6.5

This patient's wife is not making a decision based on her husband's prior expressed wishes. She wants him treated according to *her* needs. She needs to be reminded of the ethical basis for substitute decision making—in a gentle and compassionate way of course. She may still need time to grieve the loss of her husband and decisions need not be made in a ham-fisted way. Nevertheless, her husband's wishes were clear, and ultimately need to guide her and the healthcare professionals looking after her spouse.

This suggests that the professional has yet another responsibility in looking after an incapable patient: clinicians must also assess the suitability of the substitute decision maker. If the practitioner believes the proxy is acting neither on the patient's wishes nor in the patient's interests, there is a moral rationale for overruling the proxy. (The legal status of challenges to various patient proxy decision makers varies among jurisdictions.)

CASE 6.6   RISKY BUSINESS

A 60-year-old woman, hospitalized with cognitive impairment and rapidly advancing refractory Parkinsonism, is no longer able to swallow without aspirating her food. A gastrostomy feeding tube is placed with consent from her 40-year-old son. On several subsequent occasions, he is found secretly feeding his mother by mouth. Moreover, after visits to her home, she returns to hospital with injuries not easily explained by the son.

What ought her clinicians do?

DISCUSSION OF AND FOLLOW-UP TO CASE 6.6

The clinicians involved in her care must carefully assess the son's ability to protect his mother from harm. The healthcare team has good reasons to doubt that the son is a suitable proxy for the patient. In the absence of evidence about her prior wishes, her care has to turn on what seems to be in her best interests. In this case, protecting her airway and physical safety are paramount. The son's actions may indicate that he is unable or unwilling to protect his mother from harm. Legal advice should be sought in order to name another proxy for the patient. In the meantime the son should not be allowed unsupervised visits with his mother.

Discussions were had with the son as to the apparent harm to which he was subjecting his mother. He saw continued oral feeding as a 'quality-of-life' issue for his mother. He was not convinced the ward paid sufficient attention to her. He seemed unable to understand the gravity of her illness and appeared motivated more by feelings of guilt than compassion. As he was sometimes absent from the ward for months and no other substitute decision maker could be found, a court-appointed guardian was sought and obtained for the patient.

II. TREATMENT OF THE VULNERABLE

The professional duty of care for patients with reduced capacity is clear in cases concerning the refusal of medical care. One legal authority has written: 'As a general rule it may be accepted that a higher duty of care to avoid acts of negligence is owed to a person of unsound mind, than to a person of full capacity. The extent that the duty is increased must depend on the circumstances of the case and the nature of the incapacity.'[20]

CASE 6.7   NO ISN'T ALWAYS NO

A 28-year-old woman, mentally challenged and living in a group home, comes to the Emergency Room with buccal cellulitis, a serious but treatable infection of the face with a tangible risk of death. She has had recurrent serious bacterial infections due to a defective immune system. The cellulitis typically requires in-patient treatment with intravenous antibiotics but she refuses this, as she is desperately fearful of needles. You are the resident doctor in Emergency to whom she expresses her wishes in a vociferous and consistent way. You are reluctant to treat her with the necessary intravenous antibiotics, feeling the patient's clear wishes should be respected despite the history of mental disability.

How ought you proceed?

DISCUSSION OF CASE 6.7

This patient's competence should be carefully assessed. The ability to express a choice is hardly an adequate criterion of capacity, especially when death may result without treatment. The patient is known to be vociferous in refusing various interventions in her life (much as a three-year-old child might be), but in general her actions are often not consistent with her wishes (she would, for example, verbally protest putting on a coat in the winter but would readily cooperate once handed her coat). Moreover, when her decision to refuse is examined in detail, it is found that she has little insight into the seriousness of her illness.

In the current circumstances, you should not be distracted by her strenuous objections. Treatment with intravenous medications is appropriate under authorization from a substitute decision maker and is required to rescue this incapable patient from harm's way. In doing so, you should still try to involve the patient as much as possible in her treatment and treat her in a respectful and polite way.

The consequence of removing an individual's right to make his or her own decisions about healthcare is sufficiently important that 'due process' must be followed in arriving at that conclusion. Where it is not, healthcare providers may find their decisions challenged and overthrown by judicial proceedings, as it was in this real-life case.

CASE 6.8   A FRACTURED HIP, A BROKEN MIND

A 76-year-old reclusive single female is admitted with a fractured hip to a large tertiary hospital. When told surgery is required, she refuses to consent, explaining she does not believe she is in a 'real hospital', as people had been rude to her and she had noticed dust on the X-ray machine. She says she doubts she has a hip fracture as she is not in that much pain. 'Just send me home with a wheelchair,' she exclaims. 'I want to discuss this with an old ladies' organization.'

The resident, finding her line of reasoning a bit unusual, deems her incapable. In contrast, the anesthetist in his pre-operative assessment writes in her chart that he found her 'entirely competent' to refuse surgery, specifically highlighting the patient's score of 30/30 on the MMSE (Mini-Mental State Examination—a brief battery of tests that assesses orientation, recall, and concentration) that had been part of the resident's evaluation.

A psychiatric evaluation is therefore requested. On the basis of several visits to the patient, the Psychiatry team concludes that while the patient understands the nature of hip fractures and so on, she is unable to apply that knowledge to herself and acknowledge that, if she had a hip fracture, surgical treatment might help her. She is deemed incapable on those grounds. Told she can challenge the finding of incapacity, the patient does so. The review board finds the patient capable as there is conflicting evidence in her chart from various professionals about her mental status.

DISCUSSION OF CASE 6.8

This case clearly illustrates that the onus is on health professionals to prove incapacity. A disturbing aspect of this case, however, is that the review board made its pronouncement without seeing or hearing from the patient. Such hearings are treated as quasi-judicial processes wherein the patient does not have to give evidence that might appear 'self-incriminating'. Better suited for criminal proceedings, such a review process will be ill-designed to capture the intricacies of some incapacity evaluations—such as 'failure to appreciate' evaluations. The anesthetist's pronouncement was not helpful, of course, and may have swayed the board to think there were some reasonable grounds for finding the patient capable. While the MMSE has its uses, it has nothing to do with testing a patient's capability to make treatment decisions. Before going to a review board, a team looking after an incapable patient should first ensure its own house is in order; that is, that all are agreed with the capacity assessment.

III. WHEN NOT TO RESCUE: MESSRS GALLAGHER AND REID VERSUS DR FLEMING

Dr Fleming must have many difficult days. As a chief psychiatrist at one of Canada's main forensic facilities, his name appears time and again in the newspapers in public cases of involuntary treatment of the mentally ill. The result of at least some of these cases has been to set limits to what physicians may do for patients under their care.

Messrs Gallagher and Reid, involuntary patients at Penetanguishene Medical Health Centre, both had long histories of schizophrenia and criminal behaviour. Both were determined by their in-patient physician, Dr Fleming, to be incapable of consenting to treatment with antipsychotics. On the grounds of their best interests, he requested authorization to treat them with such medications despite their expressed wish, while competent, not to receive such drugs. Both patients had previous experience with the drugs and considered them to be non-beneficial or harmful.

Right to refuse reaffirmed

These cases reached the highest court in Ontario, where they were decided along the *Malette v. Shulman* lines: mentally disordered patients may not be administered treatment they refused while competent. The court wrote:

> With very limited exceptions, every person's body is considered inviolate, and, accordingly, every competent adult has the right to be free from unwanted medical treatment. The fact that serious risks or consequences result from a refusal of medical treatment does not vitiate the right of medical self-determination. The doctrine of informed consent ensures the freedom of individuals to make choices about their medical care. It is the patient, not the doctor, who ultimately must decide if treatment—any treatment—is to be administered.[21]

This judgment seems clear enough: by the doctrine of consent, the right of refusal must extend to psychiatric patients. The paradoxical result is that the principle of autonomy—self-determination, the right to refuse—is being used to maintain a person in a non-autonomous (the untreated schizophrenic) state. In effect, such refusals of treatment are 'psychiatric living wills'. Serving as a 'reverse Ulysses' contract (see the discussion of Case 1.4, 'To feed, or not to feed'), based on the principle of autonomy, they allow patients to reject psychiatric treatment they dislike and subject themselves to clearly foreseen harm which may preclude the restoration of autonomy and free choice.

Implications of right to refuse

Allowing patients to refuse treatment means patients can be committed to an institution but not be treated. This makes no sense, the American psychiatrist Paul Appelbaum has argued.[22] It turns physicians into jailers. As well, allowing such patients greater freedom to refuse medication may lead to problems in psychiatric hospitals such as increased assaults and greater use of restraints or solitary confinement. (This case also raises issues of justice. For example, untreated schizophrenia may result in extended obligations of care in an institution. Is this fair given that, with treatment, such care and its costs might be less?)

Respecting a psychiatric patient's right to refuse treatment may be, in principle, no different than not transfusing a Jehovah's Witness who is hemorrhaging. In each case, physicians have to find some other way to manage the patient's problem, rather than abandon the person because he or she has set certain limits to care. However, the logic behind involuntary commitment of psychotic patients is not just to restore their autonomy by treatment or rehabilitation, but also, at least sometimes, to protect others. While such patients may be able to refuse neuroleptic administration on autonomy grounds, they can still be institutionalized on the grounds of public safety.

A cruel world: *Starson v. Swayze*

This is the sad story behind the complex and long-drawn-out case of Scott Starson. Described variously as a brilliant autodidact in physics and as a troubled paranoid schizophrenic, Mr Starson has been in and out of psychiatric hospitals for over 20 years because of his propensity to utter death threats and appear menacing to others. When he refused antipsychotic medications, complaining they 'dulled his mind and reduced his creativity', judicial leave was sought for him to be treated against his will. This battle went all the way to the Supreme Court of Canada which, in a surprise to some, found in favour of the patient and against the judgments of lower-level tribunals that had seen Mr Starson *in vivo*. Interestingly, while other courts have allowed psychiatrically ill patients to refuse drugs on the basis of a prior competent wish, the majority for the court viewed Mr Starson's *contemporaneous* refusal as sufficient for such purposes.[23]

There are many reasons why this judgment was made, but one is critical. Central to finding someone to be capable is that the person has to acknowledge his or her illness and how treatment will impact him or her (the 'appreciation' test discussed above). In *Starson v. Swayze*, the judges found it acceptable that the patient simply admitted he was 'different'. It is hard to see how a refusal of treatment based on this view on his illness could be an informed refusal, unaffected by distracting issues. (See Case 11.3, 'No CRAP vs. No CPR', and the ensuing discussion.)

The court's view would find a psychiatric patient to be capable of *refusing* treatment when he would fail *every* criterion proposed and supported by the courts for capable medical choice. This allowance and the downplaying of the usefulness of psychiatric treatment ('the cure proposed by his physicians [is] more damaging than his disorder') suggests more than a whiff of anti-Psychiatry-ism—that mental illness is all 'in the mind' (of the physician)—at the Supreme Court level. The pluralism of values in capacity assessments—indeed, the relativity of such assessments—that the majority view espouses has not garnered much following at lower court levels.[24] All one can say to health professionals working in this area is: be meticulous in charting, be transparently clear in your reasoning, and gird yourself for the possibility of judicial review.

Patients such as Starson may end up being 'warehoused' or jailed because they do not receive active treatment for their illnesses. Empirical studies done in the United States suggest that only a small percentage of patients refuse their psychiatric medications (less than 10 per cent in most wards, but up to 75 per cent on forensic units, where the patients may be trying to avoid being jailed).[25] One reason the number remains small is that difficult patients who refuse treatment may be discharged early to 'roam the streets', even though they are 'just as ill' as before.[26] The homeless and psychiatrically ill are sometimes romanticized but, denied the benefits of modern medicine, including modern psychiatry, their reality is often a harsh and cruel one. Or, as Hobbes would have said, it is a world that is 'nasty, brutish, and short'. This is hardly a triumph of autonomy, more the triumph of *anomie*.

Limits on the right to refuse?

It is not yet clear what this Canadian judicial recognition of an involuntary patient's right of treatment refusal will mean in practice. In the United States, although committed patients may refuse their treatment, most get it anyway.[27] Their refusals are usually overridden by review boards or courts that accept the physician's view of appropriateness.

In Canada, there may be similar deference to professional wisdom. As well, there is federal legislation allowing the courts to order treatment of the mentally unfit accused so that the accused may come to trial.[28] Thus, there are other social interests—such as the administration of justice—that limit a patient's right of treatment refusal in specific circumstances. Also, patients may be treated without their consent in emergencies or when they are endangering themselves or others.

IV. FAILURE TO CARE FOR SELF

Patients can fail to care for themselves for many reasons, but a common scenario is that of cognitively impaired elderly patients living at home on their own.

CASE 6.9	'I'D RATHER DIE AT HOME!'

An 88-year-old woman is hospitalized after a neighbour finds her unconscious in her home. The house itself is in a state of extreme neglect and the patient has obviously failed to look after her basic needs for food and hygiene. She presents as confused in hospital and is discovered to be suffering from anemia and pneumonia. When she is medically stable, the patient demands to be released to her home. This, the medical team is reluctant to do, fearing that she would be returning to an unsafe environment as she still appears quite cognitively impaired. The team strongly recommends she be discharged to a long-term care facility but she refuses: 'You can't make me go! If I have to die, I'd rather die in my own home!'

What should the team do?

Mental health legislation allows healthcare providers to follow best medical care and seek the best interests of a patient with a disease of the mind (such as dementia), unless the patient has previously set limits to treatment. Physicians have clinical discretion to decide whether particular patients are in need of care on the grounds of inability to care for themselves. This discretionary power has often been backed up by judicial reviews of civil commitment proceedings. In the United States such proceedings have often been swayed less by an abstract respect for rights than by a concern for the suffering of mentally deranged patients who would certainly suffer without treatment.[29]

Involuntary treatment, in non-emergencies, is often directed towards mental maladies and is given in psychiatric facilities. What of adult patients whose needs seem more exclusively physical? Many jurisdictions lack the authority to provide non-psychiatric medical services to patients who need them in non-emergencies. (See Chapter 3 on the reporting requirements for the vulnerable elderly.)

DISCUSSION OF CASE 6.9

Before placing such a patient in a long-term care facility without her permission, a careful assessment should be made of her capacity around such a decision. Even if she is at significant risk by being returned home to independent living, her choice to return home should be honoured if she is able to understand and appreciate the risks of so doing. Allowing this to happen can be distressing for her healthcare providers who have her best interests at heart and foresee she will likely get into trouble again. Nonetheless, if this is a capable choice, they must go along with this. This is not to say that the patient should now be abandoned to her fate. As much as possible, the treating team should attempt to put as many community supports in place to allow this woman to live as autonomously as possible, given her physical and cognitive limitations. Practically speaking, it may take several more crises before this patient will be able to be institutionalized.

There is now legislation, at least in Ontario, that could authorize this patient's confinement to a long-term care facility without her consent so long as (1) she is not competent to decide about her living arrangement and (2) there is consent from a substitute decision maker.[30] (In practice many such patients, so long as they don't object too strenuously, are 'placed' without much concern for the fine points of the law.) The practical issue is more how to enforce this. Do you take someone like this kicking and screaming to the home? Once in the nursing home, if she has been found incompetent, she could be confined to a locked unit.

Some jurisdictions have gone beyond the strictly mental health needs and addressed the broader medical needs of impaired adults. For example, Newfoundland passed the *Neglected Adults Welfare Act* in 1973 which allows a court to order treatment in a non-psychiatric facility for a 'neglected adult' incapable of caring for himself or herself and requiring care. In Ontario, the capacity to decide on long-term care is considered a consent to treatment issue as the long-term care admission is considered the treatment. Alberta's *Dependent Adults Act* allows limited guardianship by the courts for specific incapacities of at-risk adults in the community in order to authorize medical care in the person's best interests.[31] After a well-publicized case in which a medically ill patient, who refused help, died at home, the United Kingdom amended the *National Assistance Act* to authorize the compulsory removal from their homes of persons unable to care for themselves.[32]

Incapable of personal care

In Ontario, cases like 6.9 are, however, covered under legislation that allows the Public Guardian and Trustee's Office to intervene if a person without relatives is incapable of personal care.[33] This office will investigate such circumstances, it may be appointed to act as the patient's guardian, and it is given 'custodial powers' over the person and the authority to 'search and remove the person [from his or her premises] using such force as may be necessary'.[34] Although this office must select 'the least restrictive and intrusive course of action that is available, and appropriate in the particular case', confinement, restraints, and monitoring of the incapable person are authorized if needed 'to prevent serious bodily harm to the person or to others, or to allow the person greater freedom or enjoyment'.[35] Despite this legislation, many vulnerable patients remain in the community, perhaps because it requires someone to identify and care about such persons at risk. As well, the current concern about legalese and due process can lead practitioners to forget their professional skills and do only what they think the law requires or allows. This can leave vulnerable patients without care.[36]

V. CASES INVOLVING MINORS

May children make their own decisions about the medical care they receive? The answer to this question is yes, if the child has the capacity to appreciate fully the consequences of consenting or not consenting to the various medical options.[37] Rather than age, what is important is the child's mental competence regarding the proposed procedure. Regulations setting an age limit to capacity ('a minor is anyone under the age of 18 . . .') for purposes of estate ownership or drinking and voting may be overshadowed by case law permitting juvenile decision making as regards healthcare. At common law, for example, when a minor is capable, no parental consent is necessary and the state cannot protect him or her, as with an adult, from his or her own wishes to accept or refuse care. (Adolescents may also be permitted to make their own decisions if they fall under a so-called mature minor rule: if, for example, they have left home and live independently or are married. This will not be considered here.) In the UK, similarly: 'As a matter of law, the parental rights to determine whether or not the minor child below the age of 16 will have medical treatment terminates if and when the child achieves sufficient understanding and intelligence to fully understand what is being proposed.'[38]

Despite this Gillick ruling, British courts have not permitted a minor to bring about his or her own death by refusing treatment.[39] Gillick, the leading UK case on consent in minors, established that children, as they become more capable of understanding what is involved in making treatment decisions, acquire greater rights to make those decisions autonomously. By these lights, for example, a doctor may accept a young teen's informed decision about birth control if she does not want her parents to know. On the other hand, the prudent physician would attempt to obtain the parents' involvement for procedures that are of great import for the minor's health and welfare. Here, the involvement of other healthcare professionals can be critical for understanding a child's seeming estrangement from his or her family. If a child refuses parental involvement, the physician should fully discuss such refusals before following the minor's wishes.

Right of minors to refuse life-sustaining treatment

In New Brunswick in 1994, 15-year-old Joshua Walker, a Jehovah's Witness with acute leukemia, was allowed to refuse life-sustaining transfusions.[40] The Court of Appeal found him to be extremely capable and therefore able to be the author of his own actions. New Brunswick, unlike other provinces, has codified the capable-minor doctrine into law.

In a case involving another young Jehovah's Witness, an Ontario Provincial Court in 1985 allowed a 12-year-old girl with acute myeloid leukemia to refuse life-sustaining care.[41] When she refused further blood transfusions, the Children's Aid Society sought court protection for the child. This application was denied because the court found that previous transfusions had infringed upon the girl's right to 'security of the person' and the right not to be discriminated against on the grounds of age and religion.

The patient had 'wisdom and maturity well beyond her years' and 'a well-thought-out, firm and clear religious belief'. The court ruled she ought to have been consulted before the transfusion. In the eyes of the court, the hospital's proposed treatment dealt with the disease only in a physical sense and failed 'to address her emotional needs and religious beliefs; it fail[ed] to address the whole person'. The patient died two weeks later.

Different fact situations have led to different decisions by the courts. A 16-year-old Jehovah's Witness in Alberta who refused blood transfusions on account of her beliefs was ordered to have them anyway.[42] Although found by psychiatric examination to be capable, the court found her decision to be non-voluntary as she was considered to be under the 'undue influence' of her Jehovah's Witness mother. This undue influence was in part due to false information provided by her mother.

Adultlike capacity not enough

The important feature of juvenile consent is that the criteria by which we judge adult capacity—the cognitive and emotional capacity of the individual to consent to treatment—may be insufficient to establish a child's capacity. Children are usually in a vulnerable position vis-à-vis adults. They can more readily be influenced by adults on account of their lack of power and less easy access to independent information. One wonders, for example, whether a 12-year old can independently grasp the nature of a decision such as the non-provision of life-saving care. What sources of support for such a decision could a child have? Wouldn't we want and expect the child to look to and rely on his or parents? If so, this natural dependency should make us look long and hard at a child's volitional and informational autonomy before one follows a child's choice regarding treatment. Some authorities—and the *Civil Code* in Quebec—recommend that children be at least 14 before being allowed to make major treatment decisions.[43]

CONCLUSION

Despite the importance of patient autonomy, healthcare professionals are still expected to exercise their professional judgment and carefully assess and protect mentally incapable patients who are in harm's way. More difficult for clinicians to manage are situations where such patients refuse to be helped and seem to do so for inappropriate reasons.

The extent of healthcare professionals' obligations to rescue or help will be examined in the subsequent two chapters on beneficence and professionalism.

CHAPTER 7 | HELPING AND NOT HARMING: BENEFICENCE AND NON-MALEFICENCE

It is common for helping professionals to feel responsible for meeting their clients' every need . . . it can be difficult indeed to sort out the differences between a 'healthy' giving, born of our deepest desires to love, and an 'unhealthy' giving, springing from unfulfilled psychological needs—for approval, for achievement, to appear more saintly than we really are.

David Hilfiker, 1994[1]

Beneficence is the commitment of healthcare professionals to the well-being of their patients. Once a practitioner takes an individual on as a patient, that person is owed a special duty of care. For that duty to be fulfilled, the clinician is expected to meet the standard of a competent practitioner's care and skill in similar circumstances. However, beneficence in medicine involves more than competence in caring for one's own patients. It also entails a commitment to professionalism (explored in Chapter 8). Beneficence requires minimizing the harms of care, setting appropriate boundaries and sometimes preventing harm to others who may not be patients of the practitioner.

CASE 7.1   A TREATABLE DEPRESSION

You are a psychiatrist who is seeing a new referral, a 45-year-old man with a nine-month history of feelings of sadness, apathy, poor sleep, and lack of appetite. His mood has not changed despite several courses of antidepressants. He is not suicidal and is not

abusing drugs. You diagnose a treatment-resistant depression and recommend a course of electro-convulsive therapy (ECT). After receiving an explanation of the various treatment options, the rationale for these interventions, as well as their possible risks—including the risks of short-term memory loss with ECT—the patient accepts your recommendation.

Is there an ethical dilemma here?

I. THE PRINCIPLES OF BENEFICENCE AND NON-MALEFICENCE

The Oath of Hippocrates directs physicians to use all their skills to benefit their patients and keep them from harm. The principles of beneficence and non-maleficence are the oldest and most important guiding tenets of medicine. Modern medical codes of ethics retain that link with the past. For example, the Canadian Medical Association's Code of Ethics, like many other professional codes, directs doctors to: 'Consider first the well-being of the patient.'[2] The right place to start is with the option(s) most likely to promote the patient's welfare.

Beneficence means doing good or showing active kindness to or assisting others in need. For the medical professions, helping others is not an option ('Hmm . . . shall I help my next patient get better or not?') but a role-mandated requirement. At a minimum, by their interventions—meant to make people better or to prevent harms and setbacks to patient interests—health professionals should not make patients *worse off* than they were before the interventions. This principle of 'non-maleficence' or 'doing no harm' requires health professionals to refrain from doing evil or making anyone ill.[3]

There are standards for practice that all healthcare professionals must meet:

> Every medical practitioner must bring to his task a reasonable degree of skill and knowledge and must exercise a reasonable degree of care. He is bound to exercise that degree of care and skill which could reasonably be expected of a normal, prudent practitioner of the same experience and standing.[4]

Most medical interventions, despite their therapeutic power, do entail *some* risk to the patient: drugs can harm unpredictably and predictably, surgeons can wound unintentionally, psychotherapy can lead to boundary violations, hospitals can be the source of new and dangerous 'superbug' contagions. The professional's 'duty of care' is not to throw up his or her hands in despair but to work to minimize the risks and maximize the benefits of any proposed interventions for patients. Thus, non-maleficence requires healthcare providers to take seriously the problem of medical error, for example, and to learn from their mistakes and to improve their skills.

DISCUSSION OF CASE 7.1

In this case the medical imperative is to help the patient do and feel better, to improve his quality of life, and to reduce the risks of self-harm. The medical facts of the case suggest the diagnosis and prompt the recommendation of a medical intervention most likely to benefit the patient. You must weigh the potential hazards of the intervention against its likely benefits in order to make your recommendations. In making a recommendation, you have made an implicit use of the principles of beneficence and non-maleficence. There is no apparent ethical dilemma in this case—and in most other cases in medicine—because these two principles coincide with the patient's wishes.

In exercising the duty of beneficence, medical professionals are expected as well to offer only *proportionate* treatment—treatment whose likely good outweighs the risk of harm. If the stakes are high, treatment should offer a magnitude of risks of harm that is not greater than the anticipated chance of benefit.

CASE 7.2   NO SURGERY WANTED

You are a surgeon with an 81-year-old female patient who has just been diagnosed with pancreatic cancer, a malignancy that, as of this writing, has a dismal prognosis—most patients die of the disease within a year of diagnosis. Surgery is the only option that is life-prolonging but involves a significant risk of morbidity and short-term mortality. Informed of the diagnosis and treatment options, the patient refuses the operation. She explains she has always been terrified of surgery but adds that she feels she has lived a full life.

Should you accept her refusal of surgery?

Healthcare professionals must judge the benefits and harms of any interventions they propose (see Box 7.1). They are constrained by the principle of beneficence to examine how illnesses and interventions may result in pain and suffering (both physical and mental), disability, and possibly death. Quality of life issues for the patient are frequently unavoidable, and sometimes one must risk a trade-off of life's quality for its duration—such as the patient with cancer who chooses potentially life-prolonging chemotherapy at the expense of (at least in the short-term) a reduction in quality of life. This calculation involves considering less easily quantified issues such as the possibility of restoring the patient's independence, maintaining the ability to relate to others, capacity for happiness and satisfaction, capacity for awareness, loss of dignity, loss of privacy, and loss of control over bodily functions such as urinating and defecating.

BOX 7.1

The principle of beneficence requires the healthcare professional to consider*

- the patient's pain;
- other kinds of suffering, both physical and mental;
- the possibility of disability;
- the possibility of death;
- the patient's quality of life as seen from the patient's perspective; and
- the patient's expectations regarding treatment.

*This list is not exhaustive but does illustrate some major issues to consider.

Although beneficence towards the patient is the standard that should guide medical practice, this does not mean doing everything conceivable. One should do and recommend what seems 'right' for the patient, all things considered—and central to that must be the kind of life one's patient has led and wants to lead.

The 'best interests' standard

Beneficence is not quite the same as the 'best interests' standard. The best interests standard suggests that there is some objectively right course of action that is most likely to help the patient: it is in the patient's best interests that a certain medication be taken or a specific procedure carried out in order to alleviate threats to his or her well-being. Matters are nonetheless not always so simple. At a minimum we presume that something is in a person's best interests if it minimizes pain and suffering and prevents untimely or premature death. Just how these outcomes should be weighed against quality of life factors will depend intimately on a patient's personal values, something that a healthcare provider (and often family members) cannot always predict for a patient. It is this subjective side of beneficence that makes well-being dependent on the principle of autonomy (see Box 7.2).

BOX 7.2

In deciding what is in someone's best interests, healthcare professionals should take into account not only whether the proposed medical intervention is actually likely to improve the person's condition, but also the person's values, beliefs, and expressed wishes.

Doing nothing is sometimes better

Sometimes, when the chance of harm is high and the likelihood of benefit low, it is better to recommend the patient do nothing, recalling the adage 'Don't just do something, stand there!' Judging when one should just stand there can be difficult, often because of uncertainty and the lack of evidence regarding outcomes. Thus, doing nothing should not be confused with non-maleficence because it involves risks of its own. For example, watchful waiting is an acceptable option in early stage prostate cancer but the risk is, despite proper vigilance, the patient's cancer may advance to an incurable stage. Some people are prepared to take this risk in order to avoid the more immediate risks of active treatment.

DISCUSSION OF CASE 7.2

Quite frankly, the only possibly curative option for this patient is surgery but how far should you push this option? If you push too far, it might be at the expense of the patient's views. In your role as the patient's advocate, you must consider not only her best interests but also her preferences. This role requires leaving no stone unturned in exploring both her expressed wishes—especially where they might put her in harm's way—and the various treatment options.

First of all, is the diagnosis correct? How good was the pathology opinion? Should you recommend the patient consult with another colleague? As an octogenarian, what are her chances with surgery? Are there any medical options and how ultimately useful would they be? Does she truly understand her situation? Does she appreciate her limited lifespan without surgery? Is there any evidence the patient might not be competent to make this decision? Further questioning should be directed at why this patient is so afraid of surgery. Has she had some personal experience with bad outcomes of surgery in the past? Is her fear preventing her from appreciating the benefits of the proposed surgery? Is her family doctor reluctant to push the surgical option?

The discussion should ultimately target what the proposed surgery would accomplish and whether such goals are consistent with the patient's preferences. For example, while her physicians might be happy to prolong her lifespan by another year, is this what is important for her? What quality of life does she desire? Has she discussed her situation with other family members and thought about the impact of her decision on them?

While one must respect an informed and competent patient's wishes, even if not 'optimal' medically, one also must ensure there are not 'ageist' assumptions on anyone's part (the family doctor, the family, and even the patient) that might deny an elderly patient beneficial care.

Respecting autonomy

Acting beneficently must therefore also mean respecting the patient's autonomy. Medical care is most successful when it combines the illness perspective of the patient with the disease perspective of the healthcare practitioner. Sometimes healthcare professionals cannot achieve what they take to be the 'best course' but must settle for what the patient will accept. This is perhaps not always ideal, but it is better than nothing and better than dismissing the patient because he or she will not accept one's recommendation. One ought to be humble about these matters, however, because the patient is likely to be right about which choice is best for him or her.

Benefit can harm

Inexperience or unrestrained therapeutic zeal can sometimes cause clinicians to do 'too much' good.

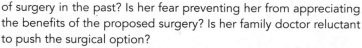

CASE 7.3   TOO MUCH OF A GOOD THING?

It is the last day of the last week of a resident's training program. He eagerly looks forward to becoming a full-fledged doctor in one week. On his last half-day it is nice to see a favourite couple on his patient list. A lovely couple, both in their eighties, they have each survived major medical maladies and are finally doing well. They appreciate the resident's attention to them and his diligence. On that day, he decides to examine the wife's circulation because she has coronary artery disease. He is surprised to hear a bruit over her carotid arteries. Although she has never had strokelike symptoms, he decides to send her for neck Dopplers (ultrasound). These reveal a close to 90 per cent bilateral carotid artery blockage. An endarterectomy is recommended, to which she reluctantly agrees. 'Oh, do I have to, doctor?' The surgery is successful and blood now flows through her carotid arteries. She is sent home four days later.

On her third day at home, she suddenly collapses and is unable to be revived. A postmortem reveals that she died of a massive cerebral hemorrhage.

Was anything wrong done here?

DISCUSSION OF CASE 7.3

The resident is distraught over this outcome. Trying to be a good and thorough clinician, he had, he feels, sent this patient to her doom. Hardly a predictable outcome (but it does happen in 1/400 cases of endarterectomies—due to the high flow of blood rushing through old arteries), he nevertheless feels responsible for this death.

The resident should be reassured that just as it is hubris to believe he can save everyone, so it is hubris to think he, as the medical professional, is always responsible for deaths of patients under his care. Some people just have 'bad physiology', others have plain ill luck, and yet others die because of bad disease. There was nothing 'wrong' done in this case, but one must always remember that medical interventions are two-edged swords. One justification for the use of such dangerous weapons is the informed consent of the patient. Did the patient appreciate the true risks or did she just go along so as not to disappoint her doctors?

Clinicians need to learn to deal with and accept limits—for themselves and for their patients. Wanting to do everything for patients may be noble but, sometimes, one has to ask the healer: 'Are you doing this for the patient, or for yourself?' This, too, is part of the uncertain art of medicine: knowing when the most beneficent thing to do is to do nothing.

Perfection not expected

It is expected that physicians will follow what is 'approved practice' or what a 'substantial' number of practitioners would do.[5] Unanimity of practice and good outcomes are not expected of physicians—but where the outcome is poor (the patient suffers serious harm) or where their practices are deviant, physicians may have their practices scrutinized by the courts or peer organizations to see if they have tried to act in the patient's best interests: 'A doctor is not guilty of negligence if he has acted in accordance with a practice accepted as proper by a responsible body of medical men. [A] doctor is not guilty of negligence merely because there is a body of opinion that takes a contrary view.'[6]

Thus, the courts recognize that the appropriate exercise of medical benefi-cence must allow for different diagnostic and therapeutic interventions, the choice among which may be determined by professional judgment.

CASE 7.4	A BAD NIGHT IN THE ER

An alert 54-year-old man presented late one night to the Emergency Room giving a history of severe headache and syncope. He was belligerent and seemed inebriated. It was the custom in this ER to have such patients 'sleep it off' overnight and be examined by the physician the next morning. After a brief examination the next morning, the patient was sent home with a diagnosis of migraine. Following his discharge from the Emergency Room, the patient's headache progressively worsened, and he was eventually taken to another physician the following day. There a diagnosis of cerebral bleeding was made which resulted in the patient undergoing emergency surgery. The patient subsequently made a complaint to the first physician's regulatory body.

Did the ER physician's care fall below the standard expected of a reasonable physician?

DISCUSSION OF CASE 7.4

The answer will depend on the particular circumstances of the case. Even though an error in diagnosis was made, if the physician did a thorough examination and took the patient's complaints seriously, it is unlikely that liability would be found. In this case, a finding of failing to meet the standard of the profession was made by the physician's regulatory body because the physician was seemingly dismissive of the patient. (The family overhead the physician mutter something about the 'big, drunk baby in cubicle 1. . . ')

Behind the failure to diagnose the problem, and probably at the root of the patient's complaint to the College, was poor communi-cation with the patient and his family.[7]

II. THE 'DUTY TO RESCUE' THE PATIENT

The duty to rescue is an encapsulation of the healthcare professional's obligation to serve the needs of his or her patients—to rescue patients from harm's way, as it were. While the emergency or casualty room best exemplifies this role-mandated duty, medical professionals every day are trying to alleviate the harms or threats to patients. Sometimes the task is to know when one should not attempt a 'heroic' rescue, when an action is disproportionate to the duty (it expects too much of the professional), and other times, by contrast, when one should go out of one's way to save a person at risk. There is a fine line between 'going overboard' for one's patients and 'abandoning' them to their fate. (See Chapter 8 on boundary violations.)

CASE 7.5	NOT LIKE HIMSELF

You are a visiting nurse who does a house call on a 90-year-old previously independent and somewhat reclusive bachelor. Having no family, he lives alone in his own bungalow. Neighbours have been used to seeing him shovelling snow, raking leaves, bent over, not complaining. In recent weeks, the man has taken to his bed and, unlike his usual self, now seems somewhat pale, disoriented, and dishevelled. His fridge is bare other than for a few eggs and some soup. After examining him, you feel he is seriously ill due to anemia of unknown cause and should be admitted to hospital for further investigation. This the patient adamantly refuses to allow. 'It's my heart,' he exclaims, 'I'm ready to die at home.' You respond, 'Well, yes, it might be your heart, but I think your hemoglobin is well below normal and maybe we can do something about that . . .'

How can you best help the patient?

Patients can have mental and physical disorders—delirium, dementia, and depression—that impair their ability to be autonomous and act autonomously. As a result, they may be left quite vulnerable. The principle of beneficence implies a 'duty to rescue' such individuals under an acceptable (indeed, a praiseworthy) version of 'paternalism': taking 'due care' of those in harm's way.[8] This duty authorizes healthcare professionals to act in a patient's best interests without that person's consent in an emergency or when the patient is incapacitated. (The issue of substitute decision making is covered in Chapter 5 on Consent.)

DISCUSSION OF AND FOLLOW-UP TO CASE 7.5

Should you simply accept the patient's 'right to refuse' treatment? Obviously not—at least, not yet. You should explore his views further. Healthcare practitioners are granted the professional discretion to try to educate and persuade patients to accept appropriate medical care. Where patients are markedly impaired, nurses or doctors have an added obligation: they must do what is necessary to prevent foreseeable harm to such patients (for example, seek ways to detain the depressed patient with active suicidal intentions). The duty of care in such cases is to ensure that people will receive necessary medical care when they are incapacitated by illness. Once their autonomy is restored, capable patients can again determine the nature of their medical care.

The question that needs to be asked here is this: is the patient's refusal of treatment reasonable, or merely eccentric, or does it reveal someone whose illness is so severe that it undermines his ability to make an informed choice regarding treatment? If the patient's competence is impaired, as seems likely, the decision to hospitalize him should not depend on his wishes but rather on what course of action is most likely to rescue him from danger. If appropriate home care cannot be arranged or the patient continues to deteriorate, he should be hospitalized against his wishes for his own protection.

This patient's command of English was quite poor, so a translator was involved. After much cajoling, the patient reluctantly agreed to hospitalization. It turned out he was extremely anaemic and septic and had a tumour in his colon. His condition stabilized after convalescing for six weeks in hospital. However, no amount of discussion could persuade the patient to agree to surgery for his tumour.

It was questioned at the time whether his refusal of surgery was a capable one, owing to his language problems and his seeming denial that he had a tumour (he insisted he only had a kidney problem). Despite this, his refusal was respected—probably in part because of his advanced age, and perhaps also due to a feeling of futility—and he returned home one month later. He died there of metastatic colon cancer the next year. In retrospect it can certainly be asked whether he should have been more carefully examined for his decision-making capacity and whether his 'rescue' was not prematurely truncated.

An incapable patient's expressed wishes should not be taken at face value; rather, the healthcare professional will be expected to act in a 'paternalistic' manner. This kind of paternalism simply means making, or helping others make, beneficial decisions (and taking beneficent action) for someone who cannot make authentic decisions and actions and has 'lost' his or her autonomy.

CASE 7.6   NO FOOLS ALLOWED

The patient is 84 years old and as fiercely independent as she can be—she's outlasted several husbands and considers most men incompetent fools. An inveterate smoker, she likes nothing better than lying in bed in silken pyjamas, imbibing her single malt scotch, reading magazines, and smoking cigarette after cigarette. To make a house call on this patient is like taking a trip back in time to some smoky 1950s lounge bar. The patient also hates most aspects of aging—she cannot stand the way it has gradually stripped away her dignity, her smooth complexion, her muscle strength, her stamina, her joie de vivre, and now her memory. Most frustratingly, she is finding it difficult to cope with the requirements of living on her own. Bills are accumulating, papers and magazines are in piles everywhere, the bathrooms are filthy, food is rotting in the fridge, stale air hangs like a thick haze about her house, and cigarette burns have punctured her bedroom carpet, her sheets, and even her usually immaculate pyjamas. Will she accept any help or consider moving? No way. She is, in her view, 'perfectly fine'.

What should her primary care provider do?

This case is about the refusal of care by a failing person at home. The legislation enabling the duty to rescue vulnerable adults varies in different jurisdictions and so medical professionals must confirm what their options are. In Ontario, for example, if one is concerned about a cognitively impaired elderly person's ability to live safely on own, one could: (1) use mental health legislation to force such a patient (under a 'Form 1') into a hospital Emergency Room for assessment (by virtue of dementia being considered a mental illness and the patient being in imminent danger to the self); or (2) arrange to have an evaluation of that person's capacity to make a long-term care decision and enable his or her placement in a long-term care facility on an urgent basis, if he or she is found incapable; or (3) as a last resort, access the Office of the Public Guardian and Trustee which can, under guardianship legislation, make decisions for the individual.[9]

DISCUSSION OF AND FOLLOW-UP TO CASE 7.6

Obviously an assessment of this patient's capacity to make a decision about her place of residence needs to be made. As well, an overall assessment of her mental status is called for. How imminent are the risks to her well-being? Can any supports be put in place that would minimize these risks and allow her to stay home? Can any family members assist with this? These avenues are explored but the patient's fierce independence slows the whole process down considerably. Everyone bends over backwards to try to accommodate her. She agrees to have help and then does not let the help in; she agrees not to smoke in bed and new burn marks are later found; her licence to drive is revoked and she is seen driving anyway. She is just capable enough to barely cope and . . .

Then one day she fails to answer the door. The police are called, break in, and find her lying at the bottom of the stairs with a broken arm and hip, barely conscious. She is admitted to hospital and later discharged to a nursing home. There was something inevitable about her ultimate fate. It is unlikely that any other course of action would have had a better outcome.

III. THE DUTY TO PROTECT THE PUBLIC

The duty of beneficence expected of clinicians may extend beyond serving the interests of one's own patients. Hospitals and physicians, for example, have a duty to protect the public and third parties from harm that might be caused by their mentally ill patients if not 'appropriately supervised and controlled. . . . The psychiatrist's duty to protect will depend on such factors as the particular risk posed by the patient, the predictability of future behavior giving rise to the risk, and the ability to identify the person or class exposed to the risk' (see Box 7.3).[10]

BOX 7.3

A clinician has a duty to protect under the following circumstances:

1. The clinician has a duty of care towards a patient who has made a serious threat of harm.

2. An identifiable person(s) is (are) in danger of grave harm from that patient.

3. That harm may be ameliorated or alleviated by an intervention.

4. There is a special relationship of care between the person(s) in danger and the physician.

Strictly speaking, there need not be a direct relationship of care between the endangered person and the physician in order to find a duty to protect. The dangerousness of the physician's direct client engenders duties to take due care and prevent harm to members of the public that could, predictably, be expected to occur were not proper precautions taken (see Box 7.4). A clinician, for example, who does not attempt to confine or seek to restrain (by involving the police) a homicidal mentally ill patient could be liable for failing to provide due care if the patient should harm another person—even if that victim were unknown to the clinician. In the so-called 'Tarasoff II' ruling, the California Supreme Court reminded physicians that their primary duty regarding dangerous patients was to protect the public.[11] Protecting may be best achieved with appropriate conventional clinical interventions such as committal, assessment, and changes in medication.[12] Physicians have met a statutory duty of care when they hospitalize such patients.[13]

BOX 7.4

Requirements for involuntary assessment or committal:

(1) Dangerousness. Namely, the patient

- has attempted to or threatened to harm himself bodily, or
- has behaved or threatens to behave violently towards another or causes another person to fear bodily harm from him, or
- has shown or is showing a lack of competence to care for himself.

And is suffering from:

(2) A mental disorder likely to result in

- serious bodily harm to the person, or
- serious bodily harm to another person, or
- imminent and serious physical impairment of the person.

Dangerous to others and oneself

Suppose in Case 7.1 the patient were brought to the Emergency Room, depressed and actively suicidal, but refused to be voluntarily admitted or to see a psychiatrist. Virtually all present-day mental health legislation in almost every jurisdiction in North America and the United Kingdom allows hospitals to commit patients (1) who have a mental disorder and (2) who constitute a danger to themselves or to others. Such legislation affirms the importance of the duty of rescue and the protection of third parties in looking after the mentally ill.

Criteria for dangerousness exist and are broadly considered to be justification for intervention. It is not enough that the patient be a danger—he or she must also have a mental disorder that appears to underlie the behaviour. Were it not for the mental disorder, the dangerous person would be taken into police custody rather than to a psychiatric facility.

Legislation allowing involuntary admission and assessment is often interpreted narrowly by physicians, who may have too restrictive an understanding of such terms as 'mental disorder' or 'imminent harm'.[14] Imminent means 'more likely than not' that it will occur—for example, a serious threat of harm to another that can be alleviated only by an urgent medical intervention, such as an emergency assessment. People with 'mental disorders' include, not only those who are acutely depressed or psychotic, but also individuals who have personality disorders or who are delirious or are irreversibly cognitively impaired. Great leeway is allowed in the interpretation of such terms. Morally, it seems preferable to protect patients or others from serious harm rather than allow an individual to refuse necessary care because of a mistaken desire to respect patient autonomy.[15]

Professional's liability

Professionals have worried that the duty to protect intended victims might impose unfair burdens on them (see Box 7.5). In general, such fears have been unwarranted.[16] Where the courts have found a professional liable, the circumstances have usually involved a failure to follow appropriate clinical practice—such as neglecting to look over available medical records for evidence of past violence or failing to examine a patient. Additionally in such rulings, the patients had made a specific threat of violence, and so the harmful outcomes would seemingly have been foreseeable if the professional had taken into consideration all the relevant factors.[17] This is clearly the crux of the matter, since predictions of dangerousness are far from certain. As long as healthcare professionals perform comprehensive and careful assessments of their patients, they are unlikely to be held liable if someone is injured by their patients. Prognostic error is allowed so long as they have exercised 'due skill and care' in their assessments.

The clinical duty to protect may be an evolution of a more basic morality concerning the duties 'citizens owe each other when one is in danger and a second can provide assistance'.[18] This common-sense morality—an expanded version of the beneficence principle—seems a fitting way to explain our basic professional obligations as healthcare providers.

BOX 7.5

Ways for clinicians to fulfill their duty to protect:

- Warn the intended victim or the relevant authorities, such as the police.
- Hospitalize the patient voluntarily.
- Seek involuntary commitment of the patient.[17]

A duty to attend?

As a healthcare professional, how far does one's duty to serve the welfare of others extend? A Canadian physician was found in breach of professional standards when he failed to attend to a patient in the ER, despite having completed his regular shift.[19] An Australian doctor was found negligent for refusing to attend to a person, not his patient, who collapsed outside his office.[20] In each of these cases the courts felt there was some professional requirement— in emergencies—for doctors to attend to patients if it could be done at no great personal cost and if what seems to be required is within the physician's sphere of competence.

The extent of this retrospective court-mandated 'duty to attend', however, is not clear legally or morally. Legally, one is not forced to be a 'good Samaritan', even if one is a doctor. Likewise, physicians are not usually obliged to take anyone on as a patient (although it is expected that they will not exclude patients on discriminatory grounds—see Chapter 8 on Professionalism).

So, when the call goes out, 'Is there a doctor in the house?' those who respond do so now largely out of moral sentiment. There is no legal requirement to rescue those in harm's way nor is there a requirement to do so when this would put oneself, as the medical professional, directly in harm's way. There can be situations—during epidemics, wars, and disasters—that exceed the dangers of ordinary civil life, however. Because of their commitment and special training, it is expected that healthcare professionals may have to put themselves in harm's way *to some degree*. Extreme situations can tax a professional's commitments to serve patients and the public. Is exposing oneself to such increased hazards morally required or simply allowable? Certainly, healthcare professionals are not required to sacrifice themselves—and ought not to allow themselves to be sacrificed—in emergencies. A patient waving a gun in the ER is a job for the police, not the medics. Healthcare professionals cannot avoid taking on some extra risk, but just how much risk is hard to quantify. They are also expected to take 'reasonable precautions' to look after their own safety (such as not re-capping needles or double-gloving to prevent exposure to contaminated fluids).[21] The healthcare professional who looks after patients only if there is no personal risk would be seen as acting in an unprofessional way.

IV. MINORS AND NECESSARY MEDICAL CARE

The care of young children is another area where beneficence as a guiding principle comes to the fore. Recommended treatment ought to reflect that which seems to be in the juvenile patient's best interests, that is, the course of action entailing the most benefit and the least harm. Although children may not be able to express competent wishes, they may have very strong preferences that cannot be ignored. The striking difference in the care of young children, as opposed to adult medicine, is that healthcare professionals usually cannot have independent, if any, recourse to the patient's wishes in deciding what to do. Someone—parent or healthcare professional—must make the decision for the child. In cases of conflict, whose view as to what is in the child's best interests should prevail? How should the young child's preferences regarding others' views about his or her best interests be taken into account?

What is seen to be in the juvenile patient's best interests can vary depending on the perspective of the beholder. The interests of a minor would seem to be inextricable from those of the family—it may be hard to determine what the child wants or even needs except through the filtering lens of the parents. Parents may have important cultural, religious, and ethnic beliefs and customs that may influence how they and their offspring view the various medical options. Such parental or family factors should be considered in medical decision making but may not be paramount where the child is critically ill and capable of being rescued by standard medical intervention. One must also always bear in mind what is on the child's mind: what are his or her hopes and fears?

Parents, for example, may refuse the best medical therapy for their child. Is this acceptable? The brief answer to this question is yes—but only under certain conditions.

Discretionary therapy

Our society regards the family as an important, semi-autonomous locus of individual power and decision making, not to be readily supplanted by others such as healthcare professionals. If a medical therapy is discretionary, that is, not required to save a child's life or prevent serious injury or disability, parents can take the physician's recommendation under advisement. (An example of this would be whether or not to take antibiotics for an ear infection.) Even if we think parents' choices for their children are poor, we do not usually interfere.

For example, we allow parents to enroll their children in hockey leagues, even though we know that every year some children are seriously injured in this sport. That does not mean clinicians cannot voice their professional opinion as to what they think is in the child's interests (such as being immunized). Only if parental refusal of best treatment imperils the child is there legal authority to intervene. Child welfare authorities may also be called in for assistance in situations of lesser gravity—poor parenting skills—to help parents cope with the responsibility of raising children.

Necessary treatment

If the medical therapy will, on best medical evidence, prevent death or serious injury to the child, the parents' discretionary power to refuse treatment is reduced. In Canada, the United Kingdom, and the United States, legislation obliges parents to provide their children with the necessities of life. If parents, whether by design or through neglect, mistreat their children, the children can be removed by the child welfare authorities so that the needed treatment can be given.[22] In some jurisdictions, a court hearing must take place before treatment may be given.[23] Where the situation is a true emergency, however, healthcare professionals should not wait for judicial approval before instituting emergency care.[24]

Children cannot be martyrs

The limits to parental authority were at issue in 1923 in a classic US case, *Prince v. Massachusetts*. In that case, a Jehovah's Witness was charged with violating child-labour laws in allowing her nine-year-old niece to sell religious pamphlets on the street. The court held that the rights of parenthood are limited by the state's authority to act in the interest of children:

> The right to practice religion freely does not include liberty to expose the community or the child to communicable disease or the latter to ill health or death. . . . Parents may be free to become martyrs themselves. But it does not follow that they are free . . . to make martyrs of their children before they have reached the age of full and legal discretion when they can make that choice for themselves.[25]

This much-quoted decision serves as the basis for limiting the right of parents to refuse treatment for their children. Thus, while adult Jehovah's Witnesses may refuse necessary blood transfusions for themselves, they may

BOX 7.6

A parent may not deny a child—even for religious reasons—medical treatment judged necessary by a medical professional and for which there exists no legitimate alternative.

not do so for their children. In January 1995, the Supreme Court of Canada unanimously upheld the judgments of lower courts that a Jehovah's Witness couple had no right to refuse a blood transfusion for their infant (see Box 7.6).[26]

Where parents refuse therapy—typically, life-saving—statutes and legal precedent exist to allow the authorities to apprehend the child and provide the treatment. (In some cases, the child is not physically removed from the parent's custody, rather consent for needed treatment is given by a temporary court-appointed guardian.) Criminal charges may also be laid if necessary. For example, in the United States, Christian Science parents who have allowed their children to die of treatable diseases by foregoing medical care in favour of prayer have been charged with manslaughter, felony, child endangerment, and reckless endangerment.[27] A classic Canadian case that raised this entire issue in a more complex way was the Stephen Dawson case.

The Dawson case: parents not free to expose child to risk of permanent injury

Stephen Dawson was a seven-year-old boy, severely mentally and physically handicapped as a result of infantile meningitis. At the age of five months, a shunt had been inserted to drain off excess cerebrospinal fluid. The child was blind, partly deaf, and incontinent and could not feed himself, walk, stand, or talk. He suffered seizures and, to his parents, seemed to be in pain. When his shunt became blocked, his parents refused consent for remedial surgery on the grounds it would be better to allow Stephen to die than prolong a life of suffering. The child was apprehended by the child welfare society and the British Columbia Supreme Court authorized the surgery.[28]

The court accepted medical evidence that life was not so gloomy for the child, that he was happy despite his handicaps. It did not believe that Stephen would be better off dead: 'This would mean regarding the life of the handicapped child as not only less valuable than the life of a normal child, but so much less valuable that it is not worth preserving.'[29] Troubled by the seemingly 'imponderable' quality of life issue, the court was also worried that without surgery an even worse fate might await the child: without the shunt he might continue to live but with more pain and disability. In allowing the surgery the court followed the UK judicial principle 'not to risk the incurring of damage to children which it cannot repair'.[30]

Even on the best odds, mandated therapy may not guarantee success. However, it should be a treatment that has some reasonable chance of rescuing the child. In a 1981 Saskatchewan case concerning a parental refusal of blood transfusion, it was noted that while parents 'are not obliged to provide the best and most modern medical care for a child, they must provide a recognized treatment that is available'.[31] A treatment less likely to succeed and requiring more suffering on the child's part may be seen as within the parent's discretion to refuse.

Experimental treatment not mandatory

In 1989, the parents of a seven-month-old child with biliary atresia refused authorization for liver transplantation. At that time, of the children who received this treatment, 65 per cent lived at least five years. Representatives of Saskatchewan's Ministry of Social Services sought legal authorization for the treatment on the grounds that not doing the surgery might constitute child abuse.

However, at trial, a majority of the doctors who testified defended the rejection of surgery as a reasonable option because of its long-term uncertain outcome and the burdens it would impose upon the child. Although recognizing that it might save the child's life, the provincial court judge refused to order transplantation, agreeing that the parents' refusal was 'completely within the bounds of current medical practice'. He believed that the parents' rejection of treatment was not a rejection 'of the values society expects of thoughtful caring parents' but based on their concern for the child's best interests.[32]

There is thus some discretion allowed in deciding when parents' rejection of treatment is inappropriate.[33] Refusal by parents of life-saving care is clearly not an option, unless defensible by a 'reasonable body' of medical opinion. Refusal by parents of 'ordinary care', such as childhood immunization, is allowed in many jurisdictions, if the refusal is an 'informed' one. In general, where the treatment is complicated, the 'right' (or best possible) decision should be made consensually by parents and healthcare providers and should take into account not only technical factors but also the practical, psychological, and emotional aspects of the situation. In particular, close attention must be paid to the child's informational and emotional maturity and independence. The closer the child is to adult capabilities in these regards, the closer the decision taken ought to cleave to the child's preferences (see Chapter 2 on Autonomy).

Child abuse and neglect

| CASE 7.7 | **FASTING UNTO DEATH** |

CASE 7.7   **FASTING UNTO DEATH**

A nine-year-old child was placed on a 40-day fast for chronic otitis media by her grandmother, who was her caregiver. A child-protection agency worker found the child severely emaciated, crying, and vomiting. The agency asked a general practitioner to attend the child. He did so with some delay, diagnosed the child only as mildly dehydrated, and failed to consult a specialist despite the worries of the child-protection worker. The latter did subsequently call in a pediatrician, who hospitalized the child, assessing this as a clear case of child abuse. Unfortunately, the child died of meningitis. The general practitioner was found guilty of professional misconduct for failing to attend properly to the child.[34]

By contrast with the previously discussed difficult decisions—made with the child's best interests at heart—child neglect or abuse means not looking after the basic needs of children and directly harming them or putting them in danger of readily avoided grave harm. The healthcare professional's moral and professional responsibility in clear cases of neglect and abuse is to notify the child welfare authorities. (See Chapter 3 on Confidentiality for further discussion of mandatory reporting.) Those who do not do so may be disciplined by their professional body for professional misconduct or prosecuted for failing to comply with the law concerning child abuse. Although it may be difficult to challenge the authority of parents or guardians by reporting them to child welfare authorities, it is better for healthcare professionals to err on the side of safety if the child's interests are at stake.

DISCUSSION OF CASE 7.7

Child neglect and maltreatment are often underreported owing to a failure to recognize or report the abuse.[35] The general practitioner was lucky not to be suspended, since his failure to protect this child was implicated in her death. The requirements of beneficence entail clinician responsibility to protect those patients, such as children, who are vulnerable and dependent.

V. PARENTAL REQUESTS FOR TREATMENT

What about the opposite situation: may parents choose whatever therapy they wish for their dependent children? The answer to this question is, in general, yes, if the therapy is medically appropriate and consistent with beneficence. The classic Canadian legal case that limited parental choice was *E (Mrs) v. Eve*. Eve's mental age was that of a very young child, hence, it would seem that the ethical principles behind this decision ought also to apply to the care of young children generally.

| CASE 7.8 | E (MRS) V. EVE |

Eve was a 24-year-old mentally handicapped woman with a communication problem who was looked after by her parents, but quite capable of interacting socially with others. The parents, who felt that she (and they) would not be able to cope with a pregnancy, requested she be sterilized for contraceptive purposes. Eve (on the basis of precious little evidence) was considered by the courts too handicapped to give consent and could not express her wishes regarding sterilization. The Supreme Court of Canada believed the parents were requesting the sterilization for the convenience of themselves and not for the benefit of the patient. The court ruled in 1986 that sterilization could never be authorized for such non-therapeutic purposes. The parents' request for sterilization was refused.[36]

Was this an appropriate decision?

DISCUSSION OF CASE 7.8

This is clearly a difficult case. Lacking at trial was any medical evidence that the effect of any pregnancy would be so bad as to justify preventative sterilization. There was also insufficient evidence of no other less intrusive method than surgical sterilization for preventing conception. However, the court's ruling that surgery was not in Eve's best interests, and therefore not therapeutic, seems a narrow one. While there may have been no strictly physiological benefits to this patient from sterilization, there could have been social and psychological benefits to her. From a wider psychological perspective it is possible that she indeed could not have coped with a pregnancy.[37] *As a result of the Eve decision, the courts require that sterilization—indeed any medical procedure—may be done on persons incapable of consenting only for clear, medically approved reasons.*[38] Hailed by some as a victory for disabled persons, it may be a hollow victory due to its restricted consideration of the needs of Eve as a whole person. The needs of a disabled person and their fulfillment may depend on the attention of others, something that might be diverted were, for example, pregnancy to intervene.[39]

Medical interventions must help child

In cases of elective medical intervention for children, the courts require clear evidence that the procedure is necessary for preserving the dependent child's life or safeguarding his or her health. Non-therapeutic interventions, especially ones that are irreversible and pose some risk of harm, should not be carried out on children (or other dependents) just because the parents authorize them (see Box 7.7).

BOX 7.7

The litmus test for childhood intervention: is this intervention in the child's best interests?

Thus, parental consent is insufficient justification to carry out a medical procedure on a child. Just how far to extend the Eve decision is unclear.[40] Is circumcision of the male permissible? (Probably it is—the risks are small, and it is defended on medical grounds by a substantial section of the medical community.) What about bone marrow donation by one sibling to another? (Probably it is—if the best-interests standard takes psychological benefit into account.) Cosmetic surgery for a child with Down's syndrome? (Suspect—is it of direct benefit to the child or to the parents? How do we weigh the importance to the child of looking like others?) What about cochlear implants for a deaf child who can sign? (Dubious—if the child does not wish it and seems happy and well-adjusted. Acceptable if the child is very young.)[41] Enrolling the child in a research trial? (Sometimes acceptable—see later in this chapter.)

CASE 7.9   THE PILLOW ANGEL

A six-year-old girl has a severe and untreatable neurological disorder that has left her profoundly impaired, with the mental life and physical abilities of a three-month-old child. She is looked after by her parents at home. They inquire as to the possibility of ceasing their child's physical maturation—specifically, they would like her bone growth halted and her sexual maturation prevented to avoid menstruation and pregnancy. They argue that she will never benefit or understand her sexual development and that a smaller size will make her easier to care for (a 'pillow angel') and less likely to develop pressure sores and feeding problems and require institutionalization. Keeping her small will make looking after her easier and more comfortable for all.[42]

Is the parents' request for such treatment of their child a legitimate one?

DISCUSSION OF CASE 7.9

This real-life case is rather astonishing and elicited a storm of public controversy. Is it in this child's 'best interests' to be kept small and immature so that others can look after her more easily? On the other hand, if her parents' request were to be allowed, what are the short-term risks from the surgery and the long-term risks of medications needed to stunt her growth?

The basic issue for many people is that this child would be undergoing invasive treatment for her parents' convenience. It also suggests that the lives of the disabled are only tolerated if they conform to the needs and tolerances of the fully abled. The proposed solution seems to be a modern version of Procrustes' 'one-size-fits-all' bed in ancient Greek mythology. Welcoming strangers into his home, Procrustes offered them food and lodging. Once on the special bed, however, the poor stranger was tortured: stretched if too short or, if too long, had his legs chopped off. The message to the disabled would seem to be: you're welcome to stay but only on condition that you are easy to look after and not overly demanding.

Complex calculations: beyond simple best interests

Because the answers in all these situations are not entirely clear, physicians need to think carefully about parents' requests for interventions before complying with them. In complex cases, such as transplantation from one sibling to another, it is important to consider the less easily weighed factors, such as emotional benefit and family impact, in the determination of a child's best interests.[43]

Resist the clearly harmful

It should go without saying that one should never comply with a parental request for therapy that promises clear harm and no benefit to a child. Such is the case with all forms of female circumcision, which is mutilating, always harmful, not medically justifiable, and certainly illegal under North American and European child-abuse laws.[44]

In other cases of questionable—but less clearly harmful—requests for therapy, the wise healthcare professional will discuss with the parents the reasons for their requests, rather than dismissing them out of hand. It would also be important to include the child's views, if possible. It is professionally prudent and respectful of parental authority (and also respectful of the child) to try to understand their perspectives and attempt to negotiate a mutually acceptable solution. This may involve looking at other options—less hazardous and more readily correctable ones first—that will try to meet the needs and concerns of all involved. Particularly contentious disputes can be helpfully addressed by multidisciplinary teams designed to examine the ethical, legal, and medical facets of the problem.

The problem of determining what is in the child's best interests is not unique to medicine: the courts must make such determinations in child custody disputes. The wishes of the parents and child, the quality of the relationship between the child and the parents and any significant others, the child's special needs and developmental requirements are some of the factors that must be taken into account. Assessors on behalf of the court are encouraged to assess the child and parents separately and together seek 'convergent validity' by assessing the factors from different perspectives: the parents, the child, the child's teachers, and so on.[45]

Research involving children

It can be argued, following the *Eve* decision, that medical research should not be done on children given its lack of 'therapeutic benefit' for the participating subjects.

The evidence for this is not clear, however. While any research requires consent or substitute consent, research can be done on children (and other incapable persons) where

1. research results cannot be obtained from capable subjects,
2. the research results will be relevant to the class of incapable patients enrolled, and
3. the research's expected risks of harm are not disproportionate to its anticipated benefits.[46]

The beneficence principle would not allow the researcher to use incapable subjects for his own purposes or for mere convenience. Parents or guardians must never consent to research that might compromise a child's best interests. In all such research, there must be scrupulous attention paid to protecting the research participants. Children who resist the study's procedures or burdens ought to have their inclinations respected and be withdrawn from the study. As one author has put it, 'research should never be carried out on children, but *with* them'.[47]

Conclusion

Beneficence and non-maleficence are key principles that inform medical care today. Relevant to all healthcare professionals, they speak to the expectations the public has of healthcare and the codes of conduct by which health professionals measure their own performance and those of their peers. In emergencies or where patients lack alternatives for care, however, there may be an evolving duty to attend even if one is not a casualty officer. The next chapter will cover the evolving issues of healthcare professionalism.

Unfortunately, despite our best efforts, some patients are harmed by what we do to them. In Chapter 8 I will also examine the professional issues involved in medical error and medical mishaps.

8 | CONDUCT BECOMING: MEDICAL PROFESSIONALISM AND MANAGING ERROR

In all dealings with patients, the interest and advantage of their health should alone influence the physician's conduct towards them.
Robert Saundby, 1907[1]

There are less than optimal situations—gaps between 'ought' and 'is', between how things should be and how they are, between expectation and experience—that a healthcare professional must be cognizant of and care about. Ethics can help provide the tools and rules to recognize and bridge these gaps. This chapter will address two connected areas—what it means to be a professional and how professionals ought to respond to error in healthcare—that should be high on the agendas of every professional and every healthcare institution and association.

I. PROFESSIONALISM IN HEALTHCARE

It seems somehow anachronistic to write about professionalism at a time of seeming postprofessionalism.[2] Expertise seems to be only a click away on the Internet. Knowledge, of course, is a necessary component of being a professional but attitude is as important, if not more crucial. A constellation of knowledge, skills, and attitudes establishes the core competencies of any healthcare professional.[3] But professionalism can be eclipsed by all sorts of distractions, from the obvious—such as the lure of money and fame—to the merely pedestrian—such as family issues and personal likes and dislikes. Buoyed by the appropriate aptitudes, professionals are like those unsinkable bath toys for kids—push them under the water as hard as you like, they always bounce back up.

CASE 8.1   A PAIN IN THE BACK

A 54-year-old male patient is admitted for the fourth time in two months for complaints of severe radicular pain following several attempts at decompressive back surgery. His pain has been sub-optimally controlled with very high-dose narcotics and other adjuvant pain-management medications. The nursing staff takes his vital signs at the start of every shift but otherwise only appear when his medications are due or he rings the call bell. The pain waxes and wanes but is so severe at times that he cries out. The medication ordered for breakthrough pain is ineffective. When he tells one nurse this, she responds, sighing, 'You've had your pain medication and you'll just have to wait three hours for your next dose. I'm going on break, so don't bother to ring the bell.'

What's wrong in this scenario?

Hard to define, almost anyone who has been a patient recognizes what is a professional attitude and what is not. Compare the nurse who says, 'I haven't looked at your chart yet, but here are your pills' to the nurse who cares enough to know that a particular patient likes his pills with ice water. Compare the medical trainee who begins her interview with a patient by saying, 'We have only 10 minutes today and so can only deal with one concern' to the learner who converses with a cancer patient by asking, 'Tell me how things have been for you lately. Did anything occur that you weren't expecting?' Contrast the attitude of a physician who doesn't work evenings or weekends and instructs his patients to attend the local ER if they have an out-of-hours problem with the physician who shares call with other clinicians and makes house calls on those too ill to venture out.

Something important is lacking in the attitude of some practitioners—they seem uninterested in truly understanding their patients. They will do their job, work the requisite hours, meet minimal standards for competence—the 'legal' requirements for their position. But true professionals go beyond the minimum to ensure that patients receive what they are due. This does not mean they must be altruistic heroes; instead, they can simply be ordinary, everyday clinicians who do their work well. The professional is someone who cares about what is done and how it is done and responds to patients in ways that are reasonable, mindful, and achievable by ordinary mortals. He or she has an aptitude to focus in on the unique needs of a patient in situations where another would be distracted and stray.[4]

DISCUSSION OF CASE 8.1

There are many comments that could be made about this case. The patient feels abandoned, with the sense there is no one to stand up for or care for him. The nurse's notion of caring seems to end with 'doing her job'. She is following the 'rules'—doling out the medications as ordered—but not doing more than that. Something has happened to the professionalism of this nurse. Does the problem have to do with this particular nurse alone or is it a 'systems issue'? Is the workload too heavy? Do the allied healthcare professionals on that floor not feel respected by the attending physicians? Is there a ward 'culture' that does not consider the individuality of patients and their unique needs?

Anyone can dole out pills according to a schedule (and robots can do it even better)—but only a dedicated professional can ask, 'What's gone wrong here? What can I do better for the patient?'

Professional manners

It is the attitude to shortfalls in care that distinguishes the professional from the unprofessional provider. There is more to being a professional than knowing rules, precedents, and duties. It also requires attitudes such as civility, tolerance, patience, competence, and accountability. As Peabody said, 'The secret of caring is caring about the patient.'[5]

Politeness and kindness are attitudes that reveal one's true commitment to the principle of respect due persons. Rudeness and just plain bad manners—not respecting a patient's privacy, leaving a patient in distress, failing to apologize for lateness, screaming at staff or patients, not saying please or thank you, not listening, not returning messages, neglecting to provide explanations to patients for maneuvers—can lead to patient disappointment and may prompt complaints to the regulatory authorities.[6] In one study a clue to malpractice actions was the failure of the surgeon to convey to patients, in his or her voice, his or her anxiety or concern about the patient's plight.[7] Firmly shaking hands is preferred by most patients and a sign of mutual respect in many cultures.[8] Other expected behaviours include a friendly smile, making eye contact, making the patient feel prioritized—all ways to lessen the patient–professional distance in an age of technology and anomie.

CASE 8.2   A QUESTION OF ATTIRE

You are on call one weekend with a resident, covering several wards of adult internal medicine patients. It is busy and both you and she have been up for much of the night admitting patients from the backed-up ER. It is now Saturday morning and time to round on all the admitted patients. The resident turns up a half-hour late, dressed in an outfit that includes a short top revealing her lower torso and her bejewelled navel. As you round on the patients, most of them fix their eyes on the resident.

Should you say anything to the resident?

DISCUSSION OF CASE 8.2

Many people would say, do, nothing. After all, we live in a diverse and modern society and people should be allowed to dress in any way they see fit. Others would argue that, as professionals, we should be concerned about the impact of what we say or do upon our patients. In this case an argument could be made that the resident's attire is distracting and interfering with the work that has to be done. As the attending staff, you should say something—tactfully explore with the resident whether she is aware of the impact her clothing has upon others and whether something a little more modest might be better suited to the clinical setting. It's a simple matter, but it is also a matter of professionalism—dressing in a way that shows respect for patients and that encourages respect from the patient for the professional in training.

Virtues

The distance between knowing what one ought to do—to bridge the gap between how things are and how they should be—and knowing how to do it may make it hard for a professional to act properly. Moral virtues are the habits of the heart and reason that impel people to overcome moral inertia and act properly. These virtues and their importance to the practice of medicine have been described admirably by Pellegrino.[9] Compassion, honesty, responsibility, benevolence, self-motivation, and trustworthiness are some of the virtues that can encourage and allow healthcare professionals to achieve the ideals of professional practice. Without proper moral motivation—a genuine concern for others—it is unlikely that decisions taken will be either trustworthy or the 'right' ones.

Is the opposite the case? Can you be a perfectly good healthcare professional so long as you are guided by an internal moral compass? If so, perhaps you need not be explicit about your ethics (just as you can ride a bike without knowing how you can do so).[10] The reality, though, is that we live in an ethically diverse society. Medical advances in therapy and diagnostics add to this complexity and make intuition, good old common sense, and kindly intentions less reliable guides now to solving moral problems than they might have been in the past. Something more is needed, and this, among other things, is the place for an explicit attention to professional ethics.

A new charter

In response to the concern that modern medicine was losing its moral mooring, a 'new professionalism' initiative was launched in 2002 by various internal medicine societies for physicians. The American Board of Internal Medicine (ABIM), American College of Physicians-American Society of Internal Medicine (ACP-ASIM), and the European Federation of Internal Medicine (EFIM) adopted the 'Medical Professionalism in the New Millennium: A Physician Charter'. This charter is based on the three principles underpinning the practice of medicine, namely, the primacy of patient welfare, patient autonomy, and 'social justice'. The charter is intended to 'promote an action agenda for the profession of medicine that is universal in scope and purpose'.[11]

The charter's principles could, quite frankly, apply to any of the healthcare professions. According to the charter, physician obligations include the commitment to:

- professional competence
- honesty with patients
- patient confidentiality
- maintaining appropriate relations with patients
- improving quality of care
- improving access to care
- a just distribution of finite resources
- scientific knowledge
- maintaining trust by managing conflicts of interest
- professional responsibilities, such as regulating members and setting standards

These themes and principles are ones this book has tried to iterate. Medicine's ability to help and to heal requires an atmosphere of trust, something the courts remind us time and again. 'The essence of a fiduciary relationship . . . is that one party exercises power on behalf of another and pledges . . . to act in the best interests of the other.'[12] This is the crux of professionalism and of ethics in medicine. The clinician owes his or her patient: 'loyalty, good faith, and avoidance of conflict of duty and self-interest'.[13]

The following case is not typical of what professionals do but is a reminder as to how wrong things can go when clinicians are distracted by outside interests or activities. *At the heart of unprofessional behaviour, whether egregious or mundane, is a practitioner using the patient or the encounter for his or her own ends.* The practitioner's own issues or concerns come to eclipse the patient's needs and expectations.

CASE 8.3   CAVEAT EMPTOR

A 73-year-old immigrant labourer with metastatic renal cancer unresponsive to all forms of treatment is referred for palliative care at home. Unwilling to accept this dismal prognosis, his family searches the Internet for alternative treatments. They find a local physician who advertises unconventional treatment with a remarkable new drug. This new drug is purported to have no side-effects and is 'effective' for many malignancies. There are numerous references to cures, patient testimonials, and to other websites, but none to reputable medical journals. This drug, the website claims, has been shunned by the medical establishment which only wants to protect its own turf. It is available exclusively through this particular doctor for cancer patients who have 'failed' traditional treatment and been declared incurable.

The patient and his family visit the doctor who repeats these claims and adds, 'Of course, this treatment is not covered by private insurance or the medicare system. Because it is so hard to get and so intensive a regimen, I have to charge you $30,000 for a month's worth of treatment. Is it worth it? I can't promise you it will work and moreover medical authorities do not approve of it, but I ask you: what is your father's life worth?'

Why is this not acceptable professional practice, despite the patient and his family appearing to be freely making an informed choice?

DISCUSSION OF CASE 8.3

This case is based on a real physician who came under the scrutiny of medical regulatory authorities.[14] He was deemed to be in an irresolvable conflict of interest situation. Relying on the good faith the public invests in the medical profession, the doctor's practice was self-serving and threatened to undermine that public confidence. Offering exorbitantly expensive and unverified treatments traded on the patient's and his family's fear of death; this resulted in uninformed and semi-coerced choices. He was found to be engaging in 'conduct unbecoming a physician'.

It is said that Hippocrates refused to attend to the sick of the Persian Empire—at that time at war with Greece—despite being offered a considerable recompense by the Persian emperor. One can take this as a tale with a favourable moral: the physician ought not be swayed to do the wrong thing by the lure of money. On a less generous interpretation, Hippocrates refused to treat some patients in need because of a morally irrelevant reason—they were not Greek citizens. While a country's citizens are not duty-bound to help another country's, even on the battlefield, the modern army medic aids the enemy patients as well as those of his or her own country.[15] This is true professionalism—it is not money or nationality that should motivate clinicians but the needs of patients before them.[16]

Nowadays, it is not emperors who seek to influence healthcare professionals but private industry and large pharmaceutical companies.

II. PROFESSIONALS AND THE DRUG INDUSTRY

CASE 8.4   SUPPING WITH THE DEVIL

You are a physician with an older clientele and you have a particular interest in hypertension. You are always willing to try new drugs in your patients with resistant hypertension. A new drug, Syperia®, is released following a large international drug trial that showed it to be as safe as and as effective as the leading drugs in this area. The pharmaceutical representative from the new drug's manufacturer offers you an opportunity to take part in a Phase 4 research trial. For every patient you enrol in this trial, you will receive $100 per year and an extra $100 at the study's completion. All you have to do is to switch them to Syperia® and assess the patient's response to treatment every three months.

Is there anything of concern with your participation in this research?

DISCUSSION OF CASE 8.4

Is this is true research or just veiled marketing? While this type of 'study' is purported to assess the effectiveness of such a drug in 'real-life' patients as opposed to subjects who typically have to meet strict inclusion and exclusion criteria demanded by peer-reviewed research, it is often a not so subtle attempt to influence physician prescribing patterns.[17] By generously recompensing you

for something you would probably do anyway—such as assessing a new drug's clinical effectiveness—the study puts you in a conflict of interest situation. If in taking part in this trial you recommend that a patient switches to the new drug, Syperia®, are you doing so for the patients' interests or for your own? This situation is conflictual as it sets up the potential for you to act in ways that are not conducive to the patient's interests. Even if you convince yourself you are doing so for the patient's benefit, many people would not see it that way. Notice it is not the amount of money that is at issue but the perceived lack of independent judgment that triggers concern.

Clinicians can avoid (or at least ameliorate) conflicts of interests by

1. disclosing their recompense to their patients,
2. ensuring patients understand the research component to what they are doing,
3. ensuring that patients and their families appreciate the research by having a meticulous informed consent form,
4. accepting only reasonable recompense for work actually done and avoiding lavish or extravagant gifts from private industry, and
5. carrying out only bona fide research that has been vetted by a credible research ethics review board.[18]

That being said, there are few laws that make healthcare professional participation in such research 'illegal'. Legal it might be, but it is less than morally optimal and is another instance of threats to the trust the public puts in the profession.

You can 'sup with the devil', to paraphrase an old saying, 'but use a long spoon'. Concerns about health professionals' relationships with private industry have led to formal strategies to make the spoon longer and the meal a more open table. In the US, the Prescription Project aims to improve physician prescribing patterns by supporting legislation curbing inappropriate relationships with private industry. For example, the *Physician Payments Sunshine Act* would require drug and medical device manufacturers with more than $100 million in annual revenue to report all gifts over the amount of $25 given to physicians, clinicians, and other prescribers. This kind of legislation is encouraged by the public's perception that prescribers are 'on the take' from the drug industry. Indeed, billions of dollars are spent yearly by the drug companies on physician-directed gifts, ads, and various other promotional efforts to influence their prescribing patterns.[19] The upside is that such influence may encourage the early adoption of beneficial drugs. The downside is that prescribers may prematurely turn to unproven or expensive drugs. A further downside is that it can eclipse what should be the independent judgment of healthcare professionals, a bad outcome for all.

Similarly, in Canada, the Canadian Medical Association has supported guidelines for physicians' relations with private industry.[20] The industry has been obliged to adapt to these guidelines which strictly limit the kinds of events that can be supported by the private sector. Nowadays every speaker or writer must disclose their relations with pharmaceutical companies. Conferences must be organized for independent educational reasons. Gone are the fancy dinners and private holidays.

CASE 8.4   REDUX

You decide to join the Phase 4 Syperia® trial, confident you are immune to any untoward influence of the study on your practice. There are many alternatives, after all, for resistant hypertension. However, the new drug's apparent lack of side-effects and once-daily dosing will make it a valuable alternative in your 'resistant' patients. You see the drug rep from the pharmaceutical company before your clinic, accept drug samples for use with your patients, and attend an educational dinner sponsored by the same company at a pleasant restaurant with a speaker on resistant hypertension.

Are you doing anything unprofessional here?

DISCUSSION OF CASE 8.4: REDUX

If you are, you are in good company—many doctors routinely see drug representatives—many get useful educational information from them—many like having samples to use with their patients and many would attend a drug dinner sponsored by a reputable company. Such educational sessions are rarely simply advertisements for new drugs—speakers have their independence and attendees are not stupid. On the other hand, maybe we are kidding ourselves. Studies have shown time and again that physicians who accept certain relations with industry are more likely to use their drugs.[21]

You should periodically monitor your drug-prescribing patterns to ensure their true independence from the industry. Comparing your prescribing habits with the recommendations in evidence-based guidelines will help ensure your integrity and also lessen your reliance on industry for your education. Forming a reading group with other prescribers is another check on perceived drug company influence.

III. BOUNDARIES AND CROSSINGS

The determination of appropriate boundaries with third parties such as the drug industry is an important aspect of the New Charter for professionalism mentioned above. Even more important is the setting of appropriate boundaries with patients. Although helping patients is a primary focus in medicine, there are limits to this, such as the patient with self-destructive wishes.

| CASE 8.5 | THE DRUG TYPE |

You are a physician in a Community Health Centre. A 32-year-old man with a history of street drug abuse, including intravenous drugs, has been seeing you because of back pain. This is a result of a knife fight years ago. He gets relief only with a narcotic but requires 8 to 10 tablets a day. For the second time in six months, he claims to have lost his prescription. He now asks for more of the narcotic to get him through the day. You consider 'firing' the patient from your practice.

How ought this patient be best managed?

DISCUSSION OF CASE 8.5

It would be best not to meet this patient's request too quickly but to discuss his addictive traits since he is asking you to prescribe a controlled substance. It may well be that he is not being truthful about having lost his prescription and his request may mask a drug addiction. While many physicians would be unhappy about keeping such a patient in their practice, you should be cautious of the rush to judgment. You could use this visit as an opportunity to review his care—is his pain being adequately treated? Are there non-pharmacological means of treating it? Is the diagnosis right?

While you should not immediately give in and meet the patient's request, you should make sure that this patient is not being dismissed as a drug addict without some compassionate enquiry into his situation first; just because he seems to be 'that type' doesn't mean he doesn't deserve just as good care as your businessman with alcohol abuse!

Of course, if this patient is drug-addicted and not wrongly diagnosed, you have to set very clear rules regarding drug use and prescriptions. Breaking these rules, it should be understood, will lead to therapeutic termination. (There are procedures to follow, if one is to take the drastic route of 'firing' a patient.)[22]

Healthcare professionals' obligations to their patients arise out of the fact of illness and the commitment to healing. Professionals are expected to ameliorate or cure illness, prevent ill health and premature death, and palliate the suffering of those ill beyond saving. In doing so they must exhibit 'good faith' and use reasonable care, skill, and judgment. This does not mean they must reflexively follow every patient wish or tolerate every patient behaviour. But how far can one go in helping a patient? Can a practitioner do too much? The answer to this is yes: clinicians can indeed go too far in trying to 'rescue' patients. Although this may seem helpful to patients, it can be deleterious to the patient-professional relationship when it reflects the physician's needs. The next case is a rather extreme, but true, case.

| CASE 8.6 | A BOUNDARY TOO FAR |

A depressed 33-year-old pregnant patient of a psychiatrist was in jail awaiting trial for a serious crime she was alleged to have committed. Although eligible for bail, the patient was estranged from her family and had no one to put up the $60,000 bond. In desperation, she called the psychiatrist, pleading with him to help her. Concerned that her mood would deteriorate, he cancelled a half-day of patients to attend her bail hearing and provided a surety for her bail.[23]

Was the doctor's action a magnanimous response to a patient in need or a serious breach of professionalism?

Serving patients

The tradition of serving patients—of seeing they get the right treatment at the right time—is at the core of medical professionalism. A healthy therapeutic relationship between a clinician and patient, a major factor in determining that a particular patient receives the right treatment at the right time, requires the construction of a professional space. Such a space is defined by its borders. The professional relationship suffers and patients can be harmed where boundaries are not respected. Among other things, professionals run the risk of treating those patients differently from other patients—either in a special way or shunning them if things turn out badly. Patients, in turn, may develop inappropriate expectations of the clinician or, if things go badly, become mistrustful of all healthcare professionals.[24]

Crossings and violations

Transgressions of such boundaries fall into two categories: violations and crossings.[25] 'Crossings' are minor infractions of a boundary. These are deviations from expected professional behaviours, such as accepting tokens of appreciation from patients or attending a social function held by a patient. 'Violations' are more serious boundary transgressions, whether by intent or by the deed itself, that compromise the professional encounter, such as having sexual relations with a patient. A violation undermines the patient-centred, 'best interests' therapeutic nature of the clinician–patient encounter and replaces it with a situation where the healthcare professional's needs displace those of the patient. Some of these occurrences may be misguided attempts to be helpful to patients. These situations may speak more to the clinician's personal needs to be the 'rescuer' than the patient's need to be rescued.

Gifts from patients to professionals

Boundary violations go beyond the sexual to include other forms of personal and inappropriate infringements on the therapeutic relationship. Excessive gift receiving by healthcare practitioners can encroach upon the appropriate distance between clinician and patient. Gifts of a small nature are usually acceptable so long as they remain simply totemic representations of the therapeutic encounter—small gifts can be, for example, respectful and courteous 'thank you's' from patients and are not necessarily intrinsically wrong.[26]

More concerning are generous gifts that, in their largesse, threaten to overwhelm the requisite professional distance between patient and healthcare professional. Even seemingly trivial gifts may degrade the professional relationship and undermine the quality of care provided.[27]

Gifts from professionals to patients

What about 'gift giving' *by* healthcare professionals *to* patients? The existing literature deals with such less serious transactions as giving patients bus fare to go home or providing them with the money to buy needed drugs they cannot

BOX 8.1

'Physicians might feel compelled to give money to a patient because, fundamentally, physicians are compassionate and empathic professionals who care for and about their patients.'

afford.[28] While frowned upon, giving money to or doing favours for patients is nowhere considered unethical *per se* by regulatory authorities.

DISCUSSION OF CASE 8.6

Unfortunately, fate is unkind to many patients and deals them blows of ill fortune and harm. It is not usually the job of healthcare providers to assist patients in avoiding all the harms and stressors that non-medical ill fortune—from stock-market crashes to job losses—hands them. Healthcare practitioners may help patients cope with the outcomes or impact of such events on their lives, but they do not seek to prevent such bad events from occurring.

Some observers might see the psychiatrist's actions as entirely understandable. His motivation seems therapeutic and not obviously self-serving. At worst he may be motivated by an overwhelming desire to rescue this patient—a mistake in judgment, for sure, but not a crime deserving of punishment.[29] That he sought no supporting peer opinion as to what he was doing suggests he acted impulsively and thought little about the implications of his actions. Psychiatrists, in particular, must be careful not to get their boundaries blurred: to go too far in trying to rescue a patient undermines the requisite therapeutic space needed for patient independence and healing to take place.[30]

When faced with an unusual or inappropriate request from a patient, the astute clinician should ask for the opinion of others, such as his professional insurers and professional and regulatory authorities. This advice can help ensure that one's actions do not go beyond the normal clinical interventions that professionals use. Unusual or personal favours for patients can have pernicious results for the therapeutic encounter and can damage the reputation of medicine generally.

Sexual impropriety

CASE 8.7   AN UNCOMFORTABLE REVELATION

You are a social worker who is seeing a new patient for psychotherapy. In taking her history, you ask her about her current medical care. The patient reluctantly tells you that currently she is without primary care. She did not feel comfortable seeing her former physician as he had made, on more than one occasion, sexually explicit remarks to her. She has not told anyone else of this.

What should you do?

A variety of interpersonal encounters and transactions between healthcare practitioners and patients have been traditionally disallowed or frowned upon, with the regulatory colleges of the various groups of healthcare practitioners setting out guidelines most clearly around sexual contact with patients.

As far back as Hippocrates, sexual relationships between physicians and patients have been forbidden. Since then, a sexual relationship with a patient has been considered a misuse of the healthcare professional's power and prestige. Although there is some leeway with respect to former patients for family physicians and the like, psychotherapists in particular must adhere to more rigid prohibitions. Sexual relations with former as well as current patients are forbidden in the codes of ethics for health professionals engaged in psychotherapy (see Box 8.2).

BOX 8.2

The *Regulated Health Professional Act* in Ontario requires any health professional to report another health professional reasonably believed to have sexually abused a patient.

Sexual abuse includes sexual intercourse with a patient, sexually touching a patient, and 'behaviour or remarks of a sexual nature'.

DISCUSSION OF CASE 8.7

Sexual abuse of patients by healthcare professionals has resulted in public inquiries in two provinces.[31] Sexual abuse of patients is an egregious misuse of a health professional's authority and a breach of the rule that health professionals must act only in the patient's interests (see Chapter 6 on Beneficence). The Canadian Medical Association advises physicians to take 'every reasonable step to ensure that such behaviour is reported to the appropriate authorities'.[32] In Ontario any member of a regulated healthcare profession must report if he or she has 'reasonable grounds, obtained in the course of practising the profession, to believe that another member of the same or a different college has sexually abused a patient' and the professional knows the name of that member.[33] Failure to report could be considered professional misconduct. If this patient's allegations are true, this is clearly a case of sexual misconduct. You should do as the CMA suggests to its members. It is preferable that allegations be submitted with the consent of the affected patient. However, if the patient prefers not to register a complaint, the professional may lodge the complaint with the regulatory College of the purported offender without naming the patient.

In some cases we must be our brethren's keeper. This is true for serious infractions such as sexual impropriety with patients. The new professionalism suggests we also must be vigilant when it comes to other clinical failings of our colleagues and, indeed, of ourselves. Medicine in being more powerful is now also more dangerous, itself frequently the cause of patient harm. As a healthcare professional you will make your share of mistakes—the way in which you manage them will test your true commitment to professionalism.

IV. THE ERROR OF OUR WAYS

CASE 8.8   **'I'M JUST SO TIRED!'**

You are a busy family physician in private practice. You are seeing a 45-year-old corporate lawyer with two children who comes complaining of fatigue of several months' duration. She reports she has recently been working very long hours preparing for a case but has been additionally stressed due to her assistant having left on maternity leave. She admits she is not eating properly and is not getting enough sleep. You both agree she should try to get more balance in her life. Just to rule out other causes of fatigue, you send her for some basic labwork, telling her your office will call her only if the results are abnormal. Otherwise, she should come back to see you in three months.

Three months later, in the New Year, she returns to your office for her follow-up visit. You look over her chart just before you enter the examining room. To your horror, you see that her bloodwork from the last visit indicates a significant reduction in her platelet, red and white blood cell counts compatible with aplastic anemia. You have absolutely no recollection of ever having looked at the report. 'Doctor, I'm still feeling really exhausted even though I'm getting enough sleep and the case has been settled,' she says as you sit down.

What should you say or do?

Error, adverse events, and negligence

An error in healthcare may be broadly defined as any outcome or process that you would have preferred not to have occurred—as when one says afterwards, 'Oh, that was a mistake.' Errors are not always harmful—they may be interrupted before affecting anyone. For example, writing the wrong dose on a prescription may be an error but not cause the patient harm if the pharmacist catches the mistake before the patient receives the medication. Errors also usually entail some moral responsibility because one could have done otherwise—acted 'better' or 'differently'—in the circumstances. (If you couldn't or wouldn't, reasonably, have done differently, then there is no 'mistake', only an unfortunate event.) By contrast, adverse events in medicine are incidents caused by a medical intervention that are harmful to patients or that threaten to harm (set back the interests of) patients. About one-third to half of adverse events are considered preventable and so can be designated as errors. (An adverse event would be a rash following the first-time administration of penicillin to a patient; it would be an error if the same outcome happened due to an inadvertent second-time use of penicillin in the same patient.)[34]

BOX 8.3

Negligence requires

1. a duty of care,

2. a breach of the standard of care,

3. an injury to the patient, and

4. the injury must have been caused by the breach.

'Negligent events' refers to that smaller class of events that cause harm, are preventable, and would not have been made by a careful clinician in the circumstances in question (see Box 8.3). Perfection is not the standard of care, 'reasonableness' is if they follow the 'standard of care'.[35] For example, a practitioner may make a mistake in diagnosis despite having done everything correctly up to that moment. If a mistake could be made by a reasonably careful and knowledgeable practitioner acting in a similar situation, then the mistake may not be deemed negligent in a court of law (see Box 8.4).[36]

The scope of the problem of medical error and harm is huge. Studies done in Canada, Australia, the UK, and in the US reveal very similar adverse event and

---

BOX 8.4

'[. . .] the standard of care which the law requires is not insurance against accidental slips. It is such a degree of care as a normally skilful member of the profession may reasonably be expected to exercise in the actual circumstances of the case in question. It is not every slip or mistake which imports negligence [. . .]'

error rates.[37] If these studies are right, preventable adverse incidents are connected with the deaths of about 1 in 200 patients admitted to hospitals. This is an astonishing number and it has not gone unquestioned. Whatever the exact number, adverse events in medicine are acknowledged by all to be a serious quality of care issue for healthcare and were the subject of a major and influential US report in 1999.[38]

Honesty about error

We have always known that illnesses and their management are complex. 'Life is short, the art is long, judgment uncertain and experiment perilous,' so wrote Hippocrates or one of his followers two thousand years ago. Medicine is still perilous and difficult. All clinicians have bad days and even the best make mistakes. But what is the proper professional attitude when an error or adverse event transpires? When bad things happen to our patients, the automatic human response is often to be defensive and secretive about them. If the resultant harms to patients are serious and seemingly avoidable, the professional's reaction can be one of shame, guilt, and embarrassment.[39] Professionals involved in medical mishaps must learn how to tame such automatic responses and try to be open and honest about such events. There are now recognized to be many reasons for such honesty: public expectations, legal requirements, philosophical reasons, respect for patients, public trust, psychological reasons, and system improvement reasons. We will look at a few of these factors.

Public expectations

There are few 'laws' *per se* that require healthcare professionals to be honest about error with patients.[40] This may change as the extent of harm that can be caused by medical care becomes apparent. The cases of medical harm that prompt patient and public ire are frequently those seriously adverse events where no one has taken responsibility for the mishap and those situations where different patients have been harmed by the same hazards in the medical environment. Often, too, there is perception of a 'coverup' by the professionals and institutions involved.[41]

The failure of professionals to be thoroughly honest about such harms or hazardous situations is a violation of professionalism, considered to be particularly deserving of sanction. For example, damages of $20,000 were awarded in a 1999 British Columbia case in which a surgeon left an abdominal roll in the patient's abdomen. During the more than two months' delay in telling the patient, he took active steps to cover up the mistake (for example, by telling the nurses not to make any written record of it). The court described the surgeon's delay in informing his patient and his deliberate attempts to cover up his mistake as demonstrating 'bad faith and unprofessional behaviour deserving of punishment'.[42]

Studies of patients and families who pursue legal action reveal that a need for explanation and accountability, and a concern for the standards of care are more often motivations for suing clinicians than is a desire for financial recompense.[43] Thus, it can be helpful to provide patients and or their families with a full explanation of unexpected events, even if 'minor'. One study revealed that more than 90 per cent of patients want to be informed about even minor errors.[44] Promptly informing patients and families in a straightforward way what is known about harmful incidents fosters a healthier and more realistic understanding of medical care and may prevent later anger.

DISCUSSION OF CASE 8.8

You must be honest with the patient about the missed lab report and what the abnormal results likely mean. You should tell her what you know about pancytopenia, its causes and management. Even if she fails to ask, you should tell her of last year's missed report. A lawsuit might result but, quite frankly, this should be the furthest thing from your mind. Your mind should be turned to: how can I ensure this patient gets the best care possible without further delays? She needs to understand that part of the urgency stems from the missed lab reports. It is doubly bad to compound the original mistake by attempting to conceal it. If the patient is not told and finds out later, this might result in anger over a perceived coverup.

Reducing risk of lawsuits

Certain 'facilitative' communication styles by health professionals can be protective against suits and complaints, no matter what the patient outcomes ('Do my recommendations make sense to you?' 'Do you have any other concerns we haven't addressed today?' 'Has anything about your illness or the treatment to date been a surprise for you?'). This disclosure is difficult for clinicians to undertake.[45] A 2004 study suggested full disclosure of error may reduce a clinician's malpractice relative risk by about one-third (absolute risk reduction, 8 per cent).[46] Overall, legal advice being sought by patients or their families in the US was more likely if an error was not disclosed and if it had a life-threatening outcome for the patient.

While error disclosure may be no guarantee against suits and complaints, such honesty can reduce the punitive 'sting' that sometimes accompanies judgments against clinicians. Kraman and colleagues reported on the experience in an American Veteran's Administration hospital that routinely informs patients and their families of any error and then offers them help in filing legal claims for recompense.[47] This 'proactive' policy of error disclosure did lead to a net increase in the number of claims made against the hospital but many more were local, out-of-court settlements. As a result, this hospital had the eighth-lowest total monetary payouts out of 36 comparable VA hospitals.

Disclosure therapeutic

Honesty may be the best policy when it comes to errors but clinicians are often reluctant to disclose errors, sometimes out of fear of legal consequences, but more commonly because of their shame, the typically high standards of perfection they set for themselves, and their fear of being censured. Secrecy around error ends up being counterproductive, nevertheless, as it impedes learning and can leave the clinician who participated in the poor outcome with a never-ending negative emotional burden of guilt and shame. Case reports by clinicians remind us of the tremendous psychological strain 'healers' undergo when they appear to harm the patients they serve.[48] Clinicians need to be supported as they, too, suffer when patients are harmed.[49] Disclosure of the untoward event can be therapeutic for clinicians and prevent the corrosive effects of duplicity on one's self-esteem as a healthcare professional.

When to disclose

When should a clinician disclose error?

- The greater the impact or harm an adverse event has or may have upon a patient, the greater is the obligation to disclose the event to the patient and/or the family.
- By corollary, 'non-significant events' do not require disclosure. However, just what 'significant' means may depend on individual or subjective factors that need to be taken into account by clinicians when deciding whether they ought to disclose an unanticipated outcome to the patient.
- When in doubt, it is better for clinicians and institutions to err on the side of disclosure than non-disclosure.

As a general rule, acknowledgment and discussion of the unexpected event should be undertaken by a trusted clinician known to the patient/family. It should take place as soon as possible after it has been identified and when the patient is stable and able to understand and appreciate the information.

BACK TO CASE 8.8

You take a deep breath and begin to explain what happened with the lab report from three months ago . . .

How should you make this disclosure to the patient?

How to disclose error

Establishing rapport with the patient is the first step. Express sympathy: 'I am sorry to see that you are still feeling so tired.' Don't beat around the bush and don't wait for her to ask. Instead say, 'I have something difficult to tell you: the abnormalities were also there the last time we did bloodwork on you.'

- Once rapport has been established, provide information and offer, 'Would it be helpful for me to explain what I think happened . . . ?'
- Avoid defensiveness.
- Provide a narrative account.
- Remember, it is not helpful to lay blame on others or yourself (see Box 8.5).[50]
- Don't speculate: if you don't know, find out. 'Here's what I know now . . .'
- Empathize with/normalize the patient's feelings. Use reflective listening: 'I know this must be hard for you . . .'
- Apologize for the event and be accountable for your part in its occurrence, its satisfactory management and prevention.

BOX 8.5

The following language should be avoided when discussing 'error' as it simplifies what is usually a complex event.

- 'I dropped the ball . . .'
- 'I sure made a mess out of things today.'
- 'Yes, I know it is not your fault . . . it is all my own.'
- 'I made a mistake and now you will have to have surgery.'
- 'The events are entirely my own fault. . . .'

Cause and accountability

The etiologies of error and adverse events in healthcare are manifold and well explored elsewhere (see endnote 38). Suffice it to say that there are typically systemic and individual factors involved. An example of a 'persons' issue is a nurse, who, through fatigue or inattention, inadvertently causes the death of a patient in giving IV KCl, instead of IV NaCl. The systems issue would be the hospital stocking lookalike medications, one lethal and the other not, in the same location. The systems issue facilitated or allowed the nurse to make the error; the error was occasioned by the nurse's fallibility. As we are humans, no matter how good we are as clinicians, we will make mistakes, sometimes with grievous consequences. We need safe systems that can assume and plan for human fallibility.[51]

For example, a common error is the 'missed result'. Sometimes clinicians say such mistakes—resulting in omissions of appropriate timely treatment—happen because they are 'too busy' to follow up on all the tests they order. The courts have not been kind to such arguments. Clinicians who are so busy that they compromise patient safety should get busy getting less busy.

CASE 8.9   THE MISSED RESULT

Dr V, a hospital-based obstetrician-gynecologist, did a Pap smear on Ms B in May 1992. The smear showed evidence of pre-cancerous cells but the patient was not told about this and did not receive treatment until 11 months later when she was diagnosed with an advanced form of cervical cancer. She died of the disease one-and-a-half years later. Her estate sued Dr V for negligence.[52] Evidence was presented at trial that, shortly after doing the Pap smear, Dr V left the country for an extended period and the hospital closed the clinic he worked in—no arrangements were made to handle his reports and, as a result, the Pap smear report of Ms B was unseen by a clinician until almost a year later.

Should anyone bear liability in this case, and if so, who?

DISCUSSION OF CASE 8.9

The original trial judge was tough. The 'standard of care' for following up on an abnormal test result as in this case, he opined, did not involve 'medical skill or expertise'. Thus, this could not be a case of 'error of judgment. . . . Having an appropriate system in place fell within the ambit of his (Dr V's) personal professional responsibility.' The judge found no direct hospital liability, ruling the failure was all Dr V's.

The higher Appeals Court thought this standard was 'too high' in requiring the doctor to 'ensure' such a system was in place. Instead, the standard should be 'a duty upon the physician to see to it that

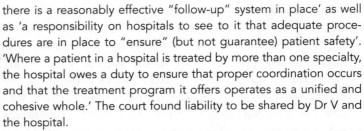

there is a reasonably effective "follow-up" system in place' as well as 'a responsibility on hospitals to see to it that adequate procedures are in place to "ensure" (but not guarantee) patient safety'. 'Where a patient in a hospital is treated by more than one specialty, the hospital owes a duty to ensure that proper coordination occurs and that the treatment program it offers operates as a unified and cohesive whole.' The court found liability to be shared by Dr V and the hospital.

I think the Appeals Court got it right. No one would defend missing an abnormal Pap smear for a year as an acceptable error, one that a reasonable physician could make. It could not be disputed that the delay in diagnosis contributed to the patient's demise. The only open question was: who should bear liability? The physician could and should have arranged coverage for his patients. The hospital also had a responsibility to its patients, so a shared liability seems appropriate.

Anonymity and cooperation

The problem today is what Balint called the 'collusion of anonymity': when different healthcare professionals are involved in the care of a patient, it is all too easy for the patient's care to fall between the cracks and for no one person to be responsible.[53] In modern healthcare, where multiple specialties and professions are almost always involved in the care of a patient, this failure to provide coordinated and comprehensive leadership can have serious repercussions for the patient. The responsibility for patient welfare does not end if one claims to be only indirectly involved in the care of a patient. If ancillary professionals have some information that bears on the patient's well-being, there is an evolving duty to see that this information is received and acted upon. For example, when significantly new and unexpected findings are seen on an X-ray, there may be liability for radiologists who do not ensure that the findings are acted upon. A radiologist's duty, for example, does not end with issuing a timely and accurate report: 'Where there is an unexpected finding which may affect patient management or where the severity of the condition is greater than expected, it is the responsibility of the radiologist to communicate this information to the clinical team either by direct discussion or other means.'[54]

If this is so, why not other professions or specialties as well: pathologists (who detect cancerous cells in a specimen) or physiotherapists (who detect a weak leg in a person still driving)? The interdisciplinary-coordination expectations regarding healthcare professionals generally, in so far as each provides information essential to the comprehensive assessment of patients, are growing. To meet these expectations, the following recommendation for radiologists could apply to any healthcare professional.[55] He or she

- must coordinate his or her efforts with those of other healthcare professionals involved in the care of the patient;
- must have a system in place whereby unusual, hazardous findings can be communicated to the patient and/or the treating team; and
- may have a duty to communicate directly with the patient if he or she is unable to contact the most responsible clinician in a timely way.

Responding to error

Corrective action as regards errors and adverse events is possible—this dangerous side of medicine is receiving attention worldwide. Every hospital now has 'quality assurance' programs and patient safety efforts. The public disclosure of hospital and even individual mortality rates has had a salutary effect on medical care—causing the seemingly less safe institutions and individuals to improve their care lest they get left in the dust. These efforts to reduce harm to patients are legion and expanding at an impressive rate. There are so many problems and possible solutions, the problem may be one of knowing where to start. The involvement of patients in improving patient care might be critical to this. Heretofore, improvement efforts relied upon mortality and morbidity rounds, chart reviews, and incident reports—all essential activities. But in the twenty-first century we need to do more. Health professionals must find new ways of encouraging patient involvement in patient safety efforts. What are the problems patients and their families see in medical care? How can we use the Internet and modern information technology to elicit feedback and time of event reporting from patients? Patient focus groups and expert patient panels can help to get to the root problems and elucidate what patient-focused solutions might look like.

CONCLUSION

Professionalism encompasses a broad scope of duties, attitudes, and behaviours by healthcare practitioners. Honesty, openness about medicine's limits and harms, and the importance of learning will all advance medicine, that 'greatest benefit to mankind'. Professionalism is being reconsidered and remodelled in profound ways by the educational, regulatory, and credentialing institutions for healthcare. This renewal may help the professions maintain their patient-focused ethos in hard times. As medicine's greatest historian, Roy Porter, explained, 'Medicine's finest hour is the dawn of its dilemmas.' There is hope. 'Many of these quandaries,' he writes, can be resolved with common decency, goodwill, and a sensible ethics committee.'[56] Hear, hear.

CHAPTER

9

BEYOND THE PATIENT: DOING JUSTICE IN MEDICAL CARE

It was the best of times, it was the worst of times, it was the age of wisdom, it was the age of foolishness, it was the epoch of belief, it was the epoch of incredulity, it was the season of Light, it was the season of Darkness, it was the spring of hope, it was the winter of despair, we had everything before us, we had nothing before us . . .

Charles Dickens, 1859[1]

The future belongs to crowds.

Don DeLillo, 1991[2]

I. JUSTICE IN EVERYDAY MEDICINE

It is certainly not the worst of times for medicine, but it is not the best either. It seems to be troubled times for medicine today—for example, patients are generally doing better than ever but many are not happier for it—they are, in the words of one observer of medicine, 'Doing better, feeling worse.'[3] Health-care professionals seem to share this malaise. The recent past seems to have been a time of optimism and unlimited potential, when any disease could be cured and price was no object. Now, things seem more complicated—diseases are more challenging, and care is more complex, more expensive, and less readily available. Concerns about cost and scarcity give rise to questions of allocation and fairness or justice. In this chapter we will explore in greater detail the principle of justice and how it affects healthcare and healthcare practitioners. The focus will largely be on 'distributive justice' from the practising clinician's perspective.

Though not often consciously considered, questions of justice come into play every day in the clinical care of patients.

| CASE 9.1 | TIME WELL SPENT? |

You are a geriatrician for a 92-year-old widow who visits you monthly. Her main complaints are fatigue and sadness connected with her experience of aging. Although she is not physically ill in any particular way, your main reason for seeing her is simply to listen to her concerns and be supportive. Although you cannot cure her sadness, the patient feels somewhat happier knowing someone is listening to her. After a number of appointments, you wonder whether the time spent with this patient is justified, given your many other patients who also need your time. Just yesterday you had to delay seeing a patient with a seemingly more urgent medical problem rather than disappoint this patient by postponing her appointment.

Should you keep seeing this patient regularly?

To do justice

While justice has many meanings, I personally like the aspect of justice captured in the definition from the *Oxford English Dictionary*: 'to do justice to (a person or thing) a. to render (one) what is his due, or vindicate his just claims, to treat (one) fairly by acknowledging his merits or the like, hence, To treat (a subject or thing) in a manner showing due appreciation, to deal with (it) as is right or fitting.'[4]

The principle of justice in medicine is intimately connected with questions of what one fairly deserves to receive as a patient in a healthcare system and what obligations clinicians have to assure their patients are treated fairly. What the OED definition does not capture is the more morally contentious notion that clinicians must also be concerned about 'the system'—the really big picture of medical and social resources that we call upon in doing good for patients. Both patients and healthcare professionals have certain expectations of personal fairness regarding medicine. Is a particular patient's claim on the healthcare system a reasonable one? Is it even a reasonable claim to make on others, such as the patient's family? What determines whether a claim is fair and reasonable? Is healthcare a basic right or is it simply one social good among many others? How best should scarce social resources be allocated within and outside healthcare?

When resources are limited, we need to ensure that access to such resources is fair or just. The notion of distributive justice addresses that issue: what does it mean to ensure the fair distribution of social resources among the various endeavours in which people are engaged? In this chapter I will consider justice mainly from the clinician's perspective, but will also consider the bigger questions of resource allocation and distributive justice.

Questions of justice

Justice has many definitions. For example, there is 'retributive' justice and 'punitive justice' that deal with meting out punishment or reward to fit an action. There is 'distributive' justice and 'redistributive justice'—concerned with allocating or reallocating wealth. All concern the 'fairness' or legitimacy of any particular state of affairs. By this I mean: is the arrangement of things morally acceptable? What can patients fairly expect from a healthcare system and what role ought healthcare professionals play in ensuring patients get what they deserve?

More than money is at stake in debates over scarcity and justice in medicine. There are questions of priorities, of which medical care to fund and which not to fund. There are questions of the time and resources of healthcare professionals, which are also limited. Spending more time with one patient means less time for all other patients waiting to be seen. The practitioner's waiting room becomes an arena for testing various theories of justice. Should it be first come, first served? Should everyone get his or her 10 minutes of the doctor's time? Or should access to the doctor be prioritized by medical need? What is medical need and who determines it?

There are no universally accepted answers to these questions. Claims on a health professional's time and services continue to be determined inconsistently. Sometimes it is the sickest patient or the one who complains the loudest who is seen first, sometimes it is the 'likeable' patient or the patient with the most easily solved problem who comes first. All these responses involve an implicit rationing of healthcare at a personal level, according to criteria which are often undisclosed and even unconscious. Prioritizing some patients, however, means posteriorizing others.[5]

DISCUSSION OF CASE 9.1

As her clinician, you *do* have a duty of care to her, but how far does it extend? The patient can expect you, as her clinician, to spend the time on her that is proportionate to her medical needs. These do not have to be physical—they can be her psychosocial needs as an aging person. To attend to these is to show her respect as a person, and is a necessary part of the effective medical care of a human being.

If your patient benefits from these visits and your time is not so stretched that questions of priorities arise, then you should continue seeing this patient. What makes her visits to you beneficial? You may consider that they allow you to address psychological and social needs that are part of her medical well-being, or that they allow you to monitor her physical condition or her medical condition as a whole, or that they are necessary for you to decide what social services or referrals are appropriate for her. However, if and when you know your time will be limited, you should inform her that at times other patients with more urgent needs will take precedence and she may have to wait longer between visits. Determining what need is 'more urgent' is another issue; if she is seriously depressed or suicidal, her need may not be less urgent than another patient's. And her claim on the healthcare system is hardly excessive. One could argue from a utilitarian perspective that a little deontological caring shown by her doctor may help prevent more serious (and ultimately costly) illnesses.

Lessons from the field of battle

During war, resources are often scarce and rationing is common: some people are denied resources that might help them. This is so even more on the field of battle. When not everyone can be saved, triage decisions must be made: the sickest are often treated 'expectantly' (that is, left to die) while those most readily salvageable and able to be returned to combat are treated first.[6]

Healthcare is not unlike modern warfare, in one significant sense. When extreme situations prevail, those for whom treatment is simple and likely to work are prioritized first for treatment. Others join a queue. Managed care is like this, too: providers become gatekeepers to the system and reimbursed if they follow pre-designed care paths to provide economically 'efficient' care. This can put clinicians on a collision course with patients.[7]

Some contend that this awareness of the need to balance economic costs of care against the benefits of interventions is appropriate and *should* change the nature of physicians' obligations to their patients. The clinician's single-minded focus on the patient's needs ignores the bigger picture.[8] Compromises in care must be made—not everyone can get or needs the most expensive artificial hip, cheaper drugs are just as good for hypertension as the latest most expensive designer pills, generic drugs as effective as name-brand ones.

CASE 9.2   PLANNING FOR DISCHARGE

A widow of advancing years was admitted three days ago due to dehydration and cognitive impairment. The former was treated but her mental deficits cannot be: she has problems with planning and judgment and cannot make a capable decision about her place of residence. You are the social worker assigned to plan her discharge. The patient is adamant about returning home and refuses to consider any alternatives. Her two grown children are not prepared to take her home with them and demand that she stay on the ward until her ideal nursing home has a bed. The medical team is getting impatient: 'She has already overstayed her welcome,' says the nursing unit director. 'There are other patients in the ER waiting to be admitted. Let's get things rolling!'

What ought you, as her social worker, do?

DISCUSSION OF CASE 9.2

Not a pleasant place to be in, but one that social workers find themselves in every day. Caught among other healthcare professionals, patients, and families, as a social worker you have to be well versed in the arts of tact and compromise. You may wish to diplomatically remind the family that the patience of the unit cannot be infinite, that a suitable place of residence will be found with or without the patient's assent, and that the latter is, of course, the best route. The daughters must put their mother on a waiting list for a long-term care institution—yes, the ideal nursing home can be one of them, but not the only one. They and the patient must accept the first bed available. If her daughters do not like this, they always have the option of taking her home.

II. MINIMAL AND OPTIMAL JUSTICE

Distributive justice is often used interchangeably with 'fairness' and 'due rewards'. This idea of justice can be defined in a 'minimal' or negative way: to be treated fairly means to be free from barriers, such as prejudice or unfair rules that interfere with receiving what one deserves. Justice can also be defined in an 'optimal' or positive way: to be treated fairly means obtaining or gaining access to the goods and services, the 'just rewards', that one deserves and should be entitled to claim.[9]

Injustices: discriminatory treatment

Dialysis machines were introduced in Seattle, Washington, in the late 1950s. As there were not enough machines for every patient with kidney failure, the first ever ethics committee was set up to decide who should receive treatment. In an article by Shana Alexander in *Life* magazine in 1962, the deliberations of that committee were described.[10] Age and sex, marital status, net worth, income, occupation, and educational background were factors the committee members took into account in making their decisions. Not surprisingly, the elderly, women, blacks, and the poor were unlikely to receive dialysis.

Until the mid-1990s age limits were still common for access to dialysis for end-stage kidney disease.[11] In the United Kingdom, there was a dramatic drop-off in dialysis for patients over 55.[12] This started to change in the late 1990s with the realization by nephrologists that dialysis was a viable option in the elderly.[13] Until this was recognized, their exclusion could be deemed *unfortunate*, but not unfair ('It's too bad, but we cannot help anyone over 75 . . .').

Similarly, gender bias seems still evident in cardiac care. It has been claimed that 'women with ischemic heart disease [receive] less than a fair deal.'[14] For example, women presenting to the ER with acute coronary syndromes are less likely than men to be hospitalized or undergo coronary revascularization.[15] However, these practices are unfair only if systematic bias is behind such differential treatment—it is not unfair, however, if women do have different coronary syndromes than men and require different treatment than men.

CASE 9.3	TOO OLD TO SAVE?

An active 80-year-old man with coronary artery disease is admitted with a serious but survivable self-inflicted gunshot wound. He had become despondent as the primary caregiver for his dementing spouse. There was no previous history of depression and he had never been treated for a psychiatric disorder. As he is sedated at the time of his admission to the ICU, consent for the surgical repair of his injuries is sought from his only capable kin, his two grown children. They refuse consent on the grounds that he had 'suffered enough' and that, at his age, further intensive treatment would not work. They request that all treatment be withdrawn and he be allowed to die.

Should his children's wishes be followed?

Unjust care

Patients may be the subjects of unfair and discriminatory attitudes and practices. At a minimum, all patients are due access to beneficial treatment regardless of age, race, gender, faith, culture, class, or sexual orientation.

Discrimination is an unjust distinction, whether intentional or not, that

- is based on grounds relating to personal characteristics of an individual or group; and
- imposes burdens, obligations, or disadvantages on such individuals or groups not imposed on others, or that withholds access to opportunities, benefits, and advantages available to other members of society.[16]

While some gender-biased decision making can be explained away by physiological differences, this may not always be the case. In a Canadian study of men and women presenting to physicians with equally arthritic knees, men were twice as likely as women to have surgery recommended.[17] The authors speculate this may be because of unconscious biases against women. If so, this is an example of Aristotelian injustice: likes being treated as unlikes and the latter receiving less than appropriate care.

Acceptable use of patient factors

The use of patient-specific factors is ethical and *not* discriminatory when it reflects a *real* difference in patient populations. It also appropriate when it accords with the patient's own wishes and values. For example, it would be acceptable to put limits on life-saving care such as dialysis for the elderly if the patients themselves choose to forego life-sustaining treatment. Indeed, when asked, the very old often do decline medical interventions, especially when accurately informed of the less than positive outcomes.[18]

DISCUSSION OF AND FOLLOW-UP TO CASE 9.3

Although the patient's offspring may have had several motives for refusing treatment, one feeling they expressed was pessimism about the treatment for depression in an octogenarian; who wouldn't want to die at his age with his problems? One should not make peremptory assumptions that he could not be helped. Depression in an 80-year-old can be just as amenable to treatment as depression in a younger person. A suicide attempt is often a cry for help which does not necessarily indicate a competent refusal of care or an inevitable reaction to difficult circumstances.

Discussion with the children should be initiated to ensure the necessary immediate clinical interventions, such as surgery, are undertaken so that more definitive management of their father's mood disorder and home situation can be initiated.

After much cajoling and discussion, the children finally assent to the needed surgery for their father. Surgery is long but successful. Unfortunately, postoperatively the patient's bowel is accidentally punctured when a feeding tube is inserted and he quickly becomes quite ill from peritonitis. As the patient is still obtunded, consent is once more sought from the children who once again refuse surgery.

Lacking consent from the children, a consultant GI surgeon refuses to intervene. The first surgeon quarrels with the GI surgeon. An ethicist is called in who tries to mediate this discussion by asking the disputing surgeons: 'What would you do if it were *your* father?'

The first surgeon immediately says of course he would do the operation while the GI surgeon, surprisingly, says she would not do so. It appears she is reluctant to get involved because she feels this patient is on a downward spiral. Surgery is not performed and the patient expires several days later, never regaining consciousness.

Was this an appropriate outcome?

DISCUSSION OF THE FOLLOW-UP TO CASE 9.3

This question is hard to answer—judgments about futility are often complex clinical judgments. Expense or resource shortfall (for example, availability of personnel or OR space) was not an issue, so in one sense the case's resolution was not unjust. But the outcome could still be unjust if age alone was used to deny the patient potentially beneficial care. If the team felt the best interests of the patient were being thwarted by the children, legal counsel could have been obtained to have them replaced as decision makers for their father.

III. MEDICALLY NECESSARY TREATMENT

The difficulty with achieving 'optimal' justice is that resources are never infinite: individuals cannot always get what they want and trade-offs must always be made. Where and how might we fairly draw this line?

CASE 9.4   TO B12 OR NOT TO B12

You have taken over the care of an independent and somewhat reclusive 83-year-old widow whose family physician of many years has recently retired. She tells you she has received regular B12 injections since her husband died 10 years ago.

The chart indicates she does not have pernicious anemia, the only clear physiological rationale for B12 injections. She asks that these continue because they have 'kept me going all these years'. She also requests that a Home Care nurse give them to her at home because she is too old to get out much. You comply with her request and fill out a Home Care referral form. The next day the Home Care coordinator calls to ask how you can justify this service.

Is this a service to which the patient is entitled in an optimally just system?

Public healthcare systems, such as Canada's medicare system and the UK's National Health Service, aim to provide all citizens equal access to (their fair share of) essential healthcare resources. Whether or not citizens have a right to *all* 'necessary medical care' is another question—nowhere in the Canadian constitution, for example, does it say to which, if any, medical care all citizens have a right. In the real world, of course, different people have different access to healthcare treatments.

In the *Canada Health Act*, care that must be provided includes those 'services medically necessary for the purposes of maintaining health, preventing disease or treating an injury, illness or disability'. Necessary medical care is 'any medically required services rendered by medical practitioners'. This would cover just about anything practitioners are willing to provide! But what healthcare professionals do in practice cannot reliably solve the problem of distributing medical resources fairly.

Necessity defined

Necessity is defined in the *Oxford Dictionary* as that which is indispensable or requisite for or to, that which must be done, a constraint or compulsion, that which is inevitable (a 'necessary evil'), a thing without which life cannot be maintained ('the necessities of life') or would be unduly harsh.[19] These definitions are quite strong. It is not clear that much of what we do in medicine is necessary in these senses. Instead of defining necessity, the *Canada Health Act* simply guarantees access to care.

DISCUSSION OF CASE 9.4

The Home Care coordinator may not realize it, but she is asking a question of justice: are the resources the patient requests her due? The patient wishes her B12; with it she has remained remarkably well.

The B12 may have helped her because of an unrecognized vitamin deficiency or because of a placebo effect.[20] Her use of B12, however, probably belongs to the old days when clinicians provided a 'tonic' to pick up a patient's energy. No doubt, evidence-based medicine would consider this a waste of resources. In addition,

unless backed up by tests to show she cannot absorb B12 orally, its continued provision as a publicly funded healthcare service could be considered deceitful and fraudulent. Nonetheless, there may be a benefit of this service, although it may be less tangible—perhaps it is the social contact engendered by the home visits that has kept this patient going. It would seem reasonable or at least respectful to continue the B12 (for now anyway, until you get to know her better). To be prudent, the clinician should honestly document in the patient's chart the true purposes of the B12 injection visits—really as an alternative form of home support. In that respect it may be a bargain.

Gaming the system

Under strain to allocate resources efficiently and equitably, the medical system may not easily provide all services requested by patients. Clinicians, acting as patient advocates, can try to access scarce services by 'gaming the system'— fudging or breaking rules of access by means of personal influence. Of course if *everyone* did this, there would be no system to game and we all would be worse off. (This is the Kantian test of moral acceptability: can you imagine your action to be a 'universal maxim' that everyone could follow? If not, it is an unacceptable rule of moral conduct.)

Do not trade off due care

At a minimum, all patients deserve non-discriminatory care. Beyond that, in the way of positive benefits, patients deserve non-negligent care, care without which they will come to avoidable harm. The standard by which treatment benefit is judged is the best interests of the patient, that is, the care that a reasonable professional would, under the circumstances, provide to the patient. Patients cannot fairly expect that they will receive a disproportionate share of the healthcare resources but they can expect to receive access to care that is proportional to their needs (see Box 9.1).[21] Of course, given the scarcity of resources, each individual patient may not get what he or she needs. In such cases, justice would require persons in need to have an equal *opportunity* to access that care.

> **BOX 9.1**
>
> Acceptable criteria for resource allocation among patients include
>
> - the likelihood of benefit to the patient,
> - the expected improvement in the patient's quality of life,
> - the expected duration of benefit,
> - the urgency of the patient's condition,
> - the amount of resources needed for successful treatment, and
> - the availability of alternative treatments.

Medical need, medical benefit

What is challenging about creating a just healthcare system is evaluating need and harm in objective ways—or at least in ways upon which we can mutually agree. In the optimistic view, hard rationing decisions will be avoided by getting rid of inefficiencies and useless treatments. In the pessimistic view, even if we do all this, there will still be insufficient resources to satisfy everyone. Pessimists compare the healthcare system to a balloon.[22] Squeeze it in one place and it simply expands in another. They believe that hard rationing decisions are unavoidable and we will always have to deny some patients the treatment they need.

The task of a just healthcare system is to try to meet these goals for patients without sacrificing the other needs of citizens. This is hard to achieve, but a worthy goal.

A just system requires, as the most important twentieth-century political philosopher, John Rawls, has written, 'a mutually recognized point of view from which citizens can adjudicate their claims . . . on their . . . institutions or against one another.'[23] In other words, lacking a *theory* of justice about how best to distribute scarce medical resources, we ought to seek a *just mechanism* for doing so. Rawls' political theory of justice does not require that everyone accepts the same comprehensive doctrine of justice—whether that be a rights theory or some form of utilitarianism. What we need, he suggests, is a 'system of cooperation between free and equal citizens' for making hard choices.

It's hard to say what such a system would look like—a cooperative system applied to medicine would be faced with difficult questions: how are we to make better, more just, decisions when the decision makers—administrators, government officials—often remain hidden?[24] What are core medical services and what are peripheral? What is medical need? Are the expected benefits of a proposed treatment only for the individual? Might we also want to include in the calculus the benefits for others—the patient's family and friends, the patient's social group, society as a whole—the 'crowd', as it were? What are morally relevant and morally irrelevant criteria for accessing scarce care? At the grand theory level, the answers to these questions remain unanswered, but that should not stop us from trying to arrive at just 'microsystems'. There have been, for example, notable attempts at constructing just or fair systems of allocation in some areas of medicine.

The most morally relevant criteria for fair or just access to medical services would be medical need and medical benefit. Medical care should be distributed according to the greatest need and to those most likely to benefit. This may seem utilitarian: to maximize the number of lives saved, to maximize the number of years of life saved, and to maximize the quality of life of patients. But these ends are also compatible with a deontological respect for persons if the needs of all are considered and the needs of none are ignored.

Transplantation and fairness

Organ transplantation is one medical service in North America that has gone a long way in attempting to resolve the problem of distributing scarce medical resources fairly and efficiently. Impartial criteria have been established which include likely medical benefit, time on the waiting list, and urgency of need.[25] Patients are ranked according to a complicated computerized point system taking into account factors such as how close to death the patient is, how quickly the donor organ can get to the recipient, and how likely it is that the patient will survive the operation. This system purportedly does not allow for prejudice or favouritism.

CASE 9.5	TRANSPLANTATION TOURISM

A 45-year-old well-connected businessman has been on the waiting list for a kidney transplant for three years. He has survived on home peritoneal dialysis but finds it increasingly burdensome and uncomfortable. He has no idea when, if ever, a kidney will become available for him. He decides to look into buying a kidney transplant in another country such as India. He asks your opinion of doing so.

How would you respond?

What makes organ transplantation special is that it is a closed and relatively finite system where there is a great deal of agreement about the purpose of treatment.[26] Even here there are moral problems: should an organ go to an 80-year-old, though he might die sooner without it, rather than to a 10-year-old?

Should the alcoholic patient with end-stage liver failure be considered a candidate? Should we always give preference to those who might benefit the most, or is some consideration owed to those who are less likely to benefit?[27] Even seemingly impartial standards of benefit, such as HLA-typing criteria for organ transplantation (to ensure cellular compatibility between donor and recipient), can unexpectedly result in racial inequalities in access to transplantation.[28]

Asking the public what should be done is one way of addressing these issues. Interestingly, public opinion polls do not support the position that organs should just go to the most needy or the most ill—the public thinks even those less likely to benefit should be given a chance to benefit.[29] This might indicate the average citizen cannot imagine saying no to anyone or may overestimate the availability of organs. It might also mean that, at some level, there is a deontological barrier to allocating organs by utilitarian criteria, a belief that anyone in need deserves a 'kick at the healthcare can', even if he or she is unlikely to be successful. This attempt to balance benefit against the 'right to be considered' is interesting and probably the most ethically defensible path to take.

DISCUSSION OF CASE 9.5

You might have strong feelings about 'transplant tourism' but you should restrain yourself. It would not be helpful to engage the patient in a discussion of its morality. Only those who have been so ill and kept waiting for years on a transplant list can appreciate how difficult it can be, emotionally and physically. Your first response should be empathic—acknowledging how hard the wait has been for the patient and his family. You should not presume to understand how he feels; your discussion should try to elicit his concerns. Next, you could reflect back to him the dangers he might face in going overseas for an operation and how much safer it might be to bide his time at home. Finally, you should discuss why the wait is so long at home and what might be done to hurry it up—perhaps a call to a director of the program, to see how far down the list the patient is, would be helpful. Gaming the system by using the man's connections to get him moved up the transplant ladder would not be appropriate.

Impartiality as ideal

Faced with scarce resources, will we always distribute medical services according to need? How will we ensure that the slightly less needy get their due? What about patients with difficulty advocating for themselves—the impoverished, the homeless, the very young, those without families, those rendered incapable by illness or lack of comprehension—how will their needs be recognized?

Such problems are not, I think, insurmountable. The current schemes to distribute scarce resources such as organs are better than earlier versions that made no attempt at impartiality. While perfect impartiality may be ultimately unachievable, it can still serve as a regulatory ideal that can foster the development of ethical and fair guidelines for medical practice.

IV. PRACTICE GUIDELINES: A SOLUTION FOR JUST MEDICINE IN HARD TIMES?

Research shows that a significant proportion of medical care is not appropriate, may not improve a population's health and may even detract from it.[30]

CASE 9.6	ENTITLEMENT

A couple, known to be demanding, comes to see you, their general practitioner. They have just been to the husband's new internist (his old one retired) and are disappointed. Unlike his previous internist, the new one has not done an EKG, a urinalysis, or a blood test for the prostate. On questioning, you discover that the 75-year-old husband has no new cardiac or prostate complaints. All the same, the couple has come to expect these tests to be done yearly and ask you to order them.

Should you comply with the couple's request?

Guidelines defined

To help healthcare professionals evaluate clinical practice and make more appropriate care decisions, there has been great interest in outcomes research and the development of clinical practice guidelines (see Box 9.2).[31] A guideline is a systematically developed statement that assists practitioners' decisions about what is appropriate healthcare for specific clinical circumstances. Some guidelines are consensus-based but these may reflect professional biases. Better

BOX 9.2

Medicine's new ethic:

- Neither the 'Do no harm' of Hippocratic medicine;
- Nor the 'Do everything possible' of technological medicine; but rather,
- 'Do only what makes a [good] difference.'

guidelines are based on evidence from the outcomes of well-conducted trials. Guidelines are meant to distinguish between what works and what does not work on the basis of the best evidence.[32]

Patients deserve medicine that works

The principle that patients deserve medicine that works suggests a solution to the problem of allocating healthcare justly. A subjective patient-preference standard for appropriate care ought to be supplemented by a more impartial, evidence-based criterion of benefit. An intervention should only be employed if, according to research, it makes a significant improvement in patients' lives. In this view of medicine, patients deserve, in the sense of positive justice, what has been shown to work.[33]

DISCUSSION OF CASE 9.6

Battles over the usefulness of medical interventions are common in healthcare. Whether it's a request for antibiotics from a patient with a viral infection (see Case 1.1) or a request to do CPR on a patient unlikely to benefit (Case 1.3), differences between patients or families and healthcare professionals abound. As with any other intervention, screening tests—such as an annual EKG and prostate blood test—should be done only if there is evidence that they are beneficial. Rather than comply with this couple's request (which is not in keeping with the standard of practice for primary care), it would be better to find out why they seem so demanding. The request should be examined. Was there a failure of communication with the new internist? Is the couple overly anxious about the husband's health? Try to sympathize with their fears while not denying their requests head-on. If you have time and are a skilled negotiator, you might get away with not doing the tests. (Then again, the day is short, and you may choose to battle another day and so give in to their wishes. Just don't forget there is a war to be won even if you lose today's skirmish!)

Guidelines and autonomy

With the development of practice guidelines, some worry that the autonomy and needs of the patient may take second place to society's interest in limiting healthcare spending. This need not be. Accurate assessments of benefit allow patients and their surrogates to make more realistic healthcare choices.[34] Guidelines, as statements of beneficent care, can take accurate reflections of patients' preferences into account (see Box 9.3).[35]

> **BOX 9.3**
>
> Guidelines are most influential if they
>
> • incorporate the latest advances in medical research,
>
> • allow for clinical discretion and flexible interpretation,
>
> • are easily implemented,
>
> • are seen as aids to decision making and not as regulations,
>
> • incorporate specialists' and generalists' perspectives, and
>
> • incorporate the patient's point of view.

An example of the need to include the patient's perspective can be found in the development of a protocol for the treatment of deep-vein thrombosis (DVT). In the 1980s a panel of experts recommended that the ideal treatment for DVT should be streptokinase and heparin because together they are better at preventing the common postphlebitic syndrome than heparin alone. However, a 1994 study showed that this treatment was unacceptable to patients because it involved a small risk of a devastating stroke.[36] A better and more acceptable practice guideline for DVT treatment takes the wishes of patients, who tend to be more risk-averse than doctors, into account.

A help to patients

Some scholars, such as Wennberg, believe that once we tell our patients the true, often poor, outcomes of most interventions, many will decline them.[37] Indeed, some truly informed patients will decline interventions—such as drug treatment for hypercholesterolemia or early screening for prostate cancer—that can be overvalued by physicians but are of lesser relevance to the patient. This will save the system the expense of marginally useful, possibly harmful, and unwanted interventions. If so, it would be a nice by-product of outcomes research, since refusals of treatment by patients ('patient-choice' rationing) are the most morally defensible ones. Outcomes research would thus expand, not contract, the patient's autonomy and could also save the system money.[38]

By contrast, some patients, no matter how small the likelihood of benefit, will want such tests done regularly, such as in the last case above. What should be done about patients who cannot 'regulate' themselves? Clinicians in their role as professionals (see Chapters 2 on Autonomy and 8 on Professionalism) have to learn to just say no. The failure of clinicians to familiarize themselves with and adhere to guidelines has encouraged some to recommend that we 'pay for performance'; that is, reward those clinicians who abide by guidelines.[39] This has yet to be shown to be effective—and may detract from patient-centred medical care by pitting the physician's financial interests against considerations of the patient as a whole.[40]

Nonetheless, sticking to guidelines will not necessarily reduce costs because some patients may end up receiving *more* treatment than they do now.[41] In fact, some recommendations with less evidential basis, such as those recommending colonoscopy screening in all asymptomatic adults or mammography in women under 50, may cost the system money. While better-designed guidelines can be initially more costly by extending truly helpful care to some patients, such as women or blacks with undertreated heart disease, in the long run they may save the system money if they can prevent harm to patients.

Unfortunately, guidelines can probably capture only a very small proportion of medical practice.

V. THE HEALTH PROFESSIONAL'S MASTER

Throughout the world, rationing or priority setting seems unavoidable in the foreseeable future. In tough times the emphasis on measurable results and performance standards in guideline-oriented medicine may subtly shift medicine from its focus on individual patients.

Guidelines a legal risk?

Guidelines might seem legally risky if, in following them, the clinician loses sight of the needs of an individual patient. Indeed, a suit that was initiated against a physician in the United Kingdom attempted to suggest that, in following a procedural guideline, a doctor exhibited negligence and that the guideline he was following was 'faulty and flawed'. The judge found in favour of the physician because the judge was loath to second-guess what, on consideration of the evidence, was reasonable practice: 'Unless a medical procedure is patently unsafe or goes against a common practice or usage a court should not attempt to substitute its views for those of the profession.'[42] In Australia, it has been likewise held: 'Given their purpose and evidence-based foundation, it is unlikely that clinical practice guidelines will promote litigation. Arguably, they may well reduce it by reducing any uncertainty about what constitutes reasonable medical practice.'[43]

Guidelines themselves are unlikely to increase the risk of litigation because they may be used to define the applicable 'standard of care'. The real test for malpractice actions will be whether, in a particular circumstance, the defendant doctor's actions deviate from a widely accepted standard—something a guideline may define.[44]

Principled patient care

If guidelines are used to *limit* access to care on the basis of cost, patients should be explicitly told this.[45] The best place for the economic evaluation of healthcare, such as cost-benefit analysis, is at the level of society in general, where all the costs and benefits of an intervention can be seen, not at the patient's bedside.[46] This avoids putting the practitioner at a direct conflict of interest with his or her patients. It is at a higher level—away from the clinical encounter—that difficult healthcare choices, such as funding for new and expensive reproductive technologies, need to take place.

CASE 9.7	AN EXPENSIVE PROPOSITION

You are a hospitalist looking after an elderly bachelor who has come into hospital with community-acquired pneumonia. Because he has been critically ill in the past with interstitial pneumonia, you worry the drug provided by the pharmacy on advice of the Drug Therapeutics Committee is less than optimal for the patient. You would prefer an expensive third-line drug but your unit's drug budget is already through the roof. Indications for the use of this drug also require evidence that the patient has failed to respond to the recommended drug. You worry this requirement will create a further delay, by which time the patient will be too ill to respond.

What should you do?

It is one thing for society or an institution to decide whether or not to provide a beneficial medical intervention; it is quite another for a clinician to decide not to offer a potentially helpful service to a particular patient. Clinicians' decisions regarding individual patients must be guided by reasonable professional practice standards and by reasonable patients' preferences. Where physicians' actions are constrained by choices made by others, they may be less likely to be blamed for patient outcomes that are less than ideal. The difficulty for healthcare professionals may be in knowing when such limit-setting is acceptable and when it is not. Where decisions made by others seem to be at the expense of the patient's interests, clinicians should explore the rationale for such decisions. The healthcare professional acting as the patient's advocate is particularly important in managed care systems where there can be conflicts of interest between the managed care system and the patient. Fairness, not market-driven interests, should be the central focus of any professional working in a managed healthcare system.[47]

DISCUSSION OF CASE 9.7

You shouldn't take the Drug Therapeutics Committee's decision lying down. You have good evidence this patient needs the more expensive drug. If that committee is a fairly constituted, it will make its decision according to what has been called 'criteria for reason-ableness'; that is, its deliberations and rationale for rationing or limiting access should be transparent, the reasons used should be those recognizable as relevant by 'fair-minded' people, there should be a mechanism for appealing its decisions, and there should be a decision enforcement mechanism.[48] These criteria make allocation or distributive justice decisions under conditions of scarcity more amenable to public debate and discussion, rather than being made in secret and presented as *fait accompli*. You should advocate for your patient and hope that the 'fair-minded' members are swayed by your arguments.

System constraints

A physician who gives substandard care out of concern for limited resources may be found negligent.[49] An adult male patient in British Columbia died of a burst cerebral aneurysm after a long delay in getting a brain CT scan. At trial the physicians testified they felt constrained by the medical system to restrict their requests for CT scans as diagnostic tools. The court agreed that such tests are expensive and that there are budgetary constraints on them. These constraints, the court claimed, 'worked against the patient's interest by inhibiting doctors in their judgment of what should be done for him'. The judge was of the opinion that, 'if it comes to a choice between a physician's responsibility to his or her individual patient and his or her responsibility to the Medicare system overall, the former must take precedence in a case such as this.'

For the physician of a patient with a medical need, costs should recede into the background: 'The severity of the harm that may occur to the patient who is permitted to go undiagnosed is far greater than the financial harm that will occur to the medical system if one more CT scan procedure only shows the patient is not suffering from a serious medical condition.'[50]

In other words, where the patient may benefit from an intervention, physicians would be unwise to think of the costs to the system. Rather than act as willing door closers, physicians ought to try to obtain reasonably beneficial services for their patients. In this case in British Columbia the physicians may have too readily accepted a tacit limit to care—they were not following an evidence-based guideline developed by the profession. Their failure to obtain appropriate care for the patient resulted in injury to the patient and a finding of professional negligence. Where physicians are too constrained by decisions already made by society, they can partially discharge their fiduciary obligations to their patients by informing them of these limits and suggesting alternative treatment. Implicit or hidden rationing has its defenders (worried about social unrest from the excluded!), but it seems far more morally robust to be open with patients about the limits to care that may damage their interests.[51]

CONCLUSION

Because of uncertainties in the area of distributive justice, it is perhaps not surprising to find that clinicians will often accommodate patients who badly want scarce medical resources considered by the healthcare professionals to be unnecessary.[52] In a world of increasingly expensive care and limited resources, problems of allocation are unlikely to be simply resolved and will remain contentious. They can also be a minefield for the unwary.

If a health professional believes an access to care standard has been imposed solely to hold down costs and not to benefit patients, the professional should not adhere to that standard and should inform his or her patients of this.[53] If a treatment has been shown by well-conducted studies to lack distinct benefit or to be only marginally beneficial, it is discretionary care. In fact, it is simply good medicine not to offer one's patients treatment that cannot help them. Other ethically acceptable ways to reduce healthcare spending include taking steps to prevent illness, helping patients curb risky behaviour, and encouraging patients to set limits on futile aggressive care at the end of life.[54] Medically beneficial care may not be available to patients due to funding inequities, poor planning, and wait times. Healthcare professionals can meet their ethical obligations by acting as advocates for patients when it comes to beneficial medical care. In the final two chapters of this book we will see what this entails in terms of beginning-of-life and end-of-life issues.

10

Labour Pains: Ethics and New Life

The best course . . . is to allow the duty of the mother to her foetus to remain a moral obligation which, for the vast majority of women, is already freely respected.

Chief Justice Lamer, 1999[1]

In this chapter I will focus on ethical problems arising out of birthing and reproduction. It is impossible to examine all facets of these complex areas. There remains great diversity and disagreements that cannot be avoided. I will concentrate on topics such as abortion, women's rights, fetal rights, and assisted reproduction, where there are some guidelines for healthcare professionals.

I. Birthing and Reproductive Choice

Medical professionals are taught there are two patients in pregnancy, but are the two patients morally equivalent? How should a health professional respond to a patient's request to terminate her pregnancy? The answers to these questions may vary throughout the world, but the evolving consensus in modern medicine is that practitioners must avoid putting their own views on these issues ahead of those of their patients.

CASE 10.1   A TRIVIAL MATTER?

A 23-year-old unmarried woman who seems happily pregnant presents at 16 weeks to be screened for fetal anomalies. When the

ultrasound reveals the fetus has a cleft palate, she requests a pregnancy termination. Her clinician considers this a rather trivial reason for a therapeutic abortion and shares this opinion with her.

Is it acceptable to voice such an opinion? Or must the clinician simply shut up and fill out the referral form for the abortion? What is the status of abortion and the fetus in Canada and the United States at this time?

Modern medicine has helped make pregnancy and its termination safe and secure, giving women, at least in the West, reproductive choices. Reproductive choice in the modern era has particularly meant that women no longer need to be enslaved by biology or be mere vessels for the fetus. Some people question whether this freedom is 'natural', but the history of medicine has been about attempts to replace the 'natural' course of an illness or condition with an 'unnatural' and more felicitous, human-made course. Nature is sometimes cruel and unjust; one task of medicine is to allow humans more say over their destiny. As the great eighteenth-century philosopher Hegel argued, human beings, in constructing society, create a 'nature above nature'.[2] We must find and develop our own 'laws' or rules to govern this 'second nature'.

The progression of medical advances in reproductive and sexual rights is not without ethical and legal quandaries. These dilemmas and disagreements should not obscure certain areas of moral consensus. For most, if not all, healthcare choices, medical practitioners should not interfere with their patients' right to decide for themselves, even if we personally disagree with their choices. The dominant view of morality in a pluralistic society gives citizens a profound right to be left alone to their own choices, especially when it comes to family planning. But what happens when a person's choice entails positive actions of assistance from another? One controversial choice is the decision to end a pregnancy.

DISCUSSION OF CASE 10.1

The clinician is not wrong to express an opinion—at least insofar as it is a professional, as opposed to a purely personal, opinion. Patients' views may be questioned or probed by their clinicians, especially in cases such as this one where a patient changes her mind so quickly. Affirming the right of a patient to access a service, such as pregnancy termination, does not necessarily require agreement with the patient or acceptance of the patient's reasoning.

It seems curious, if she is 'happily pregnant', that she should now want an abortion. Why should the presence of an easily correctable lesion such as a cleft palate make this patient decide to end a hitherto wanted pregnancy? What does she know about cleft palates? Is this an excuse to end a pregnancy now unwanted for other reasons? Does she know that becoming pregnant again may not always be so easy?[3]

Notwithstanding these good questions, the clinician should be careful to separate out his or her *opinion* from 'the facts': the fact is, the decision around continuing a pregnancy is ultimately the woman's alone to make. It is not the clinician's role to prevaricate or to oppose a woman's decision in this area.

It is argued the right to choice in pregnancy arises from the asymmetry in rights of the woman versus those of the fetus. By this view, even if one considers a fetus a person, no person has the 'right' to piggy-back onto another person.[4] Just as my 'right' to your blood or your second kidney depends on your consent, so the 'right' of the fetus to its life depends on the pregnant woman's ongoing 'consent'. This is not a knockdown argument against the view that pregnancy entails responsibility. For many people, in the context of a wanted and consented to pregnancy, the woman has a moral and social responsibility to 'take care' to protect her fetus during the pregnancy. A similar situation would be one in which someone who, having agreed to donate some tissue (or provide a gift) to another person, behaves in ways that imperil the donation (or takes the gift back). We would find this morally objectionable or at least we think it morally objectionable (or at least difficult to fathom—'*Why* would they do that?') much like breaking a promise. Such moral qualms should not, however, lead to sanctions such as refusing to respect or cooperate with the would-be donor, as the donation, like a mother's support for her fetus, is a voluntary matter. Rather, the donor's (like the promise breaker's) change of heart needs to be understood.

The rights of women to control their own bodies—the paramount ones being the right to birth control and the right to terminate pregnancy by abortion—are relatively recent ones, even in the West. For example, before 1969 in Canada, abortion was outlawed completely and an abortion provider could be charged with murder or manslaughter. In 1969, Canadian criminal law was amended to allow abortions only if a 'therapeutic abortion committee' was of the opinion that the abortion was 'medically necessary'.[5]

In 1988, this law was invalidated as unconstitutional by the Supreme Court of Canada in the landmark *Morgentaler* decision. As one of the judges explained, in giving the majority reasons, the law contravened the protection of 'security of the person' guaranteed by section 7 of the *Canadian Charter of Rights and Freedoms*. Forcing a woman to endure an unwanted pregnancy, unless she met 'criteria unrelated to her own priorities and aspirations', violated her 'most basic physical and emotional condition'. Moreover, the whole process was 'manifestly unfair', violating 'principles of fundamental fairness' because many hospitals did not have therapeutic abortion committees and some refused abortions to married women unless they were in physical danger. Since that decision, Canada has remained without any law regulating pregnancy and its termination or continuance, leaving it up to a woman and her doctor—a medical decision like any other.[6]

Similarly, in the United States, restrictions on the right to abortion were struck down as unconstitutional in 1973 in the well-known *Roe v. Wade* Supreme Court decision.[7] The court reasoned that the right to privacy protected women from interference with their decision to terminate their own pregnancy up until the point of fetal viability. The court did not, however, prohibit restrictions later in pregnancy and the door was left open to permit regulation and prohibitions of late-term abortions.[8] Prohibitions on abortion do not eliminate the procedure but simply drive it underground. In North America where induced abortions have been made available, safe abortions are the rule. It is in the developing countries, where 97 per cent of the world's unsafe abortions take place, that maternal mortality is high and so a major public health problem.[9]

CASE 10.2   CLAIMS OF CONSCIENCE

A 19-year-old is 22 weeks pregnant as a result of being assaulted. Her pregnancy was only recently diagnosed and she now seeks an abortion. She attends her family physician who questions the wisdom of her decision. 'You may regret this one day, you know,' the physician states. 'I also find it ethically troublesome it being so late on in your pregnancy. It's not like flossing your teeth.' The patient persists, however, and is anxious to have the procedure soon. Her physician declines to refer her to a pregnancy termination service.

What is the right thing to do here? If a healthcare provider has a moral objection to abortion, what role, if any, must he or she play if a patient requests an abortion?

Although abortion may be controversial ethically, in Canada it is a recognized and legitimate option that healthcare providers or others delay or impede at their own and their patient's peril. Claims of conscientious objection are sometimes acceptable.[10] Healthcare providers opposed to abortion on the grounds of conscience certainly do not have a duty to participate in it. Where abortion services are easy to find, they may not have a duty to refer them. Both of these stances are controversial. If not referring puts a woman at increased risk of a bad outcome, this could be construed as patient abandonment. It all depends on the options available and known to the patient and the difficulty of accessing them without the clinician's help.

While more difficult moral issues arise if the pregnancy is past 22 to 24 weeks (the edge of fetal viability, when the fetus may be capable of independent existence) the physical and psychological risks for women increase, too, the later the termination.[11]

DISCUSSION OF CASE 10.2

The physician's remarks are condescending towards and dismissive of her patient. Her statements only make a hard decision more difficult. 'Postdecisional regret' might be a consideration, but this seems highly unlikely in this case given the circumstances of the pregnancy. Any delay now only makes the intervention more risky for the patient. The physician should be careful with her language because it does not facilitate adult decision making on her patient's part.

In general, a physician or other health professional should not act as a gate-closer to patients who opt for an available, appropriate medical service. Some studies suggest that providers of reproductive services allow their values to influence their clinical decisions.[12] Sometimes this may be quite appropriate where those values are protective of the patient's interests. But clinicians must be careful not to make decisions that properly belong to the patient. Where health professionals are unable for any reason to provide an expected service, they must know to whom to refer the patient and should provide that referral in a timely way.[13]

CASE 10.3   A FATHER'S DEMAND

A Quebec woman who became pregnant in the context of a two-year common-law relationship sought pregnancy termination. The father of the fetus obtained a court injunction preventing her from having an abortion. Clarification of the rights of the father and the fetus were sought through the appeal to the Supreme Court of Canada.

What are the rights of fathers as regards pregnancy termination?

A similar well-known case in Quebec solidified the right of a woman to decide on her own regarding her pregnancy. Until this case was heard, the rights of fathers were unclear. No point of English law offered rights to the fetus: 'The foetus cannot, in English law . . . have a right of its own at least until it is born and has a separate existence from its mother.'[14]

As for the spouse or father, specifically, when it comes to the decision about pregnancy termination, he does not have 'veto' rights: 'No court in Quebec or elsewhere has ever accepted the argument that a father's interest in a foetus which he helped create could support a right to veto a woman's decisions in respect of the foetus she is carrying.'[15]

DISCUSSION OF CASE 10.3

That men do not have a legal say in the decision over pregnancy does not mean they are free of obligations as regards pregnancy; would-be 'hit-and-run' fathers must provide support if a pregnancy they helped engender is successfully taken to term. There is an asymmetry, in this view, between the rights of potential fathers and mothers: women have the final say over a pregnancy's continuation because it is their body; men must take (at least financial) responsibility for fathering children as a consequence, as it were, of having access to the woman's body.

These judicial rulings create a space for women to make reproductive decisions on their own. However, access to abortion services remains problematic in many parts of North America. Finding someone to perform the abortion is not difficult in most provinces in Canada, at least in the larger cities, but is difficult in many American jurisdictions. Surprisingly, hospitals are *not* required to provide such needed services and many in fact choose not to provide them, making access a problem.[16] Abortion committees and archaic restrictions still exist in many other countries. In the United Kingdom, for example, a woman must still seek approval from two physicians to obtain an abortion, a requirement opposed by the majority of United Kingdom citizens and many clinicians as well.[17] This will likely change soon.

While abortion may be available 'on demand' in some countries, this does not mean that all such requests carry the same moral weight. A key question is who is making the request. In some countries abortion has been forced on women, an obviously objectionable practice from the perspective reached in Canada and other liberal democracies.[18] Sometimes, more subtle forms of coercion exist that make the choice to terminate less than free. The practitioner needs to be sensitive to these.

CASE 10.4 A RIGHT TO BE TESTED?

You are a family physician looking after a professional couple in their early thirties who have two young girls at home. The woman is in the first trimester of her third pregnancy. At low risk for congenital anomalies and accurate for time of conception, she nevertheless requests an obstetrical ultrasound or amniocentesis. Her husband admits they are primarily seeking to know the sex of the fetus. If it is a girl, he says, they will request pregnancy termination and try to get pregnant again.

Must you help them?

DISCUSSION OF CASE 10.4

For reasons repugnant to many, this couple seeks a medical service that is readily available. If their rationale for pregnancy termination seems unacceptable, you could try to gently dissuade them, being sensitive all the while to personal opinions in this area. If at all possible, there should be a discussion with the woman without the husband in the room, or a search for a third party such as a cultural or religious advisor, if there seems to be an ethnic or faith-based issue involved, who could help the couple (or at least the woman) with this decision. As long as the woman is making an authentic choice and not seemingly coerced by her spouse or her culture, her choice ought to be respected. However, 'respect' does not mean that she has an unfettered right to the test.

It may seem odd but, although abortions are allowed for *any* reason in Canada, certain restrictions are imposed on access to ultrasound for those who simply wish to know the sex of their fetus. This is to prevent sex-selection clinics from springing up and professionals from profiting from such services. So, now that the couple has admitted the true reason for seeking the test, the cat is out of the bag, so to speak, and you have a socially accepted reason for refusing the referral. It is unlikely you would be sanctioned for this because (1) this may be an inappropriate indication for an ultrasound (sex determination unconnected with disease) and (2) ultrasound services are accessible to couples by going outside medicare or crossing the border to the United States where such testing is readily available.

II. In the Interest of the Child: Being Born and Living Life

The advance of medical science creates new obligations as regards helping patients and families with reproductive choice. Healthcare providers are obliged to properly inform prospective parents about the appropriate tests that can be readily done to evaluate fetal health. Failing to provide accurate genetic screening or counselling (such as amniocentesis to detect birth defects) is one such professional deficiency.[19] Parents may claim that they would not have continued the pregnancy or even conceived the child had they been properly apprised of the genetic risks. Where negligence is found, damages have been awarded for at least some of the costs and losses to the parents in raising the child.[20] (Legal liability on the part of a physician can be claimed if it can be shown, for example, that the parents would have opted for pregnancy termination had they been properly informed of the potential risks to the fetus. See Case 4.2, 'Not to worry'.)

Wrongful birth suits have also been filed by parents when an unexpected pregnancy occurs as a result of a negligently performed sterilization. In such cases, where a healthy child is born, claims for damages—the cost of pregnancy, delivery, and the rearing of a child, healthy or disabled—have received variable recognition in Western societies. Courts have traditionally viewed awarding damages for the birth and life of a healthy child as repugnant. Laterally, however, some Canadian and UK courts have compensated simply for the negligent sterilization.[21]

By contrast, *wrongful life* suits are filed on the infant's behalf, seeking damages for the pain and suffering caused to the child by his or her very existence because of its impairment. The claim is made that the physician negligently allowed a severely handicapped child to be born. Most courts in Canada and the United Kingdom have turned down such suits. The value of death over any kind of life is not something the courts are comfortable with calculating as a matter of justice and compensation in law. They see it as a matter for 'philosophers and theologians'.[22] (Needless to say, philosophers and theologians have not come up with an acceptable price for existence either.)

The moral rationale for wrongful birth suits rests on the right of women (or couples) to decide whether pregnancies involving preventable disabilities ought to be undertaken or continued. Healthcare professionals have an obligation to see that potential parents are properly informed or at least refer them on to others who can provide the proper information.

Issues relating to the health of the fetus—such as maternal activities that may harm the fetus—must be discussed with the pregnant woman, as managing these issues most effectively and respectfully depends on her informed choice and voluntary participation in risk-abatement activities.

CASE 10.5 FETUS AT RISK

You are a social worker with a 29-year-old woman in her second pregnancy in your caseload. Her first child had fetal alcohol syndrome (FAS) and is in foster care. The woman continues to drink heavily during this second pregnancy. Alerted to this by the woman's common-law spouse, you are concerned for the well-being of the fetus. A case conference is held where you are given the suggestion to make an urgent application for court-ordered protection for the unborn child and involuntary hospitalization for the woman to treat her alcohol problem and control her alcohol intake.

Would you go along with this suggestion?

Coercing an addicted mother into treatment risks turning healers into jailors and pits the pregnant mother against her fetus in multiple ways. Would we act in similar ways with a woman who smokes during pregnancy? What if she eats excessively or decides to take a plane trip in her third trimester? There is no practical or ethically acceptable way to intervene in any of these scenarios, lacking the mother's cooperation. Of course, it is still ethical to 'intervene' with counselling, advice, even exhortations, and offers of support or assistance, referrals, and the like, all short of coercion or forcing compliance. The same is true of intervening to ensure that *fathers* make wise lifestyle choices to promote the well-being of their children. The 'blaming-the-mother' attitude ignores the studies that show that problems in mothering (antenatal and postpartum) can arise due to maternal deprivation and lack of support (for example, financial, emotional) from the father.[23]

DISCUSSION OF CASE 10.5

This is a tough case in which to be involved—tough because one knows the predictable consequence of the mother's behaviour is another child with FAS, a huge problem for society but also for the child-to-be. Tough, also, because what can one do? One cannot incarcerate the mother—no crime has been committed or even considered. Concentrating on the fetus alone, such as by giving it 'rights', as some have argued, would be unlikely to help.[24] The pregnant woman and her fetus are one interrelated biological unit. Although it is difficult for health professionals to watch pregnant women continue to engage in risky behaviours, imposing a duty of care on them would lead to intolerable and unjust intrusions into the everyday lives of women.

You need to point out to the rest of the casework team why a vindictive approach will not work. You should see what other supports—financial, social, emotional—can be found to help the woman. What is the role of drinking in her life? Does her primary care provider know how bad things are? The context is more likely to be the key to helping the pregnant woman than railing against irresponsible mothers. What seems on the surface to be an 'ethical dilemma', a clash of fundamental principles or interests, may be resolved at a practical level by the skills and training of healthcare professionals—a 'way out' of ethical conundrums can sometimes be found by clinicians working together and thinking outside the box.

Judicial decisions on abortion have clarified the legal status of the fetus. In Canada, a fetus is not considered a person and so cannot receive protection under human rights legislation. In the clear words of the Quebec Supreme Court: 'The foetus is not entitled to legal protection.'[25]

Given the serious and intimate nature of pregnancy and abortion, there seems no more legitimate and reliable person to make the decision to continue or terminate a pregnancy, and to take the responsibility for living with the decision, than the woman who is pregnant (see Box 10.1).

BOX 10.1

'Parliament has failed to establish either a standard or a procedure whereby any [state] interests might prevail over those of the woman in a fair and non-arbitrary fashion.'

III. THE NEW AGE OF REPRODUCTION

No longer must women fear becoming pregnant; they can choose if, when, and even *how* they give birth. Some women opt to terminate a viable pregnancy whereas other women go to extraordinary lengths to become pregnant. Reproduction used to be a fairly simple matter: woman, man, sex, birth, child. Infertility was less of a problem than the puerperal-related death of mother and child. As with so much else in the past century, however, the situation may now be much safer but not as straightforward. You do not, directly at any rate, need a man to be there; you do not, except initially, need a woman to be there—well, okay, a woman's uterus is still needed but almost any uterus will do. Age, sexual orientation, infertility, a lack of sperm or eggs, even death, are all no longer limitations to successful reproduction. Sperm can be provided and joined with an ovum in a Petri dish (an *in vitro* embryo); sperm can be injected directly into an ovum (ICSI: intracytoplasmic sperm injection); fertilized eggs, embryos, and blastocysts can be implanted in the mother's womb (IVF: *in vitro* fertilization); the womb may be that of a surrogate mother; sperm can be preserved from the testes prior to castrating radiation or surgery or even harvested at death. Reproduction has even been 'globalized' as reproduction is outsourced from the West to Third World women with wombs for rent.

If the continuation of one's chromosomes is the rationale for evolution, then modern assisted reproduction technology (ART) has given our genes a way of replicating almost without us. Male and female gametes (sperm and ova or eggs, respectively) and a safe place to be joined and develop are all that are needed prior to implantation in a womb. ART includes the services, techniques, and technology used to assist individuals who cannot conceive on their own—from simple artificial insemination and IVF to egg donation and pre-implanation genetic diagnosis (PGD).[26] This includes all the varied techniques of harvesting, preserving, manipulating, transferring, and conjoining gametes and the technology for analyzing, storing, sharing, and using the genetic material of gametes and embryos.

CASE 10.6   AN ARRANGED BIRTH

A childless heterosexual couple arrange for the creation of an *in vitro* embryo from an egg and sperm donated anonymously. The embryo is successfully implanted in a surrogate mother contracted by the couple to give birth to the child, whom they intend to then adopt and raise. The pregnancy successfully carries to term but the contracting couple split up just prior to childbirth. The husband now says he wants nothing to do with the birth or the child.

Who should be considered the parents for this child?

DISCUSSION OF CASE 10.6

It used to be the existence of arranged marriages that worried (and still worries) some people. Now there are arranged births with their own sets of contracts and stipulations. The language of the contract makes the legal answer seem easy: the contracting couple, as the 'ordering' couple, is designated by mutual agreement as the child's parents. Even without a formal agreement or legal contract, morally they have obligations to the child, once born, from which they cannot escape. Assuming the wife wishes to keep the child, the ex-husband should incur the expenses that a natural father would undertake.

More troubles may occur if the surrogate mother decides she wishes to keep the child—does it matter whether the child was conceived with her ovum or someone else's? It shouldn't, according to some court judgments—she is the one who has endured the burdens of pregnancy and developed the bond with the child—but there is as yet no consensus in this area. Other courts have decided against the surrogate mother if it seems the newborn child would be better off with the contractual parents.[27]

ART create dilemmas not only as to who the parents are but also as to the status of the offspring. Are the products of ART conceptions—unborn but not implanted embryos—somehow persons with rights and interests of their own or are they mere chattel, objects belonging to the highest bidder? If the ordering parents die and leave an estate, does the estate now belong to the unborn embryo or does the embryo get inherited along with the estate? No doubt these conundrums will keep the courts and lawyers busy for years.

What is a good healthcare practitioner to do in this new age of fertility and reproduction? Are there no boundaries to what is acceptable? Here, as elsewhere, there are some indicators as to what is, and what is not, ethically acceptable conduct. One thing is clear: assisted reproductive services are not for everyone.

CASE 10.7   DISCRIMINATION OR DISCRETION?

An ART clinic specializes in fertilizing the ova of women with sperm donated by unrelated men. On the roster is a woman whose partner appears to be a woman. Is this a typo? Nope—the patient's partner is indeed another woman; they have been together for 17 years and are seeking the clinic's assistance in fertilizing the patient's ova with sperm donated by a friend of the couple. They have tried the 'turkey-baster' method at home without success and now seek the clinic's help in achieving a successful pregnancy by IVF. The clinic has only ever offered its assisted reproduction services to heterosexual couples and so denies this same-sex couple access to its services.

Is there a problem with this denial?

DISCUSSION OF CASE 10.7

There is indeed. Dr Korn, a provider of ART in British Columbia, denied a female couple access to his clinic's services on the grounds that they were a same-sex couple.[28] A complaint of discrimination on account of sexual orientation was laid and upheld by the Supreme Court of British Columbia.[29] Dr Korn was found in violation of the British Columbia *Human Rights Act*. This confirmed that physicians providing any medical services must ensure there is no discrimination in their provision.[30]

Physicians can deny any medical service if there are legitimate safety concerns, such as serious threats to the welfare of patients or society. For example, they can reject the 'gift' of donation of sperm if there are safety concerns (such as, for example, infectious disease contamination) concerning the gametes. There is no 'right' of donation; health practitioners and medical facilities are not obliged to accept all and any donations of blood, gametes, or organs.[31] Thus, sperm donation, which is governed, curiously, in Canada under the federal *Food and Drugs Act*, can be denied on the grounds of sexual orientation, because there is a higher risk of serious disease with certain sexual practices.

While there is a 'right' of opportunity to access artificial reproductive services—or at least to join the queue to access ART—there is no guaranteed financial reimbursement for their use by infertile couples or individuals in Canada. Most of these services are not covered under provincial healthcare plans. The failure of governments to reimburse such services might be viewed as treating infertility differently from other medical conditions and, arguably, infringing on the infertile person's 'equality rights'. Should the 'right' to become pregnant be on par with another patient's 'right' to be free of limitations on lying flat because of Grade IV heart failure or another's 'right' to be treated for an inability to mix socially on account of a pervasive social anxiety disorder? Is infertility a medical condition akin to ulcerative colitis or Parkinson's? Why do provincial plans pay for psychotherapy of the 'worried well' when they do not for ART? All this is complicated by the fact that infertility is not one thing: it may be due to disease and injury or simply due to older age, so the preference for ART may run from the reasonable to the outlandish.

There are social issues here concerning resource allocation (see Chapter 8 on Justice) but also concerning the notions of disease and ill-health. Briefly, illnesses are, in one broadly accepted view, deviations from the normal human range of functioning which cause harm to patients, or threaten to do so.[32] Such conditions, for which there can be some helpful interventions, are seen as *unfair* and tend to be reimbursed. We do not reimburse patients for the merely *unfortunate* experiences of life, such as being born poor or short—whether or not we can change these. Many view infertility as an unfortunate occurrence, not as an illness that renders persons so afflicted any less able to take part in life. Unfair and therefore reimbursable conditions are those that disadvantage persons and stack the playing field against them. In this view, some types of infertility (such as secondary to testicular cancer or premature ovarian failure) should count as illness states justifying reimbursement. Even so, not having children of one's own genetic heritage can be partially corrected by options other than using ART (for example, adoption), whereas the options for those with disabling medical conditions are fewer (and even then we may restrict patient choices; for example, funding an 'adequate' hip prosthesis rather than the best available).

The Supreme Court of Nova Scotia has held that not reimbursing ART is a legitimate policy decision, interpreting it as a 'reasonable limit' on the provision of services that is 'demonstrably justified' in a democratic society as permitted by the *Canadian Charter of Rights and Freedoms*. 'It would be unrealistic for this Court to assume that there are unlimited funds to address the needs of all,' opined one judge.[33] This judgment misses the nuances in the causes of infertility and the rationale for seeking ART.

The proliferation of ART exists in an international patchwork quilt of regulations and regulatory vacuums. Not surprisingly, there is little harmony in this area. For example, the United States does not as yet regulate pre-implantation genetic testing on embryos, whereas the United Kingdom and Canada do. The regulations are partial, in flux, poorly enforceable, and subject to bypass through 'reproductive tourism'.[34]

The *Assisted Human Reproductive Act*

Canada, similar to many other countries, has scrambled to keep up with the advances in reproductive medicine. New legislation to provide direction in this troubled area—the *Assisted Human Reproductive Act* (the 'Reproductive Act')—was devised and passed in 2004 (see Box 10.2).[35]

This *Reproductive Act* defines certain activities as unsafe or unethical, recommending criminal sanctions if they are performed.[36] For example, human cloning is prohibited. The *Reproductive Act* governs only the use of 'embryos'.

BOX 10.2

The *Canadian Reproductive Act* is guided by five principles:

1. Respect for human individuality, dignity and integrity.

2. Precautionary approach to protect and promote health.

3. Non-commodification and non-commercialization.

4. Informed choice.

5. Accountability and transparency.

Once transferred into a woman, the treatment or use of the fetus is not governed by the Reproductive Act's *provisions.*

The *Reproductive Act* addresses concerns that unregulated ART could undermine the fundamental principle of respect for persons embodied in medicine. This principle of respect attempts to exclude monetary gain as the primary motivation for the actions of healthcare professionals working in this field. For example, in an attempt to prevent commercialization of the process and exploitation of persons involved:

- Sex selection via embryo testing is not permitted except for medical reasons—for example, to prevent sex-specific disease such as Duchenne's muscular dystrophy. (This does not prevent couples from testing for sex or anything else, once the fetus is *en ventre de sa mère*, 'in the womb of its mother'. See Case 10.4, 'A right to be tested?'.)
- Would-be egg or sperm donors cannot be paid, except for their expenses, in Canada. (This is also so in the UK or Germany.) Not paying such donors makes their giving more altruistic and so the gift safer.
- Surrogate mothers cannot 'profit' from the birth. They can only be reimbursed for reasonable costs and losses of pregnancy—this is to remove any financial windfalls to them and prevent a market-driven traffic in babies and wombs for hire. (This does not prevent generous 'gifts' to the surrogate mother.)

The provision of healthcare is meant to be based solely on the patient's best interests (as defined by the patient). This is especially important for ART cases, which are largely outside the normal confines of medicare or socially reimbursed care. Unfortunately, with ART, it is not always clear who the patient(s) is/are and what his/her/their interests is/are.

IV. Desperately Seeking Stem Cells

The use of human 'stem cells' is controversial. Stem cells are primal cells able to renew themselves through cell division and also possessing the capacity to differentiate into more specialized cells. Human stem cells exist in two main forms: embryonic, which derive from early stage embryos (about four to five days old in humans), and adult (also known as somatic) from adult tissues. The greatest differentiating capacity to date is found in pluripotent embryonic stem cells, such as in umbilical cord blood or bone marrow, although there is a limited number of pluripotent adult stem cells.

Stem cell treatments have been used for some time to treat leukemia and related types of cancers via bone marrow transplants. Stem cells offer the promise of treatment for other diseases such as Parkinson's disease, spinal cord injuries, and juvenile-onset diabetes. Infused stem cells may replenish the lost differentiated cells, such as the dopamine-producing neurons in Parkinson's disease, that cause the illness. Unproven use of stem cells for such purposes is already, controversially, taking place.[37]

CASE 10.8   TO SAVE A CHILD, CREATE A SIBLING

A three-year-old child is gravely ill with acute leukemia. Curative treatment is possible but requires bone marrow stem cell donation from a suitable donor. Without it, the child will almost certainly die when the disease recurs in several years. No suitable match is found. The parents decide to conceive a new child in the hopes that it will be a suitable donor, but they need ART because the woman experienced premature ovarian failure at age 43. The mother has a twin sister who is prepared to donate her eggs.

Are the parents acting improperly? Is this an acceptable use of ART? And what if they only wanted the fetus's embryonic stem cells and requested the creation of multiple fertilized eggs to maximize the chances of a suitable donor fetus? Would it be wrong for an ART provider to help them?

Research using embryonic stem cells has generally been more controversial than that involving adult stem cells. Some oppose using embryonic-derived cells because they seem to come with a moral tithe: the embryo may have to be created and then sacrificed to derive such cells. Because a human embryo is a potential human being, so the reasoning goes, destroying it contributes to the devaluation of human life.[38] By the same token, it seems wrong to treat gametes or embryos as mere property to be bought or sold to the highest bidder. These actions and attitudes seem morally repugnant because they treat human life as a means to an end, rather than as an end in itself. (This, as you can tell, is a deontological argument.)

Supporters of embryonic stem cell research, by contrast, point to the tremendous potential for improving the quality of human life. (This, by contrast, is a consequentialist argument.) An unimplanted embryo *in vitro* is not the same, morally, as a third trimester fetus, let alone the same as a child or an adult, they say. Most countries do not prohibit, outright, work with embryonic human stem cells. Such work, it would be argued, need not be done at the expense of a respectful view of human life, if it follows certain restrictions.

Embryos are readily available as byproducts of IVF procedures. Could these excess or abandoned embryos, created for other purposes, not be donated for research or therapy without devaluing human life? Many people would agree to using these embryos rather than simply discarding them, but there is no social consensus on this issue.

The Ethics Committee of the American Society for Reproductive Medicine has recommended that discarded or abandoned embryos be used for research but with prior consent from the donors.[39] This would make the donation of stem cells akin to parents donating the organs of their deceased children—hardly a felicitous situation—but it can give meaning to a dreadful circumstance. Consent would be especially important if it were possible—it isn't as yet—to obtain fetal gametes from fetal reproductive tissue.

Respect for things human

The renowned eighteenth-century Prussian philosopher Immanuel Kant argued that human beings should never be treated just as a means to obtain some supposed 'greater good' because this renders them mere 'stepping-stones' to someone else's welfare or happiness.[40] He believed in the intrinsic value of each individual's life.

By the lights of the Kantian view, parents ought never to see their offspring as mere extensions of themselves and their own needs. Is the Kantian view of offspring too precious, though? After all, parents have children for all kinds of emotional, economic, and cultural reasons, but our culture does not privilege one set of reasons. There is no moral litmus test prospective parents must pass—we do not question why they want a new child. So, why not, then, produce an offspring to save the life of an imperiled one? Moreover, it is sometimes argued, the embryo or fetus is not a person with rights, so why be so concerned about its fate, as compared with the fate of an imperiled person?

DISCUSSION OF CASE 10.8

Although not undertaken to serve the health interests of the donor child, there would be little reason to hesitate with sibling-to-sibling donation if the suitable donor child already existed. Presuming the risks to be undertaken by the healthy sibling are small and the psychological benefits to the family evident, were the ill child to survive, then donation could take place. To think otherwise, to pause even for a moment, is what the twentieth-century philosopher Bernard Williams has called 'having one thought too many'.[41] The 'rescue' response should be automatic.

Would it be any more wrong if the parents had to conceive a new child to save the life of their imperiled child? If doing so were acceptable to them and easy to do (for example, they wanted another child anyway, they were young, and could afford it), who would stand in their way? But, should the couple simply want an embryo for its stem cells to save the life of their three-year-old child, would it be wrong to help them? Is it better to let a child die than destroy an embryo to save the child? If common sense intuitions have any role here, it would seem that the harm caused by the loss of an actual life is greater than the harm done by the loss of a potential life.

Other people would refuse to trade one human life (the embryo's) for that of another (the child's)—this is similar to the Kantian view of human life. One worry is that using an embryo, even for a valid therapeutic purpose, might open the floodgates to raising and harvesting embryos for the purpose of being tissue or organ factories. This worry might be countered if ART were to be strictly regulated and offered only by accredited facilities, not an easy task.[42]

Optimists put faith in technology and our ability to control it; pessimists are not as sanguine about human rationality and hanker for a simpler world. I tend to the eternal-optimism view, recognizing that the path forward is rarely easily won. Many of these rather Byzantine ethical and legal conundrums may disappear with the advance of the science that induced them. Researchers have more recently been able to deprogram adult somatic cells into primordial stem cells.[43] This may eliminate concerns about the *origin* of stem cells, but not their *use*, of course.

CONCLUSION

Modern medicine has made pregnancy and its termination safe and reliable options. Reproduction can now be a matter of choice and not destiny for women and men. There will remain moral differences over these choices that ought to be explored and understood by clinicians in order to foster and enable authentic choice. Once a child is born alive, however, things change almost entirely—the priority of the interests of the child, as opposed to the wishes of the mother or the parents, predominates, as was considered in Chapter 7.

We will now go from life's beginning to life's end. I want to examine some of the most recurring and disturbing issues in modern ethics, the issues connected with the care of the dying, the dead, and the almost dead. If life's beginning is about possibility and promise, then life's end may be more about destiny and purpose.

A DARK WOOD:
END-OF-LIFE DECISIONS

. . . the life of man, solitary, poor, nasty, brutish, and short.
Thomas Hobbes, 1651[1]

We are born in open field and die in a dark wood.
Russian proverb, n.d.

The Russian proverb reflects the pessimism by which, for most of human history, death has been viewed. Although religion provides for many the promise of paradise in the afterlife, dying is something over which people have had little control and much to fear. The act and process of dying tends to be viewed (and indeed experienced) as 'solitary, nasty, brutish' and, contrary to Hobbes' statement, all too often anything but short, at least in modern times.[2]

I. ALLOWING DEATH: THE RIGHT TO SAY NO

In this chapter I will look at how the process of dying has changed in modern medicine. Here, as elsewhere, there are precedents in law and ethics that can guide the healer's hand and heart. These precedents do not take death out of the woods yet. But they do shed light on how patients, families, and healthcare providers may proceed to make dying a less forlorn journey.

CASE 11.1   'WE CAN'T LET HIM STARVE!'

A 72-year-old retired librarian is recovering from resection of advanced esophageal cancer. Although the surgery is considered a 'success'—the tumour was removed and the patient survived the operation—a number of complications ensue in the subsequent two weeks: the incision line becomes infected, the patient cannot swallow, and a wound dehiscence (partial separation of the anastamotic site between the upper esophagus and the distal stomach) develops. Further setbacks follow: renal failure, sepsis, and, most recently, cortical blindness likely due to an embolic stroke. The patient is being fed by a naso-gastric (N-G) tube but finds it painful and has removed it himself several times. It is re-inserted by the surgical team each time over the patient's vehement protests. The surgeons insist on replacing his N-G tube because without it 'he will starve to death' and this, they argue, is unacceptable.

Is the surgical team's reasoning reasonable?

DISCUSSION OF CASE 11.1

The team is skating on thin ice if the patient is competent. Unless he is so depressed that he cannot make a decision consistent with his values and beliefs, his decision to refuse N-G feeding ought to be respected. (If the surgical team is uncertain about this, they should assess his capacity.) Patients have a right to stop any treatment, even if it means 'starving to death'. This option is buttressed by the recognition that, wound upon wound, this poor man is dying and deserves some compassion.

The option to forego treatment has by now become well established in North American healthcare (see Box 11.1).[3]

BOX 11.1

'The duty of the State to preserve life must encompass a recognition of an individual's right to avoid circumstances in which the individual himself would feel that efforts to sustain life demean or degrade his humanity.'

CASE 11.2   A LIFE WORTH LIVING

Nancy B was a 25-year-old woman from Quebec who had been hospitalized for two and half years with an extremely severe form of

Guillain-Barré syndrome. This had resulted in an almost complete decay of her respiratory motor nerves, so much that she could not breathe without the aid of a ventilator. She was bedridden and hooked up to the ventilator every hour of every day. Her condition was considered incurable, but not 'terminal' (she could be kept alive by technology indefinitely).

Nancy B expressed a firm and fixed wish over a period of a year to be removed from the ventilator and be allowed to die—'life was no longer livable' for Ms B.

Ought her request be granted?

Section 215c of Canada's *Criminal Code* requires care providers to provide the 'necessaries of life' to a person under their charge 'if that person (i) is unable, by reason of detention, age, illness, mental disorder or other cause, to withdraw himself from that charge, and (ii) is unable to provide himself with necessaries of life.'[4] Moreover, section 217 concerns 'the duty of persons undertaking acts': 'Every one who undertakes to do an act is under a legal duty to do it if an omission to do the act is or may be dangerous to life.'[5]

Together these sections suggest treatment cannot be stopped if doing so might constitute a threat to the life of a patient who is dependent on others for care. If so, how do these provisions in law square with the privacy right of competent persons to be free from unwanted interventions?

Little legal risk

In Canada at least, the courts are rarely asked to rule on intimate personal matters, such as end-of-life decisions, which are usually made *consensually* by a competent patient, doctor, and family (or substitute decision maker). Section 216 of the *Criminal Code* expects clinicians, in the exercise of their due skill, to act with 'reasonable knowledge, skill and care'.[6] Objectionable acts, ones open to criminal prosecution for criminal negligence, would be those done with 'wanton or reckless disregard for the lives or safety of other persons' (section 219).[7] So, it would seem healthcare professionals can stop life-sustaining treatment, *providing* they do so carefully and exercise the 'standard of care'.

DISCUSSION OF CASE 11.2

Uncertain of her liability under sections 215 and 217, Ms B's attending physician sought explicit judicial sanction to remove her from the ventilator.

The Quebec Superior Court ruled that stopping Nancy B's ventilator would not be culpable negligence but a reasonable treatment option and therefore should be allowed: 'What Nancy B is seeking, relying on the principle of autonomy and her right of self-determination, is that the respiratory support treatment being given her cease so that nature may take its course; that she be freed from slavery to a machine as her life depends on it.'[8] This, the court recognized, would require the assistance of another person—her doctor—to remove the ventilator and this, too, the court allowed. This was not considered suicide or assisted suicide but merely allowing 'the disease [to] take its natural course'.

One can imagine a well-intentioned person saying to her: 'You should keep on living; you may change your mind.' 'You can't give up; think what an impact this might have on others!' Such responses would be, I think, inappropriate. Nancy B's life was unacceptable to *her*. Core aspects of her life—her extreme disability, her dependence on others, her loss of privacy—could not be 'palliated'. It is often very hard for others—family members, healthcare professionals, lawyers, judges, the public—to appreciate how much patients, like Ms B, suffer.

Even in the legally charged atmosphere of American medicine, there have been few successful malpractice or criminal actions related to stopping life-sustaining treatment. 'Almost everything else physicians do (or do not do) puts them at greater risk of legal liability than withdrawing or withholding treatment in appropriate cases.'[9] The courts invariably find that the laws governing suicide or homicide do not apply to such treatment decisions when made 'in good faith'.[10] That the patient does not initiate the underlying death-inducing condition distinguishes such treatment decisions from suicide (and so the actions of professionals in such instances would not be considered 'assisted suicide') (see Box 11.2).[11]

BOX 11.2

'Refusing medical intervention merely allows the disease to take its natural course; if death were eventually to occur, it would be the result, primarily, of the underlying disease, and not the result of a self-inflicted injury.'

Inappropriate requests to stop treatment

We have seen, throughout this book, cases where requests to stop potentially helpful treatment and life support have been made for various less than optimal reasons—negative transference (Case 1.4, 'To feed or not to feed?'), misunderstood consent (Case 6.8, 'A fractured hip, a broken mind'), misguided autonomy (Case 2.6, 'A man should die at home!'), and therapeutic pessimism (Case 9.3, 'Too old to save?'). Such inappropriate requests or decisions may be made by patients, families, and healthcare professionals. They are inappropriate because they fail to explore alternatives and/or too readily agree to treatment limitations—sometimes for the 'wrong' reasons.[12]

CASE 11.3   NO CRAP VS. NO CPR

A 58-year-old homeless man, with no known relatives, who looks 20 years older is admitted in respiratory distress with resistant tuberculosis. He is emaciated, dishevelled, and non-compliant. His verbal communication is minimal. Confined to a ward, he undergoes various procedures including bronchoscopy and urinary catheterization. Although he does not specifically verbalize a refusal to the procedures, he is resistant and difficult. He yells at the staff, spills his food tray ('I can get better food on the street!'), and repeatedly pulls out his tubes ('What is all this crap for? Get it off me!').

At one point during his hospitalization, he is approached about the issue of cardio-pulmonary resuscitation (CPR). If his heart stops, would he want them to try to restart it? 'What?' he said. 'What kind of crap is this? I don't want any more crap!' He turns away from the staff and refuses any further discussion. The staff takes this as meaning he does not want CPR. They do not return to discuss the No CPR order that is entered on his chart. He arrests three weeks later and dies. CPR is not performed.

Why is there cause for concern as regards this patient's care?

DISCUSSION OF CASE 11.3

Although anyone has the right to refuse potentially life-saving treatment, refusals should be properly explored. Saying one wants 'no more crap' seems a bit different than saying one does not want CPR. This patient had several 'red flags' for less than optimal management—he was homeless, was difficult medically and personally, had previously refused treatment, and looked like he was at the end of his life. Maybe he was, but his care providers could have been a little more diligent about assessing his wishes. On the face of things, it is not clear what he wanted. His refusal of 'crap' may have been less a refusal of care than an acerbic observation on the state of his care. That being said, some patients are difficult to assess and a patient who has spent a lifetime refusing assistance may get his wishes met.

End-of-life studies

Limiting life-sustaining care is now a common event. Any kind of care, be it feeding or artificial breathing, be it considered 'ordinary' or 'extraordinary', may be stopped or withheld.[13] Stopping dialysis is, for example, the second leading cause of death in patients with End Stage Renal Disease (ESRD) in Canada and the third in the United States.[14] In 2002 it was reported that in New England 28 per cent of deaths of patients with ESRD followed treatment cessation.[15] Other forms of life-sustaining treatment including cardio-pulmonary resuscitation, intravenous fluids, antibiotics, and artificial feeding are not infrequently stopped for patients with terminal malignancies, advanced cognitive impairment, coma, and other end-stage conditions. In fact, the majority of all ICU deaths are due to foregoing life support.

Variation in care

There is a wide variation in end-of-life decisions by clinicians in different countries.[16] Many countries do not recognize the right of a patient either to name substitute decision makers or to refuse life support. Some believe that the decision to withhold life support is often driven by the healthcare professional's personal values, influenced by the clinician's religious and social values.[17]

A Canadian study correlated the withdrawal of ICU life support

- with the physician's perception that the patient would not want life-support,
- with the physician's prediction that the patient would be unlikely to survive the ICU,
- with the physician's prediction that the patient would be severely cognitively impaired if he or she did survive, and
- not with age or 'objective' measures of illness severity.[18]

Although this perception by physicians of values is important, it is still not clear whose values prevail. The patient's? The family's? Or the clinician's? How can this be sorted out?

In the late 1990s, the huge US SUPPORT initiative (Study to Understand the Prognosis and Preferences of Outcomes and Risks of Treatment) examined the lives of thousands of critically ill US patients. There were dramatic shortcomings as regards quality end-of-life palliative care and poor correlation between the decisions made and the patient's wishes. Surprisingly, as well, the study's sophisticated educational intervention to improve ICU decision making by improved communication about patient preferences and prognoses failed miserably—perhaps because it required physicians to listen to nurses.[19] There is something about the 'logic' of technological care that is hard to change, especially when it depends on physician listening skills. This does not imply that meaningful conversations cannot happen.

II. WHEN NO MEANS NO

CASE 11.4   A DEATH NOT FORETOLD

A 76-year-old male patient, still handsome, a true 'gentleman' of the old school, is found unresponsive in his house by his grand-daughter. Brought to the ER, he is put on a ventilator because his respiratory status is declining. Over the next day, no cause for his decline is found. His brain CT is normal, toxic screen negative, septic workup unrevealing, and the rest of his bloodwork unremarkable. On the second day, his 51-year-old daughter requests cessation of the ventilator, saying her father would never have wanted to be kept alive by machines.

Should the care providers abide by her wish? Why? Why not?

The refusal of life-sustaining treatment by a patient (or a family, see Case 9.3, 'Too old to save?') should not always be accepted at face value as an 'autonomous' choice. The prudent and caring professional must always consider distracting features of the patient's life, such as disabilities, alcoholism, or psychiatric illness, that may undermine unbiased decision making. Sometimes treatment refusals are precipitated by problems such as unhealthy family relationships or poor communication, a lack of empathy or caring. Patients who feel uncared for may seek 'negative' ways (by appearing resistant) in order to get *more* care, not less.

On the other side, health professionals who experience patients in a negative way may collude in a patient's resistance to treatment by seeing the patient as 'deserving' of death. 'Negative transferences' are the hostile or futile reactions or 'projections' from health professionals towards the resistant, severely disabled, or 'unlikable' patient.[20] These reactions can manifest themselves as a too-ready acceptance of death by patients with severe disabilities. Negative attitudes towards the so-called hopeless case must be thoroughly explored before treatment cessation decisions are made.

Questions to ask

The following issues should be addressed prior to making a decision about continuing or stopping life-sustaining treatment:

- Have the diagnosis and prognosis been established as firmly as possible?
- Have all reasonable options been explored and goals for care and treatment options established as a team?
- Does the patient understand the illness, the treatment options, their risks and benefits, and their consequences? (Is the refusal an informed one?)
- Do you know what treatment the patient wants/refuses and why?
- Is the patient as physically comfortable as possible?
- Have psychiatric issues been identified and explored?
- Have issues of patient dignity been addressed (feelings of helplessness, being a burden to others, isolation)?
- Are you sure the patient's choice has not been unduly influenced by other factors (for example, alcohol)?
- Have religious and cultural factors been assessed?
- Have the patient's significant others been involved if he or she wishes?
- Have consultations with other specialists been obtained, as appropriate?
- Have you made a clear recommendation and explained its rationale? Can the decision be seen as defensible and reasonable? If not, the previous steps should be repeated and other appropriate consultants involved.[21]

DISCUSSION OF CASE 11.4

This real-life case was so hard because the patient had previously been well and the cause for his sudden decline was a mystery. It may be that he would not have wanted technological life support, but no living will could be produced. In uncertainty, it is unwise to 'give up' on a patient, so the caregivers explored the rationale for removing life support.

The patient's family physician and psychiatrist were contacted. Was the patient depressed? Yes, but not suicidal. Would he have wanted to be rescued in this circumstance? Not likely. He had suffered a number of losses but he had also had a recent trip to the 'old country' where he met a long-estranged offspring. They were reconciled and he felt, as he told his family doctor, that he had achieved a sense of resolution and was prepared to die. The doctor at the time put little stock in those words but it was only a month later that he was found in a comatose state. Did he cause it? No one knew but all who knew him were aware he would not thank them for saving him even if they could do so. That fact, plus his ongoing decline, was sufficient to tip the decision in favour of the daughter's request. It was not a happy decision but seemed right in the circumstances. The patient was removed from the ventilator and died peacefully within minutes.

The values driving medical decision making should be the *patient's* values and not the values of others or the 'values of technology'. How can we try to ensure this is so (see Box 11.3)?

BOX 11.3

Conditions for the 'proper' cessation of treatment include the following:

• The request is [was] made by a competent patient.

• The request is consistent with the patient's beliefs, values and attitudes.

• The patient makes [made] the decision freely without coercion by others or under circumstances such as severe depression, drug use, etc.

• Alternative forms of treatment and support have been explored and offer no further help to the patient.

• The patient has a condition or illness that would be considered by a neutral observer to be reasonable grounds for the wish to stop treatment.

III. ADVANCE DIRECTIVES

It has been thought that completing a 'living will' is one way of reducing uncertainty about end-of-life care (see Box 11.4). Living wills were originally advocated by 'right to die' groups, and included vague directives refusing 'extraordinary treatment' if the person was 'irreversibly ill'.[22] These are now mainstream. For example, in the United States, under the *Patient Self-Determination Act*, hospitals must ask patients on admission if they have such documents.

BOX 11.4

Living wills = advance directives

1. Instruction directives: *what* decisions are to be made.

2. Proxy directives: *who* makes decisions.

Living wills are also known as 'advance (*not* advanced!) directives'. They may state in writing what sort of treatment the person would accept or reject if ill (an 'instruction directive') and may name others—surrogates—prepared to make medical decisions for the person in case of incapacity (a proxy directive or a power of attorney [POA] for personal care).

Despite their benefits, living wills have never really taken off. Advance directives require what may seem like inordinate time for discussion and are not always easy for patients to use or understand. A form cannot explain to patients what various options (such as CPR) might practically entail nor can they cover every possible situation.[23]

Most importantly, perhaps, many patients do not always want their advance directives strictly followed and are willing to give surrogates the right to override their wishes.[24] This is a thorny problem with living wills generally: why should they be followed if the patient's personhood has totally changed? Therefore, in difficult cases such as continued treatment of a 'hopeless case', living wills may give us the view from a person's past, but they do not tell us if it is the right thing to do in the present. Living wills exaggerate the patient's ability to predict or control future medical care.[25]

In situations of uncertainty, healthcare professionals often look to guidelines. Indeed, guidelines can help clinicians ensure that patients get the treatments that are appropriate and beneficial for them (see Chapter 9 on Justice). One such instance is that of CPR.

IV. THE DYING, THE DEAD, AND THE ALMOST DEAD

CPR was originally designed to save people who experienced cardiac standstill, such as from drowning accidents.[26] It subsequently developed into the standard of care for *anyone* who died in hospital, no matter how expected or inevitable the death might be. The problem then became how to limit the use of CPR to patients for whom it would be truly beneficial.[27]

A 'basic national guideline for use by all those involved in the care of the terminally ill' was revamped in 1994 in the light of new information concerning the limitations and ill-use of CPR.[28] Approved by the Canadian Hospital Association, the Canadian Medical Association, and the Catholic Health Association of Canada and developed in cooperation with the Canadian Bar Association, this statement represents a professional consensus on the issue of 'no-resuscitation' orders. It continues to serve as a template for regulatory authorities as regards end-of-life care in general and can stand as a professional guide for the standard of care in this area.[29]

This document recommends that patients for whom CPR is likely to be successful or for whom CPR might or might not help should be made aware that all life-saving measures, including CPR, will be taken unless they object. Patients unlikely to return to their pre-arrest state if CPR is successful should be made aware of the limitations of CPR and their informed preferences should guide the use of CPR. Finally, patients for whom survival is unprecedented or who are permanently unable to experience any benefit should not have CPR offered as an option.

No CPR orders

To properly obtain consent for a No CPR order, CPR should be described honestly, as it really is, without raising unrealistic expectations of its potential benefits. A cardiac arrest is a devastating situation; even if CPR is successful—and success, even in best case scenarios, is far from certain—patients need to be made aware of the risks of multi-organ failure (in particular the risk of neurological injury) and the very likely (except in rare cases) necessity of life support.

The legal reliability of these guidelines has been rarely tested, but opinion would likely be that professionals who follow them in offering or not offering CPR to patients would be seen as taking 'due care'. In a Manitoba case, the Court of Appeal was asked to rule on two parents' refusal to consent to a No CPR order on their 13-month-old who was in a persistent vegetative state. The court held that parental consent for a No CPR order was not required and physicians had the exclusive authority to withhold treatment.

> Whether or not such a direction [No CPR] should be issued is a judgment call for the doctor to make having regard to the patient's history and condition and the doctor's evaluation of the hopelessness of the case. The wishes of the patient's family or guardians should be taken into account but neither their consent nor the approval of a court is required.[30]

This is generally the law of the land: where treatment is offered or not by a clinician, so long as the clinician follows 'usual care' in doing so, the courts are unlikely to question it . . . usually, anyway. The next case challenges this notion.

CASE 11.5   THE NO CPR ORDER

Mr S was an elderly resident of a nursing home with advanced Parkinson's disease and multiple other co-morbidities including previous strokes.[31] These had resulted in cognitive impairment, limited communication, difficulty swallowing, and a tracheostomy to protect his airway. There were repeated episodes of pneumonia. After one such bout, the treating physician decided Mr S's condition was deteriorating such that he would not benefit from CPR. Previous

attempts to write a No CPR order had been met with resistance from Mrs S whom some clinicians felt had an unrealistic understanding of her husband's capabilities and limitations. The physician wrote the order in Mr S's chart but did not discuss it with his wife.

Several months earlier, she had refused consent for the tracheostomy which led to the Public Trustee taking over as the substitute decision maker for her husband. The Public Trustee was contacted by the physician about the No CPR order but declined to be involved, seeing no necessity as this had to do with 'non-treatment' rather than active treatment. Upon discovering such an order had been written, Mrs S sought a court ruling to block this.

What are the aspects of this case that made the No CPR order less than optimal?

CPR should, of course, be seen not as an isolated intervention but as one element of a comprehensive plan of treatment. Therefore, the need for CPR should be considered during wider discussions of the treatment plan and the patient's condition and wishes. Patients with No CPR orders may still be candidates for various forms of emergency treatment, such as dialysis or palliative surgery. When patients have clearly asked not to be revived, their views should be respected, even in the emergency room or the operating theatre.[32]

The conversation with a family and patient regarding end-of-life care should stress what care will be done, rather than emphasizing the non-beneficial care that should not be provided. Once made, clear communication of a decision about CPR and its implications to others, such as family and other healthcare professionals, is absolutely critical. Such discussions and their conclusions should be stated openly in the patient's record in order that others may safely and readily take over the care of the patient. 'Unilateral' decisions made by physicians not to offer CPR are legally acceptable in many jurisdictions but remain controversial and should not be taken at the expense of forthright and honest communication with all parties involved (see Box 11.5).[33]

Clinicians should raise the issue of CPR in a timely way with patients, especially *those for whom it would not be a surprise if they died*—for example, those who are critically ill or whose course is marked by a steady deterioration. Relatives or hopelessly ill patients may insist upon CPR, although it may be clearly futile.[34] Most physicians would probably give in to such pressure, thinking this to be the legally prudent course. Yet, futile attempts at resuscitation deny the patient a dignified death.[35] This can also be emotionally draining for staff and demoralizing for both staff and other patients.

BOX 11.5

A decision not to resuscitate should 'not be, or even be seen to be, arbitrary. The reasoning and criteria to be applied by the physician should be sufficiently firm and clear so any decisions can be effectively supported should they later be subject to question.'

At all times, the utmost attention must be given to patients' overall dignity and well-being whether or not they will get CPR. Patients not receiving CPR must not be abandoned (or feel abandoned); they still deserve every sort of appropriate medical care and must be visited as regularly as would be all patients.

DISCUSSION OF CASE 11.5

There are aspects of the management of this case that, in retrospect, may have predicted the trip to court. First, there was a communication problem that was not resolved before the No CPR order was written. Second, to some (such as the judge in this case) it might appear there was a change in status from a patient who could benefit from an emergency intervention (a tracheostomy) to one who could not (CPR). Were the differences in these quite distinct therapies explored with Mrs S? Third, there seems to have been a lack of understanding as to the goals of treatment. Did Mrs S appreciate that the tracheostomy tube could prevent problems and maintain comfort whereas doing CPR on Mr S would do neither? Fourth, the No CPR order was written without input from other clinicians. Fifth, the order was not communicated to Mrs S in a respectful way—she only found about it after the fact, a circumstance that may have appeared to her to be surreptitious and untrustworthy. To tell her about the order would have been the respectful thing to do even if she was no longer his substitute decision maker. Had these issues been addressed, it is possible this trip to court could have been avoided (see Box 11.6).[36]

As it turned out, the court temporarily blocked the No CPR order and asked each side to obtain other opinions. Mr S was transferred to another institution before this was completed.

BOX 11.6

Working with families

- Assess understanding: Ask: 'What have you been told about your [relative]'s condition?'

- Assess feelings: Say: 'It must be very hard to see your [relative] like this.'

- Assess for guilt or fears: Listen for statements such as: 'I can't live without [relative].'

- Allow for information handling: Suggest, 'You may have more questions later. Write them down and we'll discuss them.' State a definite time and be there.

- Avoid using jargon and value-laden words and phrases that can mislead or appear to denigrate the patient, for example, 'vegetable', 'doing every-thing' (not possible), 'restart his or her heart' (rarely that easy), 'brain dead' (such a patient is simply dead).

- Avoid asking the family to shoulder too much of the burden of decision making, for example, asking families, 'Do you want to keep [your relative] alive?'

The trouble with families

Intractable disagreements with families deserve careful ethical analysis before going the legal route. What are the particular issues families have with their relative's care? Are the family's requests based on the patient's autonomous wishes and/or the patient's best interests? Or, do they arise out of family issues, for example, not being able to let go, unresolved guilt feelings that are then projected onto medical professionals, or something as venal as financial consid-erations? Healthcare professionals must step back in difficult situations with families and try to empathize with how the family is feeling rather than getting into an adversarial relationship. That said, requests made by some families can seem excessive.

An Ontario court refused to uphold a lower tribunal's ruling that two daugh-ters were acting inappropriately for their mother, an 81-year-old patient hospi-talized with end-stage dementia.[37] Despite their mother being bed-bound, unaware of her surroundings, and suffering, her daughters had refused to consider any diminution in her treatment (they refused, for example, the suggestion that she not be re-admitted to the ICU) because she had said some years previously 'Where there's life, there's hope.' This statement was taken in two entirely different ways: by her daughters to mean that health professionals should stop at nothing; by the healthcare team (and the lower tribunal) that it was too vague to direct care in any way. Lacking a patient wish applicable to the circumstances, the team wanted to treat her according to the 'best interests' standard, which would seem to call for a palliative care approach. Her daughters, by contrast, saw their mother's statement in a very uncompromising way: they could not imagine any circumstance of life in which their mother would not want to be kept alive. The court ruled that the team (and the tribunal) ought not to have dismissed the patient's expressed statement and overruled the ruling of the tribunal that had replaced the daughters as her decision makers. The practical effect of this ruling is that the patient's suffering will continue—a difficult outcome for her healthcare team.

Persons making grand statements about end-of-life care ('I want everything . . .') should be careful. They might get more than they bargained for: yoked to a Procrustean bed of technology at life's end because some relative or court takes such statements too literally. Of course, on any reasonable understanding of advance directives, patients should be able to ask only for medical options within the standard of care. Such statements should not be interpreted as a legal means to torture patients with the exquisite and extravagant technologies of 'life support'.

The courts have ruled, as in the *Malette v. Shulman* case, that deeply held objections to treatment should not be held to the 'transitory' standards of reasonableness of the day. Okay, that might be fine for *refusals* of treatment. What about requests for treatment? Refusals of treatment are easier as they involve *not* doing something, but requests for treatment involve an obligation on the part of someone to *provide* that care. How far do such obligations extend?

The dead

CASE 11.6   A VENGEFUL GOD IN THE ICU

A 44-year-old man with a large extended family is admitted to the ICU with raised intracranial pressure from an untreatable cerebral malignancy. He has been unresponsive for several days. Despite various measures, he has continued to decline and is now on a ventilator. It is obvious to the ICU staff that the patient's brain is too compressed to respond to any treatment. Despite being on no sedatives, he is in a deep coma, completely unresponsive to any stimulation. His Glasgow Coma Scale is 3—as low as you can get. His extremely religious family feels it is necessary to do anything possible to extend the patient's life, saying: 'If God wanted him to die, he wouldn't have allowed mankind to invent ventilators.'

As is standard practice, an 'apnea test' to establish brain death is arranged. This entails temporarily removing the patient's attachment to the ventilator. In response to rising carbon dioxide levels in the body, a dead person's brain will fail to initiate respiration as would normally occur. As the ICU resident is about to unhook the patient, a member of the patient's family grabs her arm and exclaims, 'Don't touch him! If you remove him from the breathing machine, we'll sue you for assault!'

What should the response of the ICU staff be?

Certain convictions can seem at odds with humane and dignified care. Healthcare professionals should not dismiss or avoid such convictions, but first of all try to explore the reasoning behind them.

- In the first instance, you should try to avoid getting your back up. Remember, our society is now a very diverse one and you are going to find yourself more and more having to deal with such issues.
- Second, in acknowledging these convictions, families are more likely to feel respected and heard. This can set the stage for further dialogue and possible compromise.
- Third, it does no good to line up one set of core beliefs (say, atheism) against another (say, religious fundamentalism) as if two warring camps. It may be that family members are overinterpreting their scriptures. In this regard, one should consult with respected religious leaders and others from the communities in question, who are more familiar with the religion's adaptation to modern society, to seek resolution and understanding.[38]

DISCUSSION OF CASE 11.6

In most jurisdictions, religious objections to brain death are not acceptable. (Even where they are 'accepted', it is only expected that clinicians will offer such families 'reasonable accommodation'.) A 'brain-dead' person is dead, full stop, and belongs in the ICU, and not in a morgue, only for exceptional reasons (coroner's or medical examiner's inquiry, awaiting organ retrieval). Out of respect for a family's wishes, one may delay transfers to the morgue—allowing relatives time for grieving and/or any religious rites to be performed. The inevitability of complete somatic collapse—usually within seven days even with cardiovascular support—following entire brain death is a natural limit on how far a body can be kept perfused after death.[39]

The ICU staff should widen the discussion to probe whether other family members might be more 'reasonable'. Gentle, but firm, explanation of various standard procedures such as apnea testing should be offered. While not being hasty in such approaches, one should do the various aspects of ICU care that are appropriate. If relatives continue to obstruct safe and proper care, discussion with hospital counsel would be wise.

The almost dead

Another area where religious and medical values can clash is in the debate over those who are 'almost dead', but not dead yet—especially those patients in a 'persistent' or 'permanent' vegetative state (PVS).[40] Obviously, without the miracles of modern medicine, such patients would never survive. With these 'miracles', such patients can exist for a long, long time.

The legal and moral acceptability of withdrawing life support from PVS patients has been recognized, however. In 1976, the New Jersey Supreme Court ruled that Karen Ann Quinlan, a young woman in a PVS for almost a year, had a constitutional 'right to privacy' to forego treatment, specifically the ventilator, given her poor quality of life ('no reasonable possibility of the patient returning to a cognitive, sapient state'). This right could be exercised on her behalf by her parents.[41]

Since Quinlan, courts and jurisdictions across North America have recognized a broad right of relatives or the courts to stop treatment in PVS patients.[42] Similar precedents have been set in Ireland and the UK.[43]

Nonetheless, the dilemma for some is that PVS patients are not yet dead and sometimes seem to recover some awareness. The latter indicates the difficulty of distinguishing true PVS from the 'minimally aware' state. Even if a PVS patient 'lightens' a little in terms of unconsciousness, he or she will remain profoundly neurologically impaired and never regain true awareness. However, there are mysteries around what patients in such states might actually experience.[44] Such unresolved issues should make clinicians wary of treating all PVS patients identically and removing them all from life support. This would obviously be inappropriate. Decisions to forego treatment should be made on a case-by-case basis.

V. PHYSICIAN-ASSISTED DEATH

Physician-allowed death—through foregoing treatment—is to be distinguished from what has been called 'physician-assisted death' (PAD). In the latter case, the physician is an active player in the death of the patient—either by 'euthanasia' or 'assisted suicide'. In true euthanasia the healthcare professional intentionally causes a patient's death by doing something directly to the patient, such as injecting a lethal drug. In assisted suicide, by contrast, while the physician may provide the means of inducing death (such as prescribing a lethal dose of medication), the final act inducing death is performed by the patient. 'Euthanasia' is defined in the *Oxford English Dictionary* as 'bringing about a gentle and easy death, especially in the case of incurable and painful disease'. This sounds innocuous enough, but it has been considered an unacceptable task for physicians since Hippocrates ('I will give no deadly drug . . .') (see Box 11.7).[45]

BOX 11.7

'Every one who

(a) counsels a person to commit suicide, or

(b) aids or abets a person to commit suicide,

whether suicide ensues or not, is guilty of an indictable offence and liable to imprisonment for a term not exceeding 14 years.'

Criminal Code of Canada

Both forms of PAD are obviously distinct from the foregoing of treatment that leads to the patient's death. They are also distinguished from palliative care. The latter uses escalating doses of drugs, such as narcotics, that have some risk of sedating and causing an earlier death of the patient. While this outcome cannot be eliminated, the distinction from PAD should also be obvious: the patient's death is not the goal of treatment, unlike PAD. If death happens, it may be a necessary consequence of easing the patient's suffering. This is known as the doctrine of 'double-effect': a bad outcome is morally acceptable if there is no other way of achieving the good effect. Fears that opioid use might hasten a patient's death deter some clinicians from effective pain control but these fears are exaggerated.[46]

CASE 11.7   SUE RODRIGUEZ

Sue Rodriguez was a 42-year-old Canadian woman in the advanced stages of amyotrophic lateral sclerosis (ALS). She knew the disease would later progress to the point where she would become totally dependent on others and unable to swallow or breathe without assistance. When life became intolerable, she hoped to be able to obtain help from a physician to end her life for her when she could not do so on her own. This wish conflicted with section 241(b) of the *Criminal Code*, which makes it an offence in Canada to help anyone commit suicide. Sue R, as she was known, went to the courts to challenge the law prohibiting assisted suicide.

As suicide itself has been decriminalized in Canada since 1972, the Supreme Court of Canada was asked to consider whether this prohibition on assisted suicide interfered with the *Charter* rights of personal autonomy (section 7), security of the person (section 7), and equality (section 15) of a person so disabled she could not commit suicide on her own.

Should Ms Rodriguez's request for professional assistance at death have been approved by the court?

The public's view

Public opinion polls since at least the early 1990s in Canada and the United States have revealed widespread support for physician-assisted death.[47] Legalizing suicide with drugs dispensed by physicians passed by popular vote in Oregon in 1994 and has since been reaffirmed.[48]

However, patients and families are prone to confusing the right to refuse treatment with the 'right to die'.[49]

DISCUSSION OF CASE 11.7

In 1993 by a 5-to-4 margin, the court voted to uphold the prohibition of assisted suicide.[50] The sad and striking aspect of the majority's decision was its acknowledgment that Ms Rodriguez would suffer as a result of their ruling. 'Although palliative care may be available to ease the pain and other physical discomfort she will experience . . . [drugs] will not prevent the psychological and emotional distress which will result from being in a situation of utter dependence and loss of dignity.' According to the majority, 'the respect for human dignity, while one of the underlying principles upon which our society is based, is not a principle of fundamental justice within the meaning of s. 7.' The majority was worried there would be no safeguards to distinguish more legitimate cases of assisted suicide, such as that of Ms Rodriguez, from illegitimate cases of involuntary euthanasia. This, in turn, could open the floodgates to the wholesale murder of vulnerable disabled persons.

The opposing judges by contrast were more swayed by the argument that the desire of patients, such as Sue Rodriguez, to control their dying was 'an integral part of living'. They felt the law contravened the *Charter* as it unfairly deprived Ms Rodriguez of her right to make decisions that affected only herself. Judge Cory wrote: 'State prohibitions that would force a dreadful, painful death

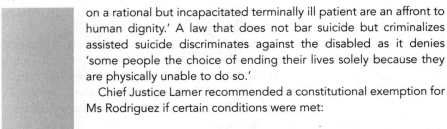

on a rational but incapacitated terminally ill patient are an affront to human dignity.' A law that does not bar suicide but criminalizes assisted suicide discriminates against the disabled as it denies 'some people the choice of ending their lives solely because they are physically unable to do so.'

Chief Justice Lamer recommended a constitutional exemption for Ms Rodriguez if certain conditions were met:

- Ms Rodriguez would have to be certified competent by two physicians.
- Her request for assisted suicide would have to be freely made.
- A physician would have to be present at the assisted suicide.
- The act causing death could only be performed by her alone.

The judgment and its surrounding arguments made no difference to Ms Rodriguez. She committed suicide with someone's assistance in 1994. No one was ever charged.

Health professionals' views

Many healthcare professionals are sympathetic to patient requests for PAD. In an Alberta study, 44 per cent of physicians surveyed supported active euthanasia and 51 per cent felt it should be legalized. If it were legalized, 28 per cent were prepared to practise it.[51] Similarly, a significant minority of surveyed US healthcare professionals have supported and are prepared to practise PAD.[52] Let us consider arguments for and against PAD.

Reasons for professionals to oppose PAD

Implications for public policy
There may be serious risks in allowing aid in dying, namely, that others might be injured by such practices for two broad reasons:

1. The challenge of how to 'draw the line': should anyone be able to access PAD or just the terminally ill? How does one define who is terminally ill? The Dutch system has legitimized assisted suicide for a physically healthy but depressed patient, suggesting that allowing PAD lowers the resistance of some practitioners to letting other 'hopeless' patients die.[53]

2. The dilemma of the 'slippery slope': what would prevent abuse? In a permissive milieu, those who cannot consent, such as the cognitively disabled and the very sick, or those who are vulnerable, such as the

depressed, the disabled, and the aged, might be coerced into accepting death. In the Netherlands, physicians perform life-terminating acts without explicit requests from the patient. (It is estimated that this happens in 0.8 per cent of deaths).[54] In new systems of 'managed care', conflicts of interest might lead institutions and doctors to encourage patients to die.[55]

Contrary to medical training

Aid in dying would be contrary to health professional training (which is to save lives), would further erode public confidence in the profession, and might cause clinicians to make less effort to save lives.

In short, professional-assisted death is a threat to the moral integrity of the medical professions.[56] According to this view, it should be condemned as being akin to medical assistance at capital punishment, which is widely regarded as unethical, even if it is legal in some jurisdictions.[57] The solution to the problem of barbaric state executions is not to train 'experts in execution'.

Cost to professionals

The emotional consequences—such as guilt or sadness—for healthcare professionals who participate in PAD cannot be ignored. As reported by Emanuel, several studies have shown 12 to 19 per cent of physicians who participated in physician-assisted death were uncomfortable afterwards, with feelings unrelated to fear of prosecution.[58]

Lack of necessity if palliative care is done properly

This may be stated in a strong version (all pain and suffering can be relieved by good palliative care) or in a weak version (much suffering can be relieved). Superb palliative care makes requests for aid in dying unusual.[59] Combined with advance care planning, high-quality end-of-life care can improve the care of the dying and have a positive impact on care providers.[60]

Reasons for professionals to support PAD

No different than accepted practice

Some of the reasons given for opposing PAD would also serve as arguments against letting patients refuse life-sustaining care. How sure can we be, for example, that someone has authentically consented to forego care? Uncertainties about foregoing care do not suggest that we end the practice, only that we exercise it carefully.

In addition, 'terminal sedation' and voluntary cessation of oral intake, palliative care options of last resort, have been largely accepted. Stopping eating will result in death in days to weeks and can be a comfortable process with good care. In terminal sedation, a patient with intractable suffering is sedated to unconsciousness and maintained there with opioids or sedatives, without feeding, until death occurs.[61] The clinician participation needed for these accepted palliative practices is little different than the type of services required for PAD.

Obligation is to the patient first

The first three arguments against PAD consider the implications for others. This privileging of third-party interests is distinct from ordinary clinical reasoning. Clinicians are used to dealing with the needs of the patient before them. Putting a particular patient's needs below the interests of others, especially when the patient constitutes no direct threat to others, is a violation of patient-focused care. Moreover, adequate palliation is not always possible.[62] Some symptoms cannot be fully controlled—pain, dyspnea, diarrhea, skin ulcers, delirium, and so on—even in palliative care units. There is also psychological suffering—from loss of dignity and loss of autonomy—that resists easy palliation.

Should be a matter of conscience

Quill provided a moving defence of physician-assisted suicide in describing his decision to give barbiturates to a woman with leukemia who decided to forego treatment.[63] Because of her fear of a lingering death, the patient asked him to give her the means to end her life when her suffering became too great. After discussing her views with her over time, he decided to grant her request: 'I . . . felt strongly that I was setting her free to get the most out of the time she had left, and to maintain dignity and control on her own terms until her death.'

Safeguards could prevent abuse

It is felt that such guidelines can limit abuse by making PAD open and accountable. Whether or not this is the case is hard to tell. Certainly, troubling cases from the Netherlands, where PAD is allowed, have come to light—in part because the patients do not have to be terminally ill, do not have to be suffering physically, and do not have to be capable at the time of the administration of the lethal medication.[64]

In Oregon the experience has been different.

Oregon's *Death with Dignity Act*

PAD may be practiced elsewhere (Switzerland, Netherlands, Belgium), but only in Oregon is it legal on account of a popular vote. If certain conditions are met, patients are eligible for a lethal prescription of drugs from a physician. Attempts by federal politicians to invalidate the Oregon law were found unconstitutional by the 9th Circuit US Appeals Court and by the US Supreme Court (see Box 11.8).[65]

BOX 11.8

Under the Oregon's *Death With Dignity Act*, eligible patients must, *inter alia*

- be adult (> 17 years old) state residents,
- be suffering from an incurable disease (life expectancy < 6 months),
- have their diagnosis confirmed by two independent physicians,
- make a verbal request and sign a written request for the prescription in the presence of two witnesses attesting that the patient is competent and acting voluntarily, and
- make their requests consistently over time.

A report on the first six years of this law noted that physician-assisted suicide was the cause of death of 1/8th of 1 per cent of the deaths in the state.[66] There are few reports of failures at assisted suicide (that might, some feared, turn it into euthanasia). The use of palliative care has increased (suggesting that the law does not undermine good end-of-life care). There also have been no reports of the inappropriate use of assisted suicide by patients who do not fit the inclusion criteria (such as psychological suffering or incapable patients). Patients who have used it have concerns that are less easy to address by palliative care—loss of autonomy and a desire to control the way in which they die.[67] Physicians grant about one in six requests for lethal medication and some patients change their mind after changes in palliative care.[68]

These are moderated results. Judging by these outcomes, it seems possible to devise guidelines that will be followed by patients and professionals. It may be that, having received support from the electorate twice, the law is well known and, Oregon being a relatively small jurisdiction, compliance easier to monitor.

CONCLUSION

In Canada, as in most places, a healthcare professional must never intentionally help a patient die. Clinicians who defy the law or professional regulations do so at the risk of attracting and being found liable for serious professional and criminal charges.[69] This legal situation should not end the moral debate on this topic. Professionals who disagree with the laws should work to change them, rather than take the law into their own hands. If patients of theirs are suffering severely or seem to be at risk of suffering severely due to lack of legal options, they could try to seek public and professional support for a means to alleviate the situation.

A UK judge commented:

> How can it be lawful to allow a patient to die slowly, though painlessly, over a period of weeks from a lack of food but unlawful to produce his immediate death by a lethal injection, thereby saving his family from yet another ordeal to add to the tragedy that has struck them? I find it difficult to find a moral answer to that question.[70]

This judge's concerns are easier to meet—death after the withdrawal of food and fluids usually occurs in less than eight days; the patient can be kept comfortable by good oral care and pain medications; a lethal injection is not needed, should never be given for the family's sake anyway, and may deprive the patient of experiencing the process of dying.

The great twentieth-century Austrian-English philosopher Wittgenstein said that we can never experience the moment of our death.[71] Maybe so, but all the moments before that ultimate one, being our last ones, may be of great import for the person dying. We interfere with this process at our peril. Do we want a quick death for the patient or for the survivors—for us? Or for the family? Perhaps we are all trying to escape from death.[72] No matter what transpires as regards PAD, we—professionals and the public—need to learn to be with individuals as they die. As professionals we need to 'suffer with' the dying and be with those who will go on living.[73]

CONCLUSION: WHERE TO GO FROM HERE?

Since this book's first edition there has been a virtual explosion of interest in medical bioethics. In fact, ethics in general is going through something of a Renaissance. People everywhere are disappointed in the cynical and often self-serving attitudes and practices of leaders in various areas of public life. Bioethics has become more sophisticated, and ethicists—experts or consultants in ethics—populate hospitals and other institutions. At my own university (Toronto), there are more than two dozen full-time bioethicists affiliated with regional and academic hospitals. The possibilities of collaboration among ethicists and healthcare professionals are enormous. Institutions of medicine, far from curtailing the growth of bioethics, have actively sponsored and supported this growth. Hospitals have significant budgets for bioethics that support thriving clinical and research ethics centres and ethics rounds and conferences, and even 'ethics weeks'.

Some, however, see such support for ethics in a less benign light and predict the demise of bioethics, suggesting it will be eaten for breakfast by the quotidian unethical realities of modern healthcare. According to these critics, truly independent clinical ethics, hemmed in by bottom-line thinking and priority setting, will either become a lapdog of administrators or wither on the vine. From my perspective, neither will happen. Patient rights and patient-based care are hard-won achievements that, I believe, will be impossible to reverse. Like democratic rights and freedoms generally, once citizens have a taste of them, they won't readily let them go.

These achievements, moral advances in my mind, are and will be buttressed by the courts, the regulatory authorities, professional associations, academies, charters, and conferences and by the millions of people who have experienced and benefited from the modern influence of ethics in healthcare. The professions of healthcare and their educational institutions—universities, colleges, examining and credentialing bodies—are also mutating in a morally positive direction. Ethics is a core curricular activity and an examinable subject, along with communication skills, necessary for entry into practice. Trainees who do well in these areas exhibit better patient care attitudes and are less likely to be the subject of professional complaints.[1]

Hard lessons have been learned by the healthcare professions out of their past failures to meet the expectations of their patients and society. Out of these disappointments a new professionalism has arisen that is all about ethics and quality patient care: the centrality of the autonomous patient, the importance of evidence-based care as opposed to clinical pragmatism, teamwork and collaboration as opposed to 'solo flying', transparency as opposed to secrecy, and a commitment to quality improvement over repeating the mistakes of the past.[2] I have stressed many of these themes throughout this book.

Ethics may ultimately be a private affair, but professional ethics is about the habits of the heart and the intellect that are a collective response to threats to the welfare and wishes of patients everywhere. Seen in this way, ethics is for all the healthcare professions and gives international unity to the human race divided still by nation and credo. Lacking a commitment to such an ethics—an ethics for everyone—we are in danger of falling back into a Hobbesian state of nature: 'Every man for himself and God against all.' Hardly a pleasurable prospect. Barring such a disaster, the modern healthcare professional simply needs to keep doing the hard work that advances in ethics require.

This book may be the beginning of a journey for you or it may be a refresher for those of you already on the journey. If you've slogged your way through it, you have some powerful tools for ethical analysis and practice, tools that can be used for good or ill but hopefully for the good of patients and the profession of medicine.

The ravenous reader should have found more than mere 'skin and bones' ethics here. Where to go now? Healthcare professionals can look to their own institutions to find help with addressing ethical issues. Professional regulatory and insurance bodies can be helpful resources for resolving troubling cases. As I suggested in the first edition, extra reading is advisable because this book can only examine briefly the concepts and controversies central to medical ethics.

Since the discussions in this book are all too short, they should be considered the beginning, not the end, of ethical reflection in clinical practice. I suggest you read at least one text on medical ethics. The classic in the field is Tom Beauchamp and James Childress's *Principles of Biomedical Ethics*.[3] Another helpful book is Albert Jonsen, Mark Siegler, and William Winslade's *Clinical Ethics*.[4] Raanan Gillon's *Principles of Health Care Ethics* touches on almost every topic in modern medical ethics.[5] The most comprehensive philosophical coverage of bioethics can be found in the superb five-volume *Encyclopedia of Bioethics*.[6]

There are so many other outstanding books on ethics that I can only list a few: Sugarman and Sulmasy's *Methods in Medical Ethics* is an excellent overview of the different approaches, theoretical and empirical, to ethics.[7] Any books by the contemporary UK philosopher Simon Blackburn are worth reading, but two in particular can be highly recommended: *Think: A Compelling Introduction to Philosophy* and *Being Good: A Short Introduction to Ethics*.[8] Their titles are self-explanatory. The musings on ethics by the contemporary US philosopher Harry Frankfurt—*The Reasons of Love* and *The Importance of What We Care About*—are stimulating and accessible as well, if a little challenging.[9]

For practical advice on research ethics, there are two long (and expensive) edited books: Amdur and Bankert's *Institutional Review Board: Management and Function* and Eckstein's *Manual for Research Ethics Committees*.[10] Cheaper and just as practical (and almost as comprehensive) is a single-authored text, *Ethics in Medical Research* by Trevor Smith.[11] The Office of the Surgeon General of the United States Army has produced a superb two-volume opus, *Military Medical Ethics*, that can be recommended as a comprehensive coverage of medical ethics with, obviously, special attention to the ethics of wartime and ethics under extreme conditions.[12] The British Medical Association has produced a very practical set of recommendations for physicians in *Medical Ethics Today*, which in its second edition has a CD-ROM as well.[13]

Other more specific topics for interested readers may be found in the following books. John Rawls' *Justice as Fairness: A Restatement* although hard-going is an elegant exploration of justice from the twentieth-century's foremost theorist of that topic.[14] Atul Gawande, a US surgeon and contributor on things medical for the *New Yorker*, has written thoughtfully about issues of import to ethics in his books *Complications* and *Better: A Surgeon's Notes on Performance*.[15] For the less felicitous side of medicine, there is Robert Klitzman's compelling study of the wounded healer, *When Doctors Become Patients*.[16] Merry and McCall Smith's book on medical mishaps, *Errors, Medicine and the Law*, is a well-written, sober account of the subject.[17] An excellent companion read would be Groopman's *How Doctors Think*.[18] Also a *New Yorker* contributor, Groopman addresses the cognitive errors to which clinicians are prone. *Almost a Revolution: Mental Health Law and the Limits of Change* by Paul Appelbaum, from which I adapted the title to Chapter 2 of this book, is an outstanding discussion of the interaction between modern health law and the practice of psychiatry.[19] Quasi-ethical and intensely interesting reflections on medicine may be found in Michael Balint's *The Doctor, His Patient and the Illness*, John Berger's *A Fortunate Man: The Story of a Country Doctor* and, more recently, the acerbically written *Hippocratic Oaths: Medicine and its Discontents* by a geriatrician, Raymond Tallis.[20]

Want to read more? Go no further than your favourite medical journals. From the *Lancet* to the *British Medical Journal*, the *Canadian Medical Association Journal*, the *New England Journal of Medicine*, the *Annals of Internal Medicine*, and the *Journal of the American Medical Association*, all medical publications carry articles on contemporary ethical issues regularly, as the footnotes throughout this book attest. Journals are probably the most easily available and relevant sources of information on ethics for healthcare professionals, house staff, interns, residents, and students. I strongly advise you to peruse such journals. Only by keeping abreast of the journals can the practising healthcare professional ensure that his or her practice is ethically acceptable and up to date.

Many journals, of course, specialize in ethics (*Ethics, Cambridge Quarterly of Healthcare Ethics, Journal of Medical Ethics*, and *Journal of Medicine and Philosophy*, to name just a few); it is worth consulting them for guidance in vexing cases and for in-depth discussions of contemporary issues. Other journals, such as *Health Law in Canada, The Journal of Legal Medicine*, and *Law, Medicine and Health Care*, cover the more strictly legal aspect of medicine.

Finally, many websites and blogs are devoted to ethics. One only has to web-search any ethics topic to discover hundreds, if not thousands, of sites. They will be of varying reliability, and readers will not want to rely on one source of information alone. In *Doing Right* I have turned frequently to Canadian law and precedent.[21] They may differ in some details, but many countries and professionals still share a similar approach to the issues addressed in this book. So, while professional ethics is increasingly international, it is often affected by local laws and regulations that this book cannot cover. You are encouraged to become familiar with those laws close to home, not just to learn what is expected of you, but also so you can work towards their change where you find them morally deficient. Local action can have bigger repercussions for healthcare professionals around the globe.

Professional ethics is not just about individual right or wrong. It's about how we—as members of the public and members of civil societies, as patients and as healthcare professionals—should make decisions, some pedestrian, some momentous. 'Doing right' is an area of continuous refinement and discernment, a public arena of thoughtful action, upon which we have improved, can further improve, and will improve even more. The advances will never be easy and are rarely predictable. Progress in professional ethics in a world seemingly riven by value and moral divides is possible but will not be made by one profession or one nation alone, but only by the combined efforts of many.

NOTES

Introduction

1. C. Dickens, *Hard Times* (London: Chapman & Hall, 1854), 1.
2. For example, the new curriculum for UK medicine 'focuses on the development of more generic professional competences such as communication, working in multi-professional teams, encouraging self-care, increasing shared decision-making between patients and healthcare professionals, and the ability to assure and improve the quality of care'. Academy of Royal Medical Colleges, *The Foundation Programme: Curriculum* (June 2007), 4.
3. T. Kuhn, *The Structure of Scientific Revolutions*, 2nd edn. (Chicago: The University of Chicago Press, 1970).
4. K. Popper, *Conjectures and Refutations: The Growth of Scientific Knowledge* (New York: Harper & Row, 1968), 322–4.
5. T. Nagel, Moral epistemology, in R. Bulger, E. Bobby, and H. Fineberg (eds.), *Society's Choices: Social and Ethical Decision Making in Biomedicine* (Washington, DC: National Academy Press, 1995), 202.
6. See, for example, H. Frankfurt, *The Reasons of Love* (Princeton: Princeton University Press, 2004), 6: 'Morality is less pertinent to the shaping of our preferences and to the guidance of our conduct . . . than is commonly presumed . . . it does not necessarily have the last word.'
7. J.S. Mill, *On Liberty* [1859] (New York: Appleton-Century Crofts, 1947), 10–11.
8. I. Kant, *The Metaphysical Principles of Virtue* [1797] (New York: The Bobbs-Merrill Company, Inc., 1964), 23, 25.
9. G. Harman, *The Nature of Morality: An Introduction to Ethics* (New York: Oxford University Press, 1977), 162.
10. K. De Ville, What does the law say? Law, ethics, and medical decision-making, *West J Med*, 160 (1994): 478–80.
11. R. Macklin, *Enemies of Patients: How Doctors Are Losing Their Power and Patients Are Losing Their Rights* (New York: Oxford University Press, 1993).
12. N. Edwards, M.J. Kornacki, and J. Silversin. Unhappy doctors: What are the causes and what can be done? *BMJ*, 324 (2002): 835–8; 'While it has been frequently suggested that the aim of professionalism and ethics preparation is not to midwife virtue or to assure sound moral character, medical students and residents themselves believe it may confer positive qualities and preservation of compassion.' L.W. Roberts, K.A. Green Hammond, C.M.A. Geppert, and T.D. Warner, The positive role of professionalism and ethics training in medical education: A comparison of medical student and resident perspectives, *Acad Psychiatry*; 28 (2004): 170–82.
13. A. Zuger, Dissatisfaction with medical practice, *N Engl J Med*, 350 (2004): 69–75; C. LeBlanc and J. Heyworth, Emergency physicians: 'burned out' or 'fired up'? *CJEM*, 9/2 (2007): 121–3.

14. R. Porter, *The Greatest Benefit to Mankind: A Medical History of Humanity* (New York: W.W. Norton & Co., 1997).

Chapter 1

1. J.S. Mill, *On Liberty* [1859] (New York: Appleton-Century Crofts, 1947), 58.
2. S. Blackburn, *Being Good: A Short Introduction to Ethics* (London: Oxford University Press, 2001), 132–3.
3. C. Del Mar, Prescribing antibiotics in primary care, *BMJ*, 335 (2007): 407–8.
4. G. Cadieux, R. Tamblyn, D. Dauphinee, and M. Libman, Predictors of inappropriate antibiotic prescribing among primary care physicians, *CMAJ*, 177 (2007): 877–83.
5. H. Frankfurt, *The Reasons of Love* (Princeton, NJ: Princeton University Press, 2004), 11.
6. K. Margittai, R. Moscarello, and M. Rossi, Medical students' perception of abuse, *Annals RCPSC*, 27 (1994): 199–204.
7. G. Cohen, *What's Wrong with Hospitals?* (Middlesex, UK: Penguin Books, 1964).
8. H. Silver and A. Glicken, Medical student abuse: Incidence, severity, and significance, *JAMA*, 263 (1990): 527–32.
9. L. Hicks, Y. Lin, D. Robertson, D. Robinson, and S. Woodrow, Understanding the clinical dilemmas that shape medical students' ethical development: Questionnaire survey and focus group study, *BMJ*, 322 (2001): 709–10.
10. S. Rennie and J. Crosby, Are 'tomorrow's doctors' honest? *BMJ*, 322 (2001): 274–5.
11. '[N]eophyte [learners] cannot perform high-stake procedures at an acceptable level of proficiency. . . . [We must] develop approaches to skills training that do not put our patients at risk in service to education.' M. Cook, D. Irby, W. Sullivan, and K. Ludmerer, American medical education 100 years after the Flexner Report, *N Engl J Med*, 355 (2006): 1339–44.
12. D. Lyons, *Ethics and the Rule of Law* (Cambridge, UK: Cambridge University Press, 1987), 7–35.
13. T. Ziv and B. Lo, Denial of care to illegal immigrants: proposition 187 in California, *N Engl J Med*, 332 (1995): 1095–8.
14. T. Beauchamp and J. Childress, *Principles of Biomedical Ethics*, 5th edn. (New York: Oxford University Press, 2000).
15. A. Jonsen and S. Toulmin, *The Abuse of Casuistry: A History of Moral Reasoning* (Los Angeles: University of California Press, 1988).
16. Oath of Hippocrates, in W. Reich (ed.), *Encyclopedia of Bioethics*, rev. edn., vol. 5 (Toronto: Simon & Schuster Macmillan, 1995), 2632.
17. T. Brewin, *Primum non nocere?* Lancet, 344 (1994): 1487–8.
18. Such was Ivan Illich's criticism of modern healthcare: 'The medical establishment has become a major threat to health', *Medical Nemesis* (Toronto: McClelland & Stewart, 1975), 11.
19. A. Esmail, Physician as serial killer: The Shipman case, *N Engl J Med*, 352 (2005): 1843–4.

20. R. Brook, Quality of care: do we care? *Ann Intern Med*, 115 (1991): 486–90.

21. C. von Gunten, Discussing Do-Not-Resuscitate status, *J Clin Oncol*, 15 (2001): 1576–8.

22. B. Lo, *Resolving Ethical Dilemmas: A Guide for Clinicians*, 2nd edn. (Philadelphia: Lippincott, Williams & Wilkins, 2000); T. Thomasma, Training in medical ethics: An ethical workup, *Forums on Medicine* (Dec. 1978): 33–6; M. Siegler, Decision-making strategy for clinical-ethical problems in medicine, *Arch Intern Med*, 142 (1982): 2178–9; L. McCullough, Addressing ethical dilemmas: An ethics work-up, *The New Physician* (Oct. 1984): 34–5.

23. W. Styron, *Sophie's Choice* (New York: Vintage Books, 1992).

24. S. Callahan, The role of emotion in ethical decision making, *Hastings Cent Rep* 18 (June/July 1988): 9–14.

25. J. Sevulescu, Conscientious objection in medicine, *BMJ*, 332 (2006): 294–7.

26. A.C. Grayling, *Meditations for the Humanist: Ethics for a Secular Age* (Oxford: Oxford University Press, 2002), 38.

27. A. Robb, T. Silber, J. Orrell-Valente, A. Valadez-Meltzer, N. Ellis, and M.J. Dadson, Supplemental nocturnal nasogastric re-feeding for better short-term outcome in hospitalized adolescent girls with anorexia nervosa, *Am J Psychiatry*, 159 (2002): 1347–53.

28. V. Levy-Barzilai, Death wish: Does an anorexic whose life is in danger have a right to starve herself to death? *Ha'aretz*, 17 Aug. 2001.

29. H. Bruch, *The Golden Cage: The Enigma of Anorexia Nervosa* (Cambridge, MA: Harvard University Press, 1982).

30. E.L. Langston, Ethical treatment of military detainees, *Lancet*, 370 (2007): 1999.

31. G. Annas, Hunger strikes at Guantanamo: Medical ethics and human rights in a 'legal black hole', *N Engl J Med*, 355 (2006): 1377–82.

32. L. Schneiderman, K. Faber-Langendoen, and N. Jecker, Beyond futility to an ethic of care, *Am J Med*, 96 (1994): 110–14.

33. S. Strauss, Death one, medicine no score, *CMAJ*, 177 (2007): 903–4.

34. P. Hébert and M. Weingarten, The ethics of forced feeding in anorexia nervosa, *CMAJ*, 144 (1991): 141–4.

35. R. Palmer, Death in anorexia nervosa, *Lancet*, 361 (2003): 1490.

36. D. Hume, *A Treatise of Human Nature, in Hume: Moral and Political Philosophy* (New York: Hafner Press, 1975), 43. Hume was pessimistic about the role of rationality in disputes over ethics: 'reason alone can never be a motive to any action of the will . . . and it can never oppose passion in the direction of the will' (ibid., 23).

37. 'What people disagree about is what is true, and not merely what is true for them. If there is no such thing as truth in a certain area people cannot disagree.' R. Trigg, *Reason and Commitment* (London: Cambridge University Press, 1974), 152.

Chapter 2

1. H. Cockerham, *The English Dictionarie* (1623), accessed in *Oxford English Dictionary* [CD-ROM], 2nd edn., Version 3.0 (Oxford: Oxford University Press, 2002).

2. *Schloendorf v. Society of New York Hospital*, 1914, 105 N.E. 92, (N.Y.C.A.).

3. P. Appelbaum, *Almost a Revolution: Mental Health Law and the Limits of Change* (New York: Oxford University Press, 1994).

4. B. Venesy, A clinician's guide to decision making capacity and ethically sound medical decisions, *Am J Phys Med Rehab*, 73 (1994): 219–26.

5. B. Dickens, Legal approaches to health care ethics and the four principles, in R. Gillon (ed.), *Principles of Health Care Ethics* (Toronto: John Wiley & Sons, 1994), 305–17.

6. 'It is time to acknowledge how far the procedures and outcomes of premodern medicine depended upon a dialogue, a co-operative relationship between the sick person and his medical attendant.' D. Porter and R. Porter, *Patient's Progress: Doctors and Doctoring in Eighteenth-Century England* (Stanford, CA: Stanford University Press, 1989), 13.

7. D. Smith quoted in *The Medical Post*, 26 Sept. 1995, 28.

8. 'Autonomy is therefore the ground of the dignity of human nature and of every rational nature.' I. Kant, *Groundwork of the Metaphysic of Morals* [1785] (New York: Harper & Row, 1956), 103.

9. W. Kaufmann, *Without Guilt and Justice: From Decidophobia to Autonomy* (New York: Dell Publishing, 1973).

10. '[T]he obligation to make all one's own decisions . . . states an unattainable and unwise standard.' C. Schneider, *The Practice of Autonomy: Patients, Doctors, and Medical Decisions* (New York: Oxford University Press, 1998), 174.

11. 'Autonomy is essentially a matter of whether we are active rather than passive in our motives and choices—whether, however we acquire them, they are the motives and choices that we really want and are therefore in no way alien to us.' H. Frankfurt, *The Reasons of Love* (Princeton, NJ: Princeton University Press, 2004), 20.

12. R. Descartes, *Discourse on Method: Discourse 4* [1637] (Baltimore, MD: Penguin Books, 1968), 53.

13. J. Brown, W. Weston, and M. Stewart, Patient-centred interviewing, *Can Fam Physician*, 35 (1989): 147–51.

14. R. Charon, Narrative medicine: A model for empathy, reflection, profession and trust, *JAMA*, 286 (2001): 1897–1902.

15. *Malette v. Shulman* (1987), 63 O.R. (2d) 243 (H.C.J.).

16. Ibid., 273.

17. *Malette v. Shulman* (1990), 72 O.R. (2d) 417 (C.A.).

18. Ibid., 27.

19. P.A. Singer and F. Lowy, Refusal of life-sustaining treatment, the Malette case, and decision making under uncertainty, *Annals RCPSC*, 24 (1991): 401–3.

20. D. Sacks and R. Koppes, Caring for the female Jehovah's Witness: Balancing medicine, ethics, and the First Amendment, *Am J Obstet Gynecol*, 170 (1994): 452–5.

21. *Fleming v. Reid* (1991), 4 O.R. (3d) 86.

22. Ibid., 75.

23. Tying the knot, *Maclean's*, 12 Nov. 2007, 51.

24. *Allen v. New Mt Sinai Hospital* (1980) 11 CCLT 299 (Ont HC) (1981) 19 CCLT 76 (CA).

25. D. Brock and S.Wartman, When competent patients make irrational choices, *N Engl J Med*, 322 (1990): 1595–9.

26. O.J. Bogunovic and S.F. Greenfield, Practical geriatrics: Use of benzodiazepines among elderly patients, *Psychiatr Serv*, 55 (2004): 233–5.

27. L. Farrell, The threat, *BMJ*, 332 (2006): 1399. 'A prescription has many fathers and physical intimidation is yet another'—on the difficulties of weaning patients from drugs.

28. 'Even if children do not have full decision-making capacity, their refusals should be taken seriously. Imposing treatment in the face of adamant refusal may traumatize children and affect their future relationships with healthcare providers.' R. Jeffries, C. Chamberlain, and W. McTavish, Child and adolescent issues, in H. Bloom and M. Bay (eds.), *A Practical Guide to Mental Health, Capacity, and Consent Law of Ontario* (Toronto: Carswell, 1996), 322.

29. M. Siegler, Critical illness: The limits of autonomy, *Hastings Cent Rep* (Oct. 1977): 7.

30. F. Ingelfinger, Arrogance, *N Engl J Med*, 303 (1980): 1507–11.

31. M. Phela, J. Dobbs, and A. David, I thought it would go away: Patient denial in breast cancer, *J Roy Soc Med*, 85 (1992): 206–7.

32. A. Coulter, What do patients and the public want from primary care? *BMJ*, 331 (2005): 1199–1201.

Chapter 3

1. G. Lyttelton, *Personal Letters* LXXIX [1744], accessed from *Oxford English Dictionary* [CD-ROM], 2nd edn., Version 3.0 (Oxford: Oxford University Press, 2002).

2. W. Shakespeare, *Troilus and Cressida* [c. 1602], Act III, Scene iii, accessed from *Oxford English Dictionary* [CD-ROM], 2nd edn., Version 3.0 (Oxford: Oxford University Press, 2002).

3. Supreme Court of Canada, *McInerney v. MacDonald* [1992] 2 SCR 138.

4. M. Ross, Subpoenas: What to do, where to go, *CMPA Information Letter*, 10 (1995): 5.

5. E. Gibson, Whither privacy of health information at the Supreme Court, in J. Downie and E. Gibson (eds.), *Health Law at the Supreme Court of Canada* (Toronto: Irwin Law, 2007), 324.

6. M. Marshall and B. von Tigerstrom, Confidentiality and disclosure of health information, in J. Downie and T. Caulfield (eds.), *Canadian Health Law and Policy* (Toronto: Butterworths Canada, 1999), 165–6.

7. Gibson, Whither privacy, 321.

8. S.D. Warren and L.D. Brandeis, The Right to Privacy, *Harv. L. Rev.*, 4 (1890): 193–220.

9. L. Gostin, J. Turek-Brezina, M. Powers, R. Kozloff, R. Faden, and D. Steinauer, Privacy and security of personal information in a new health care system, *JAMA*, 270 (1993): 2487–93.

10. *McInerney v. MacDonald*, [1992] 2 S.C.R.. 138.

11. *R v. Potvin* (1971), 16 C.R.N.S. 233 (Que. C.A.).

12. Canadian Nurses Association, *Code of Ethics for Registered Nurses* (Ottawa, 2002).
13. E. Picard and G. Robertson, *Legal Liability of Doctors and Hospitals in Canada*, 3rd edn. (Toronto: Thomson Carswell, 1996), 21. The quotation in Box 3.2 is from G. Sharpe quoted in E. Picard, *Legal Liability of Doctors and Hospitals in Canada*, 2nd edn. (Toronto: Carswell, 1984), 13 n88.
14. J. Irvine, The physician's other duties: Good faith, loyalty and confidentiality, in B. Sneiderman, J. Irvine, and P. Osborne, *Canadian Medical Law: An Introduction for Physicians, Nurses and other Health Care Professionals*, 3rd edn. (Toronto: Thomson Carswell, 2003), 224.
15. K.V. Rhodes, R.M. Frankel, N. Levinthal, E. Prenoveau, J. Bailey, and W. Levinson, 'You're not a victim of domestic abuse, are you?' Provider–patient communication about domestic violence, *Ann Intern Med*, 147 (2007): 620–7.
16. The quotation in Box 3.3 is from J. Burnham, Secrets about patients, *N Engl J Med*, 324 (1991): 1130–3.
17. Ibid.
18. *Health Protection and Promotion Act*: '26. A physician or registered nurse in the extended class who, while providing professional services to a person, forms the opinion that the person is or may be infected with an agent of a communicable disease shall, as soon as possible after forming the opinion, report thereon to the medical officer of health of the health unit in which the professional services are provided.' R.S.O. 1990, c. H.7, s. 26; 2007, c. 10, Sched. F, s. 4.
19. A. Ala, A.P. Walker, K. Ashkan, J.S. Dooley, and M.L. Schilsky, Wilson's disease, *Lancet*, 369 (2007): 397–408.
20. Adapted from W.C. Leung, E. Mariman, J.C. van der Wouden, H. van Amerongen, and C. Weijer, Ethical debate: Results of genetic testing: when confidentiality conflicts with a duty to warn relatives, *BMJ*, 321 (2000): 1464–6.
21. Oath of Hippocrates, in W. Reich (ed.), *Encyclopedia of Bioethics*, rev. edn., vol. 5 (Toronto: Simon & Schuster Macmillan, 1995), 2632.
22. P. Ubel, M. Zell, D. Miller, G. Fischer, D. Peters-Stefani, and R. Arnold, Elevator talk: Observational study of inappropriate comments in a public space, *Am J Med*, 99 (1995): 190–4.
23. Picard, *Legal Liability*, 8.
24. J. Cambell Rep. Cases King's Bench III. 81 [1814].
25. J. Irvine, The physician's other duties: Good faith, loyalty and confidentiality, in B. Sneiderman, J. Irvine, and P. Osborne, *Canadian Medical Law: An Introduction for Physicians, Nurses and other Health Care Professionals*, 3rd edn. (Toronto: Thomson Carswell, 2003), 212.
26. *Medicine Act*, O. Reg. 856/93, s. 1(1)(10).
27. *Shulman v. CPSO* (1980), 29 O.R. (2d) 40 (Ont. Div. Ct.).
28. P. Collins, P. Slaughter, N. Roos, K. Weisbaum, M. Hirtle, J. Williams, et al., *Harmonizing Research & Privacy: Standards for a Collaborative Future*, Privacy Best Practices for Secondary Data Use (SDU) (Ottawa: Canadian Institutes of Health Research, 2006).

29. '[R]ules [regarding confidentiality] (i.e., the *Quebec Charter of Human Rights and Freedoms*, the *Code of Civil Procedure*, the *Medical Act*, and the *Code of Professional Ethics for Physicians*) are rules of *protective public order*.' J. LeBel quoted in Gibson, Whither privacy, 336.

30. J. Duff quoted in *McInerney v. MacDonald* (1992) S.C.C. 12.

31. See above note 18. See also Failure to Report Communicable Disease is Negligence Per Se—*Derrick v. Ontario Community Hospital*, 47 Cal.App.3d 145, 120 Cal.Rptr. 566 (1975).

32. See *US State Laws on Mandatory Reporting of Suspected Child Abuse* <www.preventchild abusenj.org/documents/links_government/Child_Abuse_Reporting_Laws.pdf>; S.K. Loo, N. Bala, M. Clarke, and J. Hornick, *Child Abuse: Reporting and Classification in Health Care Settings* (Ottawa: Health Canada, 1998) <www.phac-aspc.gc.ca/cm-vee/publicat/rclass-eng.php>.

33. M. Lachs and K. Pillemer, Abuse and neglect of elderly persons, *N Engl J Med*, 332 (1995): 437–43.

34. Canadian Network for the Prevention of Elder Abuse, *Mandatory Reporting Requirements across Canada for Abuse and Neglect in Institutions* (2005) <www.cnpea.ca/mandatory_reporting.htm>.

35. *Toms v. Foster* (1994) OJ No. 1413 (CA).

36. D.A. Breen, D.P. Breen, J. Moore, P.A. Breen, and D. O'Neill, Driving and dementia, *BMJ*, 334 (2007): 1365–9.

37. D. Redelmeier, V. Venkatesh, and M. Stanbrook, Mandatory reporting by physicians of patients potentially unfit to drive, *Open Medicine*, 2/1 (2008): E8–17.

38. *Determining Medical Fitness to Drive: A Guide for Physicians*, 6th edn. (Ottawa: Canadian Medical Association, 2000) <www.cma.ca/staticContent/HTML/N0/l2/publications/catalog/driversguide>.

39. *The Physician and the Aeronautics Act: A Guide to Mandatory Reporting* (Ottawa: Canadian Medical Association, 1995).

40. Canadian Medical Protective Association quoted in *Newsletter of the Section on Occupational and Environmental Health* (Nov.) (Toronto: Ontario Medical Association, 1994).

41. *Mandatory Gunshot Wounds Reporting Act*, 2005, S.O. 2005, c. 9.

42. 'ME/Cs have state statutory authority to investigate deaths that are sudden, suspicious, violent, unattended, or unexplained.' D.L. Combs, R.G. Parrish, and R. Ing, Death investigation in the United States and Canada, 1995 (Atlanta: U.S. Department of Health and Human Services, CDC, 1995).

43. *V. Tarasoff, et al. v. Regents of the University of California, et al.* (1974), 329 Pacific Reporter (2d) 553–69.

44. *Smith v. Jones*, [1999] 1 S.C.R. 455.

45. *V. Tarasoff v. Regents of University of California*, (1976), 17 Cal. 3d, 131 California Reporter 26 (S.C.C.).

46. M. Mills, G. Sullivan, and E. Spencer, Protecting third parties: A decade after Tarasoff, *Am J Psychiatry*, 144 (1987): 68–74.

47. Quoted in ibid., 70.

48. L. Ferris, H. Barkun, J. Carlisle, B. Hoffman, C. Katz, and M. Silverman, Defining the physician's duty to warn: Consensus statement of Ontario's Medical Expert Panel on Duty to Inform, *CMAJ*, 158 (1998): 1473–9.
49. *Public Interest Disclosure Act* (1998) <www.opsi.gov.uk/acts/acts1998/ukpga_19980023_en_1>. Described at the time as the 'most far-reaching whistle-blower act in the world', it makes it possible for employees, including doctors, and contract and agency staff, to raise concerns without endangering their own jobs or careers. C. Dyer, UK introduces far reaching whistleblower act, *BMJ*, 319 (1999): 7.
50. D. Greene and J. Cooper, Whistleblowers, *BMJ*, 305 (1992): 1343–4.
51. K. Lennane, Whistleblowing: A health issue, *BMJ*, 307 (1993): 667–70; Blowing the whistle on incompetence: One nurse's story, *Nursing* (July 1989), 47–50. The quotation in Box 3.5 is based on A. Haddad and C. Dougherty, Whistleblowing in the OR, *Today's OR Nurse* (March 1991), 30–3.

Chapter 4

1. L. Durrell, *The Alexandria Quartet: Clea* (New York: E.P. Dutton & Co., 1961), 24.
2. *Oxford English Dictionary* [CD-ROM], 2nd edn., Version 3.0 (Oxford: Oxford University Press, 2002).
3. A. Bowling and S. Ebrahim, Measuring patients' preferences for treatment and perceptions of risk, *Quality in Healthcare*, 10/Suppl I (2001): 2–8.
4. I. Kant, *The Metaphysical Principles of Virtue* [1797] (New York: The Bobbs-Merrill Co., 1964), 90–1.
5. R. Fulford, Private secrets, public lies, *Queen's Quarterly*, 113 (Summer 2006): 187–96.
6. J. Lee, Screening and informed consent, *N Engl J Med*, 328 (1993): 438–40.
7. D. Crauford, A. Dodge, L. Kerzin-Storrar, and R. Harris, Uptake of presymptomatic testing for Huntington's disease, *Lancet*, 2 (1989): 603–5.
8. L. MacDonald, D. Sackett, R. Haynes, and D. Taylor, Labelling in hypertension: A review of the behavioural and psychological consequences, *J Chronic Dis*, 37 (1984): 933–42.
9. V. Jenkins, L. Fallowfield, and J. Saul, Information needs of patients with cancer: Results from a large study in UK cancer centres, *Br J Cancer*, 84/1 (2001): 48–51.
10. H. Bursztajn, R. Feinbloom, R. Hamm, and A. Brodsky, *Medical Choices, Medical Chances: How Patients, Families and Physicians Can Cope with Uncertainty* (New York: Dell Publishing, 1981).
11. M. Balint, *The Doctor, His Patient and the Illness*, rev. edn. (Madison, CT: International Universities Press, 1988).
12. R.B. Bausell, *Snake Oil Science: The Truth about Complementary and Alternative Medicine* (New York: Oxford University Press, 2007).
13. *Daniels v. Heskin* 1954 IR 73 at 86–87 (SC).
14. D. Nyberg, *The Varnished Truth* (Chicago: The University of Chicago Press, 1993).
15. T. Greenhalgh, Barriers to concordance with antidiabetic drugs: Cultural differences or human nature? *BMJ*, 330 (2005): 1250.

16. L. Egbert, G. Battit, C. Welch, and M. Bartlett, Reduction of postoperative pain by encouragement and instruction of patients, *N Engl J Med*, 270 (1964): 825–7.

17. A. Luck, S. Pearson, G. Maddern, and P. Hewett, Effects of video information on pre-colonoscopy anxiety and knowledge: A randomized trial, *Lancet*, 354 (1999): 2032–5.

18. S. Woloshin, M. Schwartz, and H. Welch, The effectiveness of a primer to help people understand risk: Two randomized trials in distinct population, *Ann Intern Med*, 146 (2007): 256–65.

19. S. Kaplan, S. Greenfield, B. Gandek, W. Rogers, and J. Ware, Characteristics of physicians with participatory decision-making styles, *Ann Intern Med*, 124 (1996): 497–504.

20. R. Logan and P. Scott, Uncertainty in clinical practice: Implications for quality and costs of health care, *Lancet*, 347 (1996): 595–8.

21. M. Elian and G. Dean, To tell or not to tell the diagnosis of multiple sclerosis, *Lancet*, 2 (1985): 28.

22. *Arndt v. Smith*, [1997] 2 S.C.R. 539.

23. L. Fallowfield, A. Hall, P. Maguire, M. Baum, and R. A'Hern, Psychological effects of being offered choice of surgery for breast cancer, *BMJ*, 309 (1994): 448.

24. Elian and Dean, To tell or not to tell, 27–8.

25. J. Groopman, *The Anatomy of Hope* (New York: Random House, 2005).

26. Once a dark secret [personal view], *BMJ*, 308 (1994): 542.

27. R.C. Cabot, The use of truth and falsehood in medicine: An experimental study, *Am Med*, 5 (1903): 344–9.

28. S. Bok, *Lying: Moral Choice in Public and Private Life* (Toronto: Random House of Canada, 1979), 247.

29. J. Davies and A. Bacon, When things go wrong, *Anesth Rev*, 17(1990): 50–3.

30. *Chappel v. Hart* [1998] 195 CLR 232; *Rogers v. Whitaker* [1992] 175 CLR 479, 490.

31. *Canterbury v. Spence* [1972] 464 F 2d 772.

32. *Bolam v. Friern Hospital Management Committee* [1957] 1 WLR 582, 586.

33. L. Snyder and C. Leffler for the Ethics and Human Rights Committee, American College of Physicians, Ethics Manual, 5th edn., *Ann Intern Med*, 142 (2005): 560–82.

34. The British Medical Association, *Medical Ethics Today: The BMA's Handbook of Ethics and Law*, 2nd edn. (London: BMJ Publishing Group, 2004), 37–41.

35. Canadian Medical Association, CMA code of ethics [policy], *CMAJ*, 172 (2005):1053–5.

36. D. Oken, What to tell cancer patients: A study of medical attitudes, *JAMA*, 175 (1961): 1120–8.

37. D. Novack, R. Plumer, R.L. Smith, H. Ochitill, G.R. Morrow, and J.M. Bennett, Changes in physicians' attitudes toward telling the cancer patient, *JAMA*, 241 (1979): 897–900.

38. M. Good, B. Good, C. Schaffer, and S. Lind, American oncology and the discourse on hope, *Cult Med Psychiatry*, 14 (1990): 59–79.

39. O. Thomsen, H. Wulff, A. Martin, and P. Singer, What do gastroenterologists in Europe tell cancer patients? *Lancet*, 341 (1993): 473–6.

40. R. Samp and A. Curreri, Questionnaire survey on public cancer education obtained from cancer patients and their families, *Cancer*, 10 (1957): 382–4.

41. President's Commission for the Study of Ethical Problems in Medicine, *Making Health Care Decisions*, vol. 1 (Washington, DC: US Government Printing Office, 1982), 69–111.

42. E. Erde, E. Nadal, and T. Scholl, On truth telling and the diagnosis of Alzheimer's disease, *J Fam Pract*, 26 (1988): 401–4.

43. M. Silverstein, C.B. Stocking, J.P. Antel, J. Beckwith, R.P. Roos, M. Siegler, et al., ALS and life-sustaining therapy: Patients' desires for information, participation in decision-making, and life-sustaining therapy, *Mayo Clin Proc*, 66 (1991): 906–13.

44. A. Ajaj, M.P. Singh, and A.J. Abdulla, Should elderly patients be told they have cancer? Questionnaire survey of older people, *BMJ*, 323 (2001): 1160.

45. L.J. Blackhall, S. Murphy, G. Frank, V. Michel, and S. Azen, Ethnicity and attitudes toward patient autonomy, *JAMA*, 274 (1995): 820–5.

46. E. Pucci, N. Belardinelli, G. Borsetti, and G.Guiliani, Relatives' attitudes towards informing patients about the diagnosis of Alzheimer's disease, *J Med Ethics*, 29 (2003): 51–4.

47. G. Ruhnke, S. Wilson, T. Akamatsu, T. Kinoue, Y. Takashima, M. Goldstein, et al., Ethical decision-making and patient autonomy: A comparison of physicians and patients in Japan and the United States, *Chest*, 118 (2000): 1172–82.

48. A. Akabayashi, I. Kai, H. Takemura, and H. Okazaki, Truth telling in the case of a pessimistic diagnosis in Japan, *Lancet*, 354 (1999): 1263.

49. F. Fukuyama, *The Great Disruption: Human Nature and the Reconstruction of Social Order* (New York: Simon & Schuster, 2000).

50. B. Freedman, Offering truth: One ethical approach to the uninformed cancer patient, *Arch Intern Med*, 153 (1993): 572–6.

51. A. Surbone, Letter from Italy: Truth telling to the patient, *JAMA*, 268 (1992): 1661–2.

52. T.Y. Chiu, W. Hu, S. Cheng, and C. Chen, Ethical dilemmas in palliative care: A study in Taiwan, *J Med Ethics*, 26 (2000): 353–7.

53. M. Lacroix, G. Nycum, B. Godard, and B. Knoppers, Should physicians warn patients' relatives of genetic risks? *CMAJ*, 178 (2008): 593–5.

54. G. Sigman, J. Kraut, and J. La Puma, Disclosure of a diagnosis to children and adolescents when parents object, *Am J Dis Child*, 147 (1993): 764–8.

55. Anon, Delivering bad news, *BMJ*, 321 (2000): 1233.

56. U. Kreicbergs, U. Valdimarsdottir, E. Onelov, J.-I. Henter, and G. Steineck, Talking about death with children who have severe malignant disease, *N Engl J Med*, 351 (2004): 1175–86;

57. *Hopp v. Lepp* [1980] SCR: 192; *Chester v. Afshar* [2004] UKHL 41 (14 Oct. 2004).

58. *McInerney v. MacDonald* (1992), 137 N.R. 35 (S.C.C.).

59. *Pittman Estate v. Bain* (1994), 112 DLR (4th) 257 (Ont. Gen. Div.).

60. T. Smith, *Ethics in Medical Research: A Handbook of Good Practice* (Cambridge, UK: Cambridge University Press, 1999), 159–68.

61. D. Novack, B.J. Detering, R. Arnold, L. Forrow, M. Ladinsky, and J.C. Pezzullo, Physicians' attitudes toward using deception to resolve difficult ethical problems, *JAMA*, 261 (1989): 2980–5.

62. A. Shattner, What do patients really want to know? *Q J Med*, 95 (2002): 135–6.

63. J. Brown, M. Boles, J. Mullooly, and W. Levinson, Effect of clinician communication skills training on patient satisfaction: A randomized, controlled trial, *Ann Intern Med*, 131 (1999): 822–9.

64. A. Mann, Factors affecting psychological state during one year on a hypertension trial, *Clin Invest Med*, 4 (1981): 197–200.

65. A. Jonsen, M. Siegler, and W. Winslade, *Clinical Ethics*, 5th edn. (New York: McGraw-Hill, 2002), 63. The quotation in Box 4.4 is adapted from R. Charlton, Words of sorrow, *BMJ*, 307 (1993): 1502.

66. M. Stewart, Effective physician–patient communication and health outcomes: A review, *CMAJ*, 152 (1995): 1423–33.

67. L. Fallowfield and V. Jenkins, Communicating sad, bad, and difficult news in medicine, *Lancet*, 363 (2004): 312–19.

68. *Stamos v. Davies* [1985] 52 OR (2d) 10 (H.C.); Cabot, The use of truth and falsehood, 344–9.

69. This case is adapted from A. Burrows, The man who didn't know he had cancer, *JAMA*, 266 (1991): 2550.

70. C. Feudtner, D. Christakis, and N. Christakis, Do clinical clerks suffer ethical erosion? *Acad Med*, 69 (1994): 670–9.

71. R. Buckman, *How to Break Bad News* (Toronto: University of Toronto Press, 1992).

Chapter 5

1. J.S. Mill, *On Liberty* [1859] (New York: Appleton-Century Crofts, 1947), 10.

2. *Canterbury v. Spence* 464 F.2d 772 at 784 (1972).

3. President's Commission for the Study of Ethical Problems in Medicine, *Making Health Care Decisions*, vol. 1 (Washington, DC: US Government Printing Office, 1982), 42–51.

4. Mill, *On Liberty*, 9.

5. I. Health, A wolf in sheep's clothing: A critical look at the ethics of drug taking, *BMJ*, 327 (2003): 856–8.

6. A. Akkad, C. Jackson, M. Dixon-Woods, N. Taub, and M. Habiba, Patients' perceptions of written consent: Questionnaire study, *BMJ*, 333 (2006): 528.

7. C.H. Braddock, K. Edwards, N. Hasenberg, T. Laidley, and W. Levinson, Informed decision making in outpatient practice: Time to get back to basics? *JAMA*, 282 (1999): 2313–20.

8. S.J. Weiner, B. Barnet, T. Cheng, and T. Daaleman, Processes for effective communication in primary care, *Ann Intern Med*, 142 (2005): 709–14; S. Woolf, C. Chan, R. Harris, S. Sheridan, C. Braddock, R. Kaplan, et al., Promoting informed choice: Transforming heath care to dispense knowledge for decision-making, *Ann Intern Med*, 143 (2005): 293–300.

9. C. Barry, C. Bradley, N. Britten, F. Stevenson, and N. Barber, Patients' unvoiced agendas in general practice consultations: Qualitative study, BMJ, 320 (2000): 1246–50. The quotation in Box 5.2 is from the College of Physicians and Surgeons of Ontario, *Consent to Medical Treatment Policy Statement #4-05* (Jan./Feb. 2006).

10. J. Kassirer, Incorporating patients' preferences into medical decisions, *N Engl J Med*, 330 (1994): 1895–6.

11. *Reibl v. Hughes* (1980), 2 S.C.R. 880.

12. *Reibl v. Hughes* (1980), 16 O.R. (2d) 311–12.

13. College of Physicians and Surgeons of Ontario, *Report of Proceedings, Disciplinary Committee* (June 1992), 20.

14. D. Ziegler, M. Mosier, M. Buenever, and K. Okuyemi, How much information about adverse effects of medication do patients want from physicians? *Arch Intern Med*, 161 (2001): 706–13.

15. J. Mitchell, M. Jones, and J.N. Lunn, A fundamental problem of consent, *BMJ*, 310 (1994): 43–8.

16. G. Ness and J. Menage [letters], *BMJ*, 310 (1995): 935.

17. *Marshall v. Curry* (1993), 3 D.L.R. 260: 275 (N.S.S.C.); *Murray v. McMurchy* (1949), 2 D.L.R. 442 (B.C.S.C.).

18. P. Angelos, D. DaRosa, D. Bentram, and H. Sherman, Residents seeking informed consent: Are they adequately knowledgeable? *Current Surgery*, 59 (2002): 115–18.

19. E. Picard, *Legal Liability of Doctors and Hospitals in Canada*, 2nd edn. (Toronto: Carswell, 1984), 91.

20. Based on R. Webb, The zero option, *BMJ*, 310 (1995): 1380.

21. *Kovachic v. St. Joseph's Hospital*, [2004] O.J. No. 4471 (Ont. S.C.J.) in Picard, *Legal Liability*, 92. The quotation in Box 5.7 is from *Best v. Hoskins* [2006] ABQB 58.

22. G. Sharpe, *The Law and Medicine in Canada*, 2nd edn. (Toronto: Butterworths, 1987), 57.

23. '[T]he frequency of the risk becomes much less material when the operation is unnecessary for his medical welfare.' E. Picard and G. Robertson, *Legal Liability of Doctors and Hospitals in Canada*, 3rd edn. (Toronto: Carswell Thomson Canada, 1996), 126–7.

24. General Counsel to the Canadian Medical Protective Association as quoted in ibid., 114.

25. M.K. Marvel, R. Epstein, K. Flowers, and H. Beckman, Soliciting the patient's agenda: Have we improved? *JAMA*, 281 (1999): 283–7.

26. A. Edwards, Communicating risk, *BMJ*, 3257 (2003): 691–2.

27. R. Deyo, Tell it like it is: Patients as partners in medical decision making, *J Gen Intern Med*, 15 (2000): 752–4.

28. C. Lavelle-Jones, D. Byrne, P. Rice, and A. Cushieri, Factors affecting quality of informed consent, *BMJ*, 306 (1993): 885–90.

29. *Ciarlariello v. Schacter*, [1993] 2 S.C.R. 119.

30. *Nightingale v. Kaplovitch*, [1989] O.J. No. 585 (H.C.J.; unreported; 20 April 1989).

31. '13. Consent to medical care is not required in case of emergency if the life of the person is in danger or his integrity is threatened and his consent cannot be obtained

in due time. It is required, however, where the care is unusual or has become useless or where its consequences could be intolerable for the person.' *Civil Code of Québec*, S.Q., 1991, c. 64, s. 13. Authorized by Les Publications du Québec.

32. Y. Conwell and E. Caine, Rational suicide and the right to die: Reality and myth, *N Engl J Med*, 325 (1991): 1100–3.

33. 'Suicide should be considered the response of someone, whether suffering from mental disease or not, who is unable to find a solution to a relational crisis.' F. Pochard, M. Robin, and S. Kannas [letter to the editor], *N Engl J Med*, 338 (1998): 261–2. 'Only 10 to 14 percent of persons commit suicide over the decade following a failed attempt, suggesting that in most suicidal persons, the desire to die is transient.' L. Ganzini and M. Lee, Psychiatry and assisted suicide in the United States, *N Engl J Med*, 336 (1997): 1824–6.

34. D. Kerrigan, R. Thevasagayam, T. Woods, I. McWelch, W. Thomas, A. Shorthouse, et al., Who's afraid of informed consent? *BMJ*, 306 (1993): 298–300.

35. G. Lamb, S. Green, and J. Heron, Can physicians warn patients of potential side-effects without fear of causing these side-effects? *Arch Intern Med*, 154 (1994): 2753–6.

36. M. Gattellari, K. Voigt, P. Butow, and M. Tattersall, When treatment goal is not the cure: Are cancer patients equipped to make informed decisions? *J Clin Oncol*, 20 (2002): 503–13.

Chapter 6

1. *Starson v. Swayze* [2003] S.C.J. No. 33, C.J.C. McLachlin, dissenting.

2. H. Bloom and M. Bay (eds.), *A Practical Guide to Mental Health, Capacity, and Consent Law of Ontario* (Toronto: Carswell, 1996).

3. E. Cassell, A. Leon, and S. Kaufman, Preliminary evidence of impaired thinking in sick patients, *Ann Intern Med*, 134 (2001): 1120–3.

4. President's Commission for the Study of Ethical Problems in Medicine and Biomedical and Behavioral Research, *Making Health Care Decisions*, vol. 1: *A Report on the Ethical and Legal Implications of Informed Consent in the Patient-Practitioner Relationship* (Washington, DC: US Government Printing Office, 1982), 55, 171.

5. P. Applebaum, Assessment of patients' competence to consent to treatment, *N Engl J Med*, 357 (2007): 1834–40. Box 6.1 is adapted from B.L. Beattie, Determining competency to continue driving, *Canadian J of CME* (June 1994), 81–6.

6. L. Roth, A. Meisel, and C. Lidz, Tests of competency to consent to treatment, *Am J Psychiatry*, 134 (1977): 279–84.

7. P. Appelbaum and T. Gutheil, *Clinical Handbook of Psychiatry and the Law* (New York: McGraw-Hill, 1982), 210–52.

8. The National Ethics Committee of the Veterans Health Administration, *Ten Myths About Decision-Making Capacity* (Washington, DC: National Center for Ethics in Health Care, Veterans Health Administration Department of Veterans Affairs, Sept. 2002).

9. *Consent to Treatment Act*, R.S.O. 1992, c. 31, S.G.

10. M. Farnsworth, Evaluation of mental competency, *Am Fam Physician*, 39 (1989): 182–90; J. Kutner, J. Ruark, and T. Raffin, Defining patient competence for medical decision making, *Chest*, 100 (1991): 1404–9.

11. T. Grisso and P. Appelbaum, Comparison of standards for assessing patients' capacities to make treatment decisions, *Am J Psychiatry*, 152 (1995): 1033–7.

12. T. Gutheil and H. Bursztajn, Clinicians' guidelines for assessing and presenting subtle forms of patient incompetence in legal settings, *Am J Psychiatry*, 143 (1986): 1020–3.

13. Adapted from ibid.

14. The Quebec *Civil Code* distinguishes care that a minor may consent to ('not required') and 'serious risk' care which requires the involvement of his/her parents or 'tutor'. 'A minor fourteen years of age or over may give his consent alone to care not required by the state of his health; however, the consent of the person having parental authority or of the tutor is required if the care entails a serious risk for the health of the minor and may cause him grave and permanent effects.' *Civil Code of Québec*, S.Q., 1991, c. 64, s. 17. Authorized by Les Publications du Québec.

15. Adapted from Farnsworth, Evaluation of mental competency, 186.

16. Ibid., 186–8.

17. The Quebec *Civil Code* also requires judicial involvement: 'The authorization of the court is necessary where the person who may give consent to care required by the state of health of a minor or a person of full age who is incapable of giving his consent is prevented from doing so or, without justification, refuses to do so; it is also required where a person of full age who is incapable of giving his consent categorically refuses to receive care, except in the case of hygienic care or emergency. The authorization of the court is necessary, furthermore, to cause a minor fourteen years of age or over to undergo care he refuses, except in the case of emergency if his life is in danger or his integrity threatened, in which case the consent of the person having parental authority or the tutor is sufficient.' *Civil Code of Québec*, S.Q., 1991, c. 64, s. 16. Authorized by Les Publications du Québec.

18. *Consent to Treatment Act, 1992*, S.O. 1992, c. 31, s. 13, as amended, and *Substitute Decisions Act*, 1992, S.O. 1992, c. 30, s. 66, as amended.

19. The Quebec *Civil Code*, if less elaborate, is similar: 'A person who gives his consent to or refuses care for another person is bound to act in the sole interest of that person, taking into account, as far as possible, any wishes the latter may have expressed. If he gives his consent, he shall ensure that the care is beneficial notwithstanding the gravity and permanence of certain of its effects, that it is advisable in the circumstances and that the risks incurred are not disproportionate to the anticipated benefit.' *Civil Code of Québec*, S.Q., 1991, c. 64, s. 12. Authorized by Les Publications du Québec.

20. H. Venables, *A Guide to the Law Affecting Mental Health Patients* (Toronto: Butterworths, 1975), 75–6.

21. *Fleming v. Reid by his litigation guardian, the Public Trustee; Fleming v. Gallagher*, etc. (1992), 4 O.R. (3d) 74–96 (C.A.).

22. P. Appelbaum, *Almost a Revolution: Mental Health Law and the Limits of Change* (New York: Oxford University Press, 1994), 128.

23. *Starson v. Swayze* [2003] S.C.J. No. 33.

24. S. Wildeman, The Supreme Court of Canada at the limits of decisional capacity, in J. Downie and E. Gibson (eds.), *Health Law at the Supreme Court of Canada* (Toronto: Irwin Law, 2007), 290–2.

25. Appelbaum, *Almost a Revolution*, 133–5.

26. Ibid., 143.

27. P. Appelbaum, The right to refuse treatment with antipsychotic medications: Retrospect and prospect, *Am J Psychiatry*, 145 (1988): 413–19.

28. N. Hewak, The ethical, medical and legal implications of the forcible treatment provisions of the Criminal Code, *Health Law in Canada*, 15/4 (1995): 107–16.

29. Applebaum, *Almost a Revolution*, 42.

30. *Health Care Consent Act, 1996*, S.O. 1996, c. 2, Schedule A, Part III, Admission to Care Facilities, 47.1: Crisis Admission.

31. G. Sharpe, *The Law and Medicine in Canada*, 2nd edn. (Toronto: Butterworths, 1987), 78.

32. S. Harris, J. Hepburn, J. Gray, E. Murphy, and C. Carrie, What to do with a sick elderly woman who refuses to go to hospital, *BMJ*, 289 (1984): 1435–6.

33. *Substitute Decisions Act, 1992*, S.O.. 1992, c. 30, s. 44, as amended.

34. Ibid., s. 62.

35. Ibid., s. 66 (9); ibid., s. 66 (10a).

36. M. Jones, Caring for those who refuse help, *BMJ*, 328 (2004): 1546.

37. See P. Alderson, *Children's Consent to Surgery* (Buckingham, UK: Open University Press, 1993).

38. *Gillick v. West Norfolk and Wisbech Area Health Authority* [1985] 3 All ER 402HL 31.

39. A. Elton, P. Honig, A. Bentovim, and J. Simons, Withholding consent to lifesaving treatment: Three cases, *BMJ*, 310 (1995): 373–7.

40. *Region 2 Hosp Corp v. Walker* (1994), N.B.J. No. 242 (N.B.C.A.).

41. Re L.D.K.; *Children's Aid Society of Metropolitan Toronto v. K. and K.* (1985), 48 R.F.L. (2d) 164 (Ont. Prov. Ct.).

42. *Hughes (Estate of) v. Hughes*, 2006, ABQB 159.

43. G. Sigman and C. O'Connor, Exploration for physicians of the mature minor doctrine, *J Pediatr*, 119 (1991): 520–5.

Chapter 7

1. D. Hilfiker, *Not All of Us Are Saints* (Toronto: Hill and Wang, 1994), 198–9.

2. CMA Code of Ethics, *CMAJ*, 172 (2005): 1053–5.

3. T. Brewin, *Primum non nocere? Lancet*, 344 (1994): 1487–8.

4. *Crits et al. v. Sylvester et al.* [1956] O.R. 132 (C.A.), aff'd [1956] S.C.R. 991: 143.

5. *V.G.H. v. McDaniel* (1934) 4 D.L.R. 593 (P.C.) 597; *Wilson v. Swanson* (1956), 5 D.L.R. (2d) 113 (S.C.C.) 120.

6. *Bolam v. Frien Hospital Committee* (1957), 2 All E.R. 118 (Q.B.D.) 122.

7. Adapted from Canadian Physicians and Surgeons of Ontario, *Report of Proceedings*, Disciplinary Committee (Jan. 1992), 33.

8. J. Feinberg, The child's right to an open future, in J. Feinberg, *Freedom and Fulfillment: Philosophical Essays* (Princeton, NJ: Princeton University Press, 1992), 89.

9. J. Wahl, K. Le Clair, and S. Himel, The geriatric patient, in H. Bloom and M. Bay (eds.), *A Practical Guide to Mental Health, Capacity, and Consent Law of Ontario* (Toronto: Carswell, 1996), 343–77.

10. *Fleming v. Reid by his litigation guardian, the Public Trustee; Fleming v. Gallagher, etc.* (1992), 4 O.R. (3d) 74–96 (C.A.).

11. *Tarasoff v. Regents of University of California*, 551 P2d 334 (Cal 1976).

12. M. Mills, G. Sullivan, and S. Eth, Protecting third parties: A decade after Tarasoff, *Am J Psychiatry*, 144 (1987): 69.

13. I. Kleinman, Confidentiality and the duty to warn, *CMAJ*, 149 (1993): 1783–5.

14. L. Ferris, H. Barkun, J. Carlisle, B. Hoffman, C. Katz, and M. Silverman, Defining the physician's duty to warn: Consensus statement of Ontario's Medical Expert Panel on Duty to Inform, *CMAJ*, 158 (1998): 1473–9.

15. N. Hewak, The ethical, medical and legal implications of the forcible treatment provisions of the *Criminal Code, Health Law in Canada*, 15/4 (1995): 107–16.

16. Box 7.5 is adapted from P. Applebaum, *Almost a Revolution: Mental Health Law and the Limits of Change* (New York: Oxford University Press, 1994), 96; ibid., 92.

17. Mills, Sullivan, and Eth, Protecting third parties, 71.

18. Applebaum, *Almost a Revolution*, 100.

19. *Egedebo v. Windermere District Hospital Association* [1991] BCJ No.2381 (QL) (SC), aff'd (1993) 78 BCLR (2d) 63 (CA).

20. *Woods v. Lowns* (1995), 36 NSWLR 344 (SC).

21. E.J. Emanual, The Lessons of SARS, *Ann Intern Med*, 139 (2003): 589–91.

22. L. Wissow, Child abuse and neglect, *N Engl J Med*, 332 (1995): 1425–31.

23. E. Picard, *Legal Liability of Doctors and Hospitals in Canada*, 2nd edn. (Toronto: Carswell, 1984), 47.

24. 'Consent to medical care is not required in case of emergency if the life of the person is in danger or his integrity is threatened and his consent cannot be obtained in due time.' *Civil Code of Québec*, S.Q., 1991, c. 64, s. 13. Authorized by Les Publications du Québec.

25. Quoted in P. Schroeder, Female genital mutilation: A form of child abuse, *N Engl J Med*, 331 (1994): 739–40.

26. *B.(R) v. CAS of Metropolitan Toronto* [1995] 1 S.C.R. 315, 176 N.R. 161, 26 C.R.R. (2d) 202, 78 O.A.C. 1, 122 D.L.R. (4th) 1.

27. *New York Times*, 6 Aug. 1990, 1.

28. *Superintendent of Family and Child Service v. RD and SD, etc.* (1983), 42 B.C.L.R. 173–87 (B.C.S.C.).

29. Ibid., 187.

30. Ibid., 177.

31. J. Carter quoted in Picard, *Legal Liability*, 49.

32. *Minister of Social Services v. F & L Paulette* (1991), Saskatchewan Provincial Court, Sask. D. 1568–1605 (Prov. Ct.; unreported).

33. Picard, *Legal Liability*, 50.

34. Canadian Physicians and Surgeons of Ontario, *Members' Dialogue*, 2/2 (1994): 31–2.

35. H. MacMillan, J. MacMillan, and D. Offord, with the Canadian Task Force on the Periodic Health Examination, Periodic health examination, 1993 update: 1. Primary prevention of child maltreatment, *CMAJ*, 148 (1993): 151–63.

36. *E (Mrs) v. Eve.* (1986), 2 S.C.R.: 388–438.

37. S. Wildeman, The Supreme Court of Canada at the limits of decisional capacity, in J. Downie and E. Gibson (eds.), *Health Law at the Supreme Court of Canada* (Toronto: Irwin Law, 2007), 245–7.

38. B. Dickens, No contraceptive sterilization of the mentally retarded: The dawn of 'Eve', *CMAJ*, 137 (1987): 65–7.

39. Wildeman, The Supreme Court, 266.

40. R. Solomon and B. Hoffmaster, The Eve case and the validity of substitute consent, *Westminster Affairs Newsletter* (Feb. 1987).

41. N. Cohen, The ethics of cochlear implants in young children, *Adv Otorhinolaryngol*, 50 (1995): 1–3.

42. Adapted from D. Gunther and D. Diekama, Attenuating growth in children with profound developmental disability, *Arch Pediatr Adolesc Med*, 161 (2007): 521–2.

43. W. Curran, Beyond the best interests of a child: Bone marrow transplantation among half-siblings, *N Engl J Med*, 324 (1991): 1818–19.

44. N. Toubia, Female circumcision as a public health issue, *N Engl J Med*, 331 (1994): 712–16; J. Black and G. DeBelle, Female genital mutilation in Britain and France, *BMJ*, 310 (1995): 1590–2.

45. B. Nurcombe and D. Partlett, *Child Mental Health and the Law* (New York: The Free Press, 1994), 119–21.

46. 'A minor or a person of full age who is incapable of giving consent may not be submitted to an experiment if the experiment involves serious risk to his health or, where he understands the nature and consequences of the experiment, if he objects. Moreover, a minor or a person of full age who is incapable of giving consent may be submitted to an experiment only if, where the person is the only subject of the experiment, it has the potential to produce benefit to the person's health or only if, in the case of an experiment on a group, it has the potential to produce results capable of conferring benefit to other persons in the same age category or having the same disease or handicap. Such an experiment must be part of a research project approved and monitored by an ethics committee . . .

'Consent to experimentation may be given, in the case of a minor, by the person having parental authority or the tutor and, in the case of a person of full age incapable of giving consent, by the mandatary, tutor or curator.' *Civil Code of Québec*, S.Q., 1991, c. 64, s. 21. Authorized by Les Publications du Québec.

47. T. Smith, *Ethics in Medical Research: A Handbook of Good Practice* (Cambridge, UK: Cambridge University Press, 1999), 175.

Chapter 8

1. R. Saundby, *Medical Ethics: A Guide to Professional Conduct*, 2nd edn. (London: Charles Griffin & Co, 1907), 2.
2. E. Pellegrino, Medical professionalism: Can it, should it survive? *J Am Board Fam Prac*, 13 (2000): 147–9.
3. F. Hafferty, Professionalism: The next wave, *N Engl J Med*, 355 (2006): 2151–2.
4. R. Cruess, S. Cruess, and S. Johnston, Professionalism and medicine's social contract, *J Bone Joint Surg*, 82 (2000): 1189–94.
5. F. Peabody, Care of the patient, *JAMA*, 88 (1927): 877–82.
6. 'Patients clearly and rightly feel doctors should heed minimum standards of courtesy, should acknowledge their patients' human distress, just like anyone else.' C. Schneider, *The Practice of Autonomy: Patients, Doctors, and Medical Decisions* (New York: Oxford University Press, 1998), 227. What he says about doctors should apply across the board to all healthcare professionals. Much of the examples of common rudeness in medicine are drawn from this book (see pp. 219–27).
7. N. Ambady, D. LaPlante, T. Nguyen, R. Rosenthal, N. Chaumeton, and W. Levinson, Surgeons' tone of voice: A clue to malpractice history, *Surgery*, 132 (2002): 5–9.
8. Editorial, Evidence-based handshakes, *Lancet*, 370 (2007): 2.
9. E. Pellegrino, Toward a virtue-based normative ethics for the health professions, *Kennedy Institute of Ethics J*, 5 (1995): 253–77.
10. D. Leach, Competence is a habit, *JAMA*, 287 (2002): 243–4.
11. Medical professionalism in the new millennium: A physician's charter, *Lancet*, 359 (2002): 520–2. Simultaneously published in *Ann Intern Med*, 136 (2002): 243–6.
12. *Norberg v. Wynrib* [1992] 2 SCR 226.
13. Ibid.
14. *CPSO v. R Devgan*. <www.cpso.on.ca/info_public/dis_sum/WEBDISC/2003/DevganR.pdf>.
15. D. Winslow, Treating the enemy, *Ann Intern Med*, 147 (2007): 278–9.
16. P. Surdyk, D. Lynch, and D. Leach, Professionalism: Identifying current themes, *Curr Opin Anaesthesiol*, 16 (2003): 597–602.
17. M.R. Griffin, C.M. Stein, and W. Ray, Postmarketing surveillance for drug safety: Surely we can do better, *Clin Pharm Ther*, 75 (2004): 491–4.
18. E.H. Morreim, Conflicts of interest for physician entrepreneurs, in R. Spece, D. Shimm, and A. Buchanan (eds.), *Conflicts of Interest in Clinical Practice and Research* (New York: Oxford University Press, 1996), 251–85.
19. E.G. Campbell, Doctors and drug companies: Scrutinizing influential relationships, *N Engl J Med*, 357 (2007): 1796–7.
20. Canadian Medical Association, Guidelines for Physicians in Interactions with Industry. Approved 2007-Dec-01. <http://policybase.cma.ca/dbtw-wpd/Policypdf/PD08-01.pdf>.
21. T. Brennan, D. Rothman, L. Blank, D. Blumenthal, S. Chimonas, J. Cohen, et al., Health industry practices that create conflicts of interest: A policy proposal for academic health centers, *JAMA*, 295 (2006): 429–33.

22. The following are the generally accepted conditions for ending the doctor–patient relationship and avoiding allegations of patient 'abandonment'. In certain circumstances—where there are few alternatives for care or where the patient's care is unique—more time may have to be given for the patient to find alternative care. The practitioner, in removing a patient from his or her list, should: not do so in emergencies; provide the patient with a reasonable interval to find a new doctor (perhaps one month, longer if fewer doctors available); make suggestions as to how he or she might find a new doctor; look after the patient's needs until he or she finds a new doctor; and send a registered letter informing the patient of the decision to terminate.

23. CBC News, Turner psychiatrist ordered to pay $10,000, 31 March 2006 <www.cbc.ca/canada/newfoundland-labrador/story/2006/03/31/nf-doucet-decision-20060331.html>.

24. C. Nadelson and M. Notman, Boundaries in the doctor–patient relationship, *Theor Med Bioeth*, 23 (2002): 191–201.

25. S. Rosenbloom, 'Boundary Transgressions in Therapeutic Relationships' (M.Sc. thesis, Virginia State University, 2003), 2–3.

26. L. Lyckholm, Should physicians accept gifts from patients? *JAMA*, 280 (1998):1944–6.

27. A. Spence, Patients bearing gifts: Are there strings attached? *BMJ*, 331 (2005): 1527–9.

28. The quotation in Box 8.1 is from T. Miksanek, Should I give money to my patients? *Am Family Physician*, 67 (2003): 1629. D. Krassner, Gifts from physicians to patients: An ethical dilemma, *Psychiatr Serv*, 55 (2004): 505–6.

29. T. Gutheil and G. Gabbard, Misuses and misunderstandings of boundary theory in clinical and regulatory settings, *Focus*, 1 (2003): 421.

30. A. Smolar, When we give more: Reflections on intangible gifts from therapist to patient, *Am J Psychother*, 57 (2003): 300.

31. The quotation in Box 8.2 is based on the *Regulated Health Professional Act*, S.O., 1991. c. 18, schedule 2, s. 1(3); College of Physicians and Surgeons of Ontario, *The Final Report on the Task Force on Sexual Abuse of Patients* (Toronto, 1991); College of Physicians and Surgeons of British Columbia, *Crossing the Boundaries: The Report of the Committee on Physician Sexual Misconduct* (Vancouver, 1992).

32. CMA, The patient-physician relationship and sexual abuse, *CMAJ*, 152 (1994): 1884A-C.

33. College of Nurses of Ontario, *Mandatory Reporting of Sexual Abuse* <www.cno.org/docs/ih/42006_fsMandReporting.pdf>.

34. J. Davies, C. Hoffman, and P.C. Hébert, *Canadian Patient Safety Dictionary* (Ottawa: RCPSC, 2003).

35. Lord Denning, 'We must not condemn as negligence that which is only a misadventure.' Quoted in E. Picard and G. Robertson, *Legal Liability of Doctors and Hospitals in Canada*, 3rd edn. (Toronto: Carswell Thomson Canada, 1996), 212.

36. 'If the error is one which a reasonable doctor would not have made in similar circumstances, liability will be imposed.' Ibid., 281. The quotation in Box 8.4 is taken from *Mahone v. Osborne*, [1939]2 KB 14 at 31 (CA).

37. G.R. Baker, P.G. Norton, V. Flintoft, R. Blais, A. Brown, J. Cox, et al., The Canadian Adverse Events Study: The incidence of adverse events among hospitalized patients in Canada, *CMAJ*, 170 (2004): 1678–86; R. Wilson, W. Runciman, R. Gibberd, B. Harrison, L. Newby, and J. Hamilton, The Quality in Australian Health Care Study, *Med J Aust*, 163 (1995): 458–71; An Organisation with a Memory, UK Department of Health (2000) <www.doh.gov.uk>; A. Gawande, E. Thoma, E. Zinner, and T. Brennan, The incidence and nature of surgical adverse events in Colorado and Utah in 1992, *Surgery*, 126 (1999): 66–75.

38. Institute of Medicine, *To Err is Human: Building a Safer Health System* (Washington, DC: National Academy Press, 1999).

39. 'Shame is so devastating because it goes right to the core of a person's identity, making them feel exposed, inferior, degraded; it leads to avoidance, silence.' F. Davidoff, Shame: The elephant in the room, *BMJ*, 324 (2002): 623–4.

40. Although there are few 'laws' on the books requiring honesty, there is certainly ample case law and the weight of professional opinion to make veracity a standing duty for healthcare professionals. See The duty to disclose medical mistakes, in Picard and Robertson, *Legal Liability*, 170–2.

41. Institute of Medicine, *To Err is Human*, 2–3.

42. *Shobridge v. Thomas* [1999] BCJ No 1747 (SC).

43. C. Vincent, M. Young, and A. Phillips, Why do people sue doctors? A study of patients and relatives taking legal action, *Lancet*, 343 (1994): 1609–13.

44. A.B. Witman, D.M. Park, and S.B.Hardin, How do patients want physicians to handle mistakes? A survey of internal medicine patients in an academic setting, *Arch Intern Med*, 156 (1996): 2565–9.

45. T.H. Gallagher, C.R. Denham, L.L. Leape, G. Amori, and W. Levinson, Disclosing unanticipated outcomes to patients: The art and practice, *J Patient Saf*, 3 (2007): 158–65.

46. K.M. Mazor, S.R. Simon, and J.H. Gurwitz, Communicating with patients about medical errors: A review of the literature, *Arch Intern Med*, 164 (2004): 1690–7.

47. S. Kraman and G. Hamm, Risk management: Extreme honesty may be the best policy, *Ann Intern Med*, 131 (1999): 963–7; D. Hilfiker, Facing our mistakes, *N Engl J Med*, 310 (1984): 118–22.

48. J. McMurray, Caring for Mr. Gray, *J Gen Intern Med*, 15 (2000): 144–6.

49. A. Wu, Medical error: The second victim, *BMJ*, 320 (2000): 726–7.

50. The second to fifth bullets in Box 8.5 are from *Wickoff v. James*, 324P2d 441 Cal App (1958); *Lashley v. Koerber*, 156 P2d 441 cal (1945); Robertson v. La Croix, 534 P2d 17 Okla App (1975); A Rest Home & Hospital, HDC 13293 (1999).

51. K. Vicente, *The Human Factor: Revolutionizing the Way We Live with Technology* (Toronto: Vintage Canada Books, 2004).

52. *Braun v. Vaughan Manitoba Court of Appeal* [2000] M.J. No. 63.

53. M. Balint, *The Doctor, His Patient and the Illness*, rev. edn. (Madison, CT: International Universities Press, 1988), 69–80.

54. Royal College of Radiologists, Where does the radiologist's duty end? *Lancet*, 367 (2006): 444.

55. L. Berlin, Using an automated coding and review process to communicate critical radiologic findings: One way to skin a cat, *AJR*, 185 (2005): 840–3.
56. R. Porter, *The Greatest Benefit to Mankind: A Medical History of Humanity* (New York: Norton & Co., 1997), 717–8.

Chapter 9

1. C. Dickens, *A Tale of Two Cities* [1859] (Markham, ON: Penguin Books Canada, 1976), 35.
2. D. DeLillo, *Mao II* (New York: Viking Penguin, 1991), 16.
3. A. Wildavsky, Doing better, feeling worse: The political pathology of social policy, in A. Wildavsky, *Speaking Truth to Power: The Art and Craft of Policy Analysis* (Boston: Little Brown, 1979).
4. *Oxford English Dictionary* [CD-ROM] 2nd edn., Version 3.0 (Oxford: Oxford University Press, 2002).
5. R. Tallis, *Hippocratic Oaths: Medicine and its Discontents* (London: Atlantic Books, 2004).
6. T. Beam, Medical ethics on the battlefield, in T. Beam and M. Sparacino (eds.), *Military Medical Ethics*, vol. 2 (Washington, DC: Office of the Surgeon General, 2003), 369–402.
7. J. La Puma, *Managed Care Ethics* (New York: Hatherleigh Press, 1998).
8. P. Ubel, *Pricing Life: Why It's Time for Health Care Rationing* (Cambridge: First MIT Press, 2001).
9. Aristotle, *Politica*, in R. McKeon (ed.), *The Basic Works of Aristotle* (New York: Random House, 1941).
10. S. Alexander, They decide who lives, who dies, *Life*, 9 Nov. 1962, 102ff.
11. R. Baker, Visibility and the just allocation of health care: A study of age-rationing in the British NHS, *Health Care Anal*, 1 (1993): 139–50.
12. A.Wing, A different view from different countries: UK, in C. Kjellstrand and J. Dossetor, *Ethical Problems in Dialysis and Transplantation* (Dordrecht: Kluwer Academic, 1992), 205–10.
13. K. Madhan, The epidemic of elderly patients with dialysis-requiring end-stage renal disease in New Zealand, *New Zealand Medical Journal*, 117/1195 (2004) <www.nzma.org.nz/journal/117-1195/912/>.
14. K. Clarke, D. Gray, N. Keating, and J. Hampton, Do women with acute myocardial infarction receive the same treatment as men? *BMJ*, 309 (1994): 563–6.
15. P. Kual , W. Chang, C. Westerhout, M. Graham, and P. Armstrong, Differences in admission rates and outcomes between men and women presenting to emergency departments with coronary syndromes, *CMAJ*, 177 (2007): 1193–9.
16. J. McIntyre quoted in M. Jackman, The Canadian Charter as a barrier to unwanted medical treatment of pregnant women in the interests of the foetus, *Health Law in Canada*, 14/2 (1993): 53.
17. G. Borkhoff, G. Hawker, H. Kreder, R. Glazier, N. Mahomed, and J.Wright, The effect of patients' sex on physicians' recommendations for total knee arthroplasty, *CMAJ*, 178 (2008): 681–7.

18. D. Miller, D. Jahnigan, M. Gorbien, and L. Simbartl, CPR: How useful? Attitudes and knowledge of an elderly population, *Arch Intern Med*, 152 (1992): 578–82.

19. *Oxford English Dictionary* [CD-ROM] 2nd edn., Version 3.0 (Oxford: Oxford University Press, 2002).

20. H. Naurath, E. Joosten, R. Riezler, S. Stabler, R. Allen, and J. Lindenbaum, Effects of B12, folate and vitamin B6 supplements in elderly people with normal serum vitamin concentrations, *Lancet*, 346 (1995): 85–9; D. Chaput de Saintonge and A. Herxheimer, Harnessing placebo effects in healthcare, *Lancet*, 344 (1994): 995–8.

21. Box 9.1 is taken from Council on Ethical and Judicial Affairs, AMA, Ethical considerations in the allocation of organs and other scarce medical resources among patients, *Arch Intern Med*, 155 (1995): 40.

22. S. Schroeder and J. Cantor, On squeezing balloons: Cost control fails again, *N Engl J Med*, 325 (1991): 1099–1100.

23. J. Rawls, *Justice as Fairness: A Restatement* (Cambridge, MA: Harvard University Press, 2001), 9.

24. C. Flood and M. Zimmerman, Judicious choices: Health care resource decisions and the Supreme Court of Canada, in J. Downie and E. Gibson (eds.), *Health Law at the Supreme Court of Canada* (Toronto: Irwin Law, 2007), 55.

25. See the *United Network for Organ Sharing* (UNOS) <www.unos.org>.

26. M. Benjamin, C. Cohen, and E. Grochowski, What transplantation can teach us about health care reform, *N Engl J Med*, 330 (1994): 858–60.

27. N. Daniels, Four unsolved rationing problems: A Challenge, *Hastings Cent Rep*, 24 (July–Aug. 1994): 27–9.

28. R. Gaston, I. Ayres, L. Dooley, and A. Diethelm, Racial equity in renal transplantation: The disparate impact of HLA-based allocation, *JAMA*, 270 (1993): 1352–6.

29. Ubel, *Pricing Life*, 84.

30. N.R. Hicks, Some observations on attempts to measure appropriateness of care, *BMJ*, 309 (1994): 730–3; K. Warren and F. Mosteller (eds.), *Doing More Good Than Harm: The Evaluation of Health Care Interventions* (New York: The New York Academy of Sciences, 1993).

31. D. Eddy, Practice policies: What are they? *JAMA*, 263 (1990): 877–80.

32. S. Woolf, Practice guidelines: a new reality for medicine, *Arch Intern Med*, 153 (1993): 2647. The quotations in Box 9.2 are from A. Jonsen, *The New Medicine and the Old Ethics* (Cambridge, MA: Harvard University Press, 1990).

33. K. Warren and F. Mosteller (eds.), *Doing More Good Than Harm: The Evaluation of Health Care Interventions* (New York: The New York Academy of Sciences, 1993).

34. W. Silverman, Doing more good than harm, in Warren and Mosteller, *Doing More Good Than Harm*, 5–11.

35. P. Oppenheim, G. Sotiropoulos, and L. Baraff, Incorporating patient preferences into practice guidelines: Management of children with fever without source, *Ann Emerg Med*, 24 (1994): 836–41.

36. J. O'Meara, R. McNutt, T. Evans, S. Moore, and S. Downs, A decision analysis of streptokinase plus heparin as compared with heparin alone for the treatment of deep-vein thrombosis, *N Engl J Med*, 330 (1994): 1864–9. Box 9.3 is adapted from

Colloquium Report on *Legal Issues Related to Clinical Practice Guidelines* (Washington, DC: National Health Lawyers Association, 1995); R. Brook, Implementing medical guidelines, *Lancet*, 346 (1995): 132.

37. J. Wennberg, The paradox of appropriate care, *JAMA*, 258 (1987): 2568–9.
38. '[T]o increase trust, all guidelines should include explicit information about cost-effectiveness to help physicians better assess the objectivity of the recommendations. Cost-effectiveness information enhances the credibility and usefulness of guidelines by showing their reasonableness.' E. Hummel and P. Ubel, Cost and clinical practice guidelines: Can two wrongs make it right? *Virtual Mentor*, 16/12 (2004) <http://virtualmentor.ama-assn.org/2004/12/pfor1-0412.html>.
39. L. Petersen, L. Woodard, T. Urech, C. Daw, and S. Sookanan, Does pay-for-performance improve the quality of health care? *Ann Intern Med*, 145 (2006): 265–72.
40. L. Snyder and R. Neubauer for the American College of Physicians Ethics, Professionalism and Human Rights Committee, Pay-for-performance principles that promote patient-centered care: An ethics manifesto, *Ann Intern Med*, 147 (2007): 792–4.
41. J. Swales, Guidelines for management of hypertension: Sticking to guidelines can be expensive, *BMJ*, 308 (1994): 855.
42. *Early v. Newham Health Authority* [119] 5 Med LR 214.
43. P. Dwyer, Legal implications of clinical practice guidelines, *MJA*, 169 (1998): 192–3.
44. Colloquium Report on *Legal Issues*, 20; E. Hirshfeld, Should ethical and legal standards for physicians be changed to accommodate new models for rationing health care? *U Pa. L. Rev.*, 140 (1992): 1809.
45. D. Sulmasy, Physicians, cost control and ethics, *Ann Intern Med*, 116 (1992): 920–6.
46. J. Kassirer, Managed care and the morality of the marketplace, *N Engl J Med*, 333 (1995): 50–2.
47. J. La Puma, *Managed Care Ethics* (New York: Hatherleigh Press, 1998), 166.
48. N. Daniels, Is the Oregon rationing plan fair? *JAMA*, 265 (1991): 2232–5. 'One of the best avenues to improve accountability is to make decision-making less opaque and more transparent. Unfortunately, health care decisions have been and continue to be made behind closed doors.' C. Flood and M. Zimmerman, Judicious choices: Health care resource decisions and the Supreme Court of Canada, in Downie and Gibson, *Health Law*, 54.
49. Colloquium Report on *Legal Issues*, 16.
50. *Law Estate v. Simice*, [1994] B.C.J. No. 979.
51. D. Mechanic, Dilemmas in rationing health care services: The case for implicit rationing, *BMJ*, 310 (1995): 1655–9.
52. E. Campbell, S. Regan, R. Gruen, T. Ferris, S. Rao, P. Cleary, et al., Professionalism in medicine: Results of a national survey of physicians, *Ann Intern Med*, 147 (2007): 795–802.
53. L. Snyder and R. Neubauer for the American College of Physicians Ethics, Professionalism and Human Rights Committee, Pay-for-performance principles that promote patient-centered care: An ethics manifesto, *Ann Intern Med*, 147 (2007): 792–4.

54. J. Fries, C.E. Koop, C. Beadle, P. Cooper, M. England, R. Greaves, et al., Reducing health care costs by reducing the need and demand for medical services, *N Engl J Med*, 329 (1993): 321–5.

Chapter 10

1. *Dobson v Dobson* 1999 2 SCC *per* C.J. Lamer.
2. G.W.F. Hegel, *The Phenomenology of Mind* [c. 1806]. Trans. J.B. Baillie (New York: Harper & Row), 615–27.
3. Abortion does not make future pregnancies less likely, but women should not assume it is always easy to get pregnant! J. Virk, J. Zhang, and J. Olsen, Medical abortion and the risk of subsequent adverse pregnancy outcomes, *N Engl J Med*, 357 (2007): 648–53.
4. J.J. Thomson, A defense of abortion, *Philosophy & Public Affairs*, 1/1 (Fall 1971). Reprinted in R. Munson (ed.), *Intervention and Reflection: Basic Issues in Medical Ethics*, 5th ed. (Belmont, CA: Wadsworth, 1996), 69–80.
5. B. Sneiderman, Issues in reproductive choice, in B. Sneiderman, J. Irvine, and P. Osborne (eds.), *Canadian Medical Law: An Introduction for Physicians, Nurses and Other Health Care Professionals*, 3rd edn. (Toronto: Thomson Carswell, 2003), 347.
6. *R. v. Morgentaler* (1988), 44 D.L.R. (4th) 385 (S.C.C.), 402.
7. *Roe v. Wade* (No. 70-18) 314 F. Supp. 1217, aff'd in part and rev'd in part.
8. M. Greene and J. Ecker, Abortion, health and the law, *N Engl J Med*, 350 (2004): 184–6.
9. G. Sedagh, S. Henshaw, S. Singh, E. Ahman, and I. Shah, Induced abortion: Estimated rates and trends worldwide, *Lancet*, 370 (2007): 1338–45.
10. B. Dickens and R. Cook, The scope and limits of conscientious objection, *Int J Gynecol and Obstet*, 71 (2000): 71–7.
11. R. Alta Charo, The partial death of abortion rights, *N Engl J Med*, 356 (2007): 2125–8.
12. '[T]he majority of ART programs believe that they have the right and responsibility to screen candidates before providing them with ART to conceive a child. The key value that seems to guide programs' screening practices is ensuring a prospective child's safety and welfare and not risking the welfare of the prospective mother.' A. Gurmankin, A. Caplan, and A. Braverman, Screening practices and beliefs of ART programs, *Fertil Steril*, 83 (2005): 61–7.
13. R.A. Charo, The celestial fire of conscience: Refusing to deliver medical care, *N Engl J Med*, 352 (2005): 2471–3.
14. *Tremblay v. Daigle*, [1989] 2 S.C.R. 530.
15. Ibid.
16. S. Rodgers and J. Downie, Abortion: Ensuring access, *CMAJ*, 175 (2006): 9.
17. M. Day, Nurses should be allowed to run abortion services up to nine weeks, charity says, *BMJ*, 333 (2006): 1139.
18. A. Cheng, Chinese couple sue over forced abortion. One child policy: Citizens push their rights in first case of its kind, *National Post*, 29 Aug. 2007, A16.

19. Sneiderman, Issues in reproductive choice, 323.
20. C.A. Kent, *Medical Ethics: The State of the Law* (Toronto: LexisNexis Canada, 2005), 215.
21. E. Picard and G. Robertson, *Legal Liability of Doctors and Hospitals in Canada*, 3rd edn. (Toronto: Carswell Thomson Canada, 1996), 213.
22. *Jones (Guardian ad litem of) v. Rostvig*. Between Liam Thomas Jones, an infant by his mother and Guardian ad litem, Kelly Rae Short, the said Kelly Rae Short and Leonard James Jones, plaintiffs, and Dr Lars Jeffrey Rostvig, defendant. [2003] B.C.J. No. 1840 2003 BCSC 1222.
23. I. Bretherton, The origins of attachment theory: John Bowlby and Mary Ainsworth, *Developmental Psychology*, 28 (1992): 759–75.
24. R. Mukherjee, N. Eastman, J. Turk, and S. Hollins, Foetal alcohol syndrome: Law and ethics, *Lancet*, 369 (2007): 1149–50.
25. *Tremblay v. Daigle*, [1989] 2 S.C.R. 530. The quotation in Box 10.1 is from Kent, *Medical Ethics*, 161.
26. PGD is a powerful technique that can be used on an embryo prior to womb implantation to determine its precise chromosomal makeup—including its sex and inherited characteristics such as genetic disorders.
27. G. Rivard and J. Hunter, *The Law of Assisted Human Reproduction* (Toronto: LexisNexis Canada, 2005), 125.
28. *Potter v. Korn* [1995] BCCHRD No 20.
29. *Korn v. Potter* [1996] BCJ No 692.
30. Discrimination is defined in Chapter 8 on Justice.
31. Rivard and Hunter, *Law of Assisted Human Reproduction*, 11.
32. C. Boorse, On the distinction between disease and illness, in M. Cohen, T. Nagel, and T. Scanlon (eds.), *Medicine and Moral Philosophy* (Princeton, NJ: Princeton University Press, 1981), 3–48.
33. *Cameron v. Nova Scotia (AG)* [1999] NSJ No 297 para 170.
34. A. Wolfberg, Genes on the web: direct-to-consumer marketing of genetic testing, *N Engl J Med*, 355 (2006): 543–5.
35. The quotation in Box 10.2 is from Rivard and Hunter, *Law of Assisted Human Reproduction*, 21.
36. Ibid., 31.
37. P. White, Cure or hoax in China? Stem cell therapy: 'Some get miracles'; others are skeptical, *National Post*, 23 Aug. 2007, L1, 3.
38. S. Laidlaw, Battle lines being drawn for new war over stem cells, *Toronto Star*, 25 Aug. 2007, ID6.
39. The Ethics Committee of ASRM, Financial compensation of oocyte donors, *Fertil Steril*, 88 (2007): 305–9.
40. I. Kant, *Groundwork of the Metaphysic of Morals* [1785] (New York: Harper & Row, 1956), 96.
41. B. Williams, *Moral Luck: Philosophical Papers 1973–1980* (Cambridge, UK: Cambridge University Press, 1981), 18.
42. C. Taver, International policy failures: Cloning and stem cell research, *Lancet*, 364 (2004): 209–14.

43. J. Yu, M. Vodyanik, K. Smuga-Otto, J. Antosiewicz-Bourget, J. Frane, S. Tian, et al., Induced pluripotent stem cells from adult human fibroblasts by defined factors, *Science*, 318 (2007): 1917–20.

Chapter 11

1. T. Hobbes, *Leviathan* [1651] (New York: Collier Books, 1977), 100.
2. S. Nuland, *How We Die: Reflections on Life's Final Chapter* (Toronto: Random House of Canada, 1993).
3. The quotation in Box 11.1 is from *Brophy v. New England Sinai Hospital*, [1986] Sup Jud Ct Mass 497 NE 2d 626.
4. *Criminal Code of Canada*, s. 215c.
5. Ibid., s. 217.
6. Ibid., s. 216.
7. Ibid., s. 219.
8. *Nancy B. v. Hôtel-Dieu de Québec et al.* (1992), 86 D.L.R. (4th) 385–95 (Q.S.C.).
9. L. Glantz quoted in G. Snider, Withholding and withdrawing life-sustaining therapy, *Am J Respir Crit Care Med*, 151 (1995): 279.
10. Ibid., 279–81.
11. The quotation in Box 11.2 is from *In the Matter of Claire Conroy*, 486 A.2d 1209, NJ, 1985.
12. S. Baumrucker, Withdrawing treatment for the 'wrong' reasons, *Am J Hosp Palliat Care*, 24 (2008): 509–14.
13. G. Annas, *Judging Medicine* (Clifton: Humana Press, 1990), 311.
14. C. Kjellstrand, Practical aspects of stopping dialysis and cultural differences, in J. Dossetor and C. Kjellstrand (eds.), *Ethical Problems in Dialysis and Transplantation* (Boston: Kluwer Academic, 1992), 103.
15. ESRD Network of New England, *2001 Annual Report to the Centers for Medicare and Medicaid Services* (New Haven, CT: Tyco Printers, 2002), 60–3.
16. N. Christakis and D. Asch, Biases in how physicians choose to withdraw life-support, *Lancet*, 342 (1993): 642–6.
17. R. Lin, Withdrawing life-sustaining medical treatment: A physician's personal reflection, *Mental Retardation & Developmental Disabilities Research Reviews*, 9 (2003): 10–15.
18. D. Cook, G. Rocker, J. Marshall, P. Sjokvist, P. Dodek, L. Griffith, et al., Withdrawal of mechanical ventilation in anticipation of death in the ICU, *N Engl J Med*, 349 (2003): 1123–32.
19. The SUPPORT Principal Investigators, The SUPPORT study: A controlled trial to improve care for seriously ill hospitalized patients: The Study to Understand Prognoses and Preferences for Outcomes and Risks of Treatments (SUPPORT), *JAMA*, 274 (1995): 1591–8.
20. C. Rodgers, H. Field, and E. Kunkel, Countertransference issues in termination of life support in acute quadriplegia, *Psychosomatics*, 36 (1995): 305–9.
21. C. von Gunten, F. Ferris, and L. Emanuel, Ensuring competency in end-of-life care, *JAMA*, 284 (2000): 3051–7; H. Chochinov, T. Hack, T. Hassard, L. Kristianson, S.

McClement, and M. Harlos, Dignity in the terminally ill: A cross-sectional cohort study, *Lancet*, 360 (2002): 2026–30; L. Crawley, P. Marshall, B. Lo, and B. Koenig for the End-of-Life Care Consensus Panel, Strategies for culturally effective end-of-life car, *Ann Intern Med*, 136 (2002): 673–9.

22. S. Bok, Personal directions for care at the end of life, *N Engl J Med*, 295 (1976): 367–9.

23. S. Brett, Limitations of listing specific medical interventions in advance directives, *JAMA*, 266 (1991): 825–8.

24. T. Thompson, R. Barbour, and L. Swartz, Adherence to advance directives in critical care decision making: Vignette study, *BMJ*, 327 (2003): 1011–14.

25. H. Perkins, Controlling death: The false promise of advance directives, *Ann Intern Med*, 147 (2007): 51–7.

26. W. Kouwenhoven, J. Jude, and G. Knickerbocker, Closed-chest cardiac massage, *JAMA*, 173 (1960): 1064–7.

27. Critical Care Committee of Massachusetts General Hospital, Optimum care for hopelessly ill patients, *N Engl J Med*, 295 (1976): 362–6.

28. Joint Statement on Resuscitative Interventions, *CMAJ*, 151 (1994): 1176A–C.

29. CPSO, Decision-Making for the End-of-life. Policy Statement #5-02, (May/June/July 2006).

30. *Re Child and Family Services of Central Manitoba v. Lavallee* (1997), 154 D.L.R. (4th) 409 at 413 (Man. C.A.).

31. *Sawatsky v. Riverview Health Centre Inc.* (1998), 167 D.L.R. (4th) 359 at 362 (Man. Q.B.).

32. E. Fox and M. Seigler, Redefining the emergency physician's role in DNR decision-making, *Am J Med*, 92 (1992): 125–8; M. Clemency and N. Thompson, DNR orders in the perioperative period: A comparison of the perspectives of anesthesiologists, internists, and surgeons, *Anesth Analg*, 78 (1994): 651–8.

33. T. Quill, R. Arnold, and F. Platt, 'I wish things were different': Expressing wishes in response to loss, futility, and unrealistic hopes, *Ann Intern Med*, 135 (2001): 551–5; K. Evans, *A Medico-Legal Handbook for Physicians in Canada* (Ottawa: CMPA, 2002), 36.

34. B. Lo and R. Steinbrook, Deciding whether to resuscitate, *Arch Intern Med*, 143 (1983): 1561–3.

35. T. Tomlinson and H. Brody, Ethics and communication in do-not-resuscitate orders, *N Engl J Med*, 318 (1988): 43–6.

36. Box 11.6 is taken from S. Goold, B. Williams, and R. Arnold, Conflicts regarding decisions to limit treatment: A differential diagnosis, *JAMA*, 283 (2000): 909–14.

37. *Scardoni v. Hawryluck* (2004), CanLII 34326 (ON S.C.).

38. A. Brett and P. Jersild, 'Inappropriate' treatment near the end-of-life conflict between religious convictions and clinical judgment, *Arch Intern Med*, 163 (2003): 1645–9.

39. 'Ultimately, the heart stops in brain death . . . despite full cardiovascular support, 97% of . . . brain-dead bodies developed asystole in a week.' E.F.M. Wijdicks and J.L.D. Atkinson, Pathophysiologic responses to brain death, in E.F.M. Wijdicks (ed.), *Brain Death* (Philadelphia: Lippincott Williams & Wilkins, 2001), 35. Of course, just how long one can prolong circulation in a (brain) dead person may

depend on how hard one tries and on the advance of medical science. Such perfusion never reverses the sequence of inexorable circulatory decline.

40. PVS refers to a state of the absence of awareness and the irreversible loss of higher brain function. Such patients go through sleep-wake cycles but have no purposive movements or communication and must be artificially fed and sometimes artificially ventilated. B. Jennett, *The Vegetative State* (Cambridge, UK: Cambridge University Press, 2002).

41. *In re Quinlan* [1976] 137 NJ Sup 227, 348 A2d 801, modified, 70 NJ 10, 335A 2d 647 cert denied, 429 US 922.

42. *In the matter of Claire Conroy*, [1985] 98 NJ 32; *Brophy v. New England Sinai Hospital*, [1986] Sup Jud Ct Mass 497 NE 2d 626; *Cruzan v. Director, Missouri Dept of Health*, [1990] 110 S, Ct, 2841; G. Annas, 'Culture of Life' politics at the bedside: The case of Terri Schiavo, *N Engl J Med*, 352 (2005): 1710–15.

43. *Re a Ward of the Court* [1995] 2ILRM 401 (Ir Sup Ct); *Airedale NHS Trust v. Bland* [1993] Appeal Cases 789.

44. Jennett, *The Vegetative State*, 10–23.

45. The quotation in Box 11.7 is from the *Criminal Code of Canada*, s. 241(b).

46. R. Portenoy, U. Sibirceva, R. Smout, S. Horn, S. Connor, and R. Blum, Opioid use and survival at the end-of-life: A survey of a hospice population, *J Pain Symptom Manage*, 32 (2006): 532–40.

47. S.J. Genius, S.K. Genius, and W.C. Chang, Public attitudes towards the right to die, *CMAJ*, 150 (1994): 701–2; *New York Times*, 18 Aug. 1991, E1.

48. M. Lee and S. Tolle, Oregon's plan to legalise suicide assisted by a doctor, *BMJ*, 310 (1995): 613–14.

49. M. Silveira, A. DiPiero, M. Gerrity, and C. Feudtner, Patients' knowledge of options at the end of life: Ignorance in the face of death, *JAMA*, 284 (2000): 2483–8; K. Wilson, J. Scott, I. Graham, J. Kozak, S. Chater, R. Viola et al., Attitudes of terminally ill patients toward euthanasia and physician-assisted suicide, *Arch Intern Med*, 160 (2000): 2454–60.

50. *Rodriguez v. B.C.* (A.G.) [1993] 3 S.C.R.: 519–632.

51. D. Kinsella and M. Verhoef, Alberta euthanasia survey: 1. Physicians' opinions about the morality and legalization of active euthanasia, *CMAJ*, 148 (1993): 1921–33.

52. J. Cohen, S. Fihn, E. Boyko, A. Jonsen, and R. Wood, Attitudes toward assisted suicide and euthanasia among physicians in Washington State, *N Engl J Med*, 331 (1994): 89–94; D. Meier, C.A. Emmons, S. Wallenstein, T. Quill, R. Morrison, and C. Cassell, A national survey of physician-assisted suicide and euthanasia in the US, *N Engl J Med*, 338 (1998): 1193–201; E. Emanuel, D. Fairclough, B. Clarridge, D. Blum, E. Bruera, W. Penley et al., Attitudes and practices of US oncologists regarding euthanasia and physician-assisted suicide, *Ann Intern Med*, 133 (2000): 527–32.

53. A. Ogilvie and S. Potts, Assisted suicide for depression: The slippery slope in action? *BMJ*, 309 (1994): 492–3.

54. L. Pijnenborg, P. van der Maas, J. van Delden, and C. Looman, Life-terminating acts without explicit request of patient, *Lancet*, 341 (1993): 1196–9.

55. D. Sulmasy, Managed care and managed death, *Arch Intern Med*, 155 (1995): 133–6.
56. R. Momeyer, Does physician assisted suicide violate the integrity of medicine? *J Med Philos*, 20 (1995): 13–24.
57. A. Gawande, D. Denno, R. Truog, and D. Waisel, Physicians and executions: Highlights from a discussion of lethal injection, *N Engl J Med*, 358 (2008): 448–51.
58. E. Emanuel, Euthanasia and physician-assisted suicide: A review of the empirical data from the US, *Arch Intern Med*, 162 (2002): 142–52.
59. G. Kasting, The nonnecessity of euthanasia, in J. Humber, R. Almeder, and G. Kasting (eds.), *Physician-Assisted Death* (New Jersey: Humana Press, 1994), 25–46.
60. A. Qaseem, V. Snow, P. Shekelle, D. Casey, T. Cross, and D. Owens for the Clinical Efficacy Assessment Subcommittee of the American College of Physicians, Evidence-based interventions to improve the palliative care of pain, dyspnea, and depression at the end of life: A clinical practice guideline from the American College of Physicians, *Ann Intern Med*, 148 (2008): 141–6.
61. T. Quill, B. Lee, and S. Nunn, Palliative treatments of last resort: Choosing the least harmful alternative, *Ann Intern Med*, 132 (2000): 488–93.
62. F. Miller, J. Finns, and L. Snyder, Assisted suicide compared with refusal of treatment: A valid distinction? *Ann Intern Med*, 132 (2000): 470–5.
63. T. Quill, Death and dignity: A case of individualized decision making, *N Engl J Med*, 324 (1991): 691–4.
64. G. van der Wal and R. Dillman, Euthanasia in the Netherlands, *BMJ*, 308 (1994): 1346–9.
65. *Oregon v. Ashcroft.* 368 F.3d 1118 (9th Cir. 2004), aff'd 192 F.Supp.2d 1077 (D.Or. 2002 Holding that Oregon's *Death With Dignity Act* does not violate the Federal *Controlled Substances Act*); 'Held: The Controlled Substances Act does not allow the Attorney General to prohibit doctors from prescribing regulated drugs for use in physician-assisted suicide under state law permitting the procedure.' Supreme Court of the United States. *Gonzales, Attorney General, et al. v. Oregon et al.* Certiorari to the United States Court of Appeals for the Ninth Circuit. Decided January 17, 2006 No. 04—623. The quotation in Box 11.8 is from Oregon Death with Dignity Act. Or Rev Stat 127.800–127.897 (1994).
66. S. Okie, Physician-assisted suicide: Oregon and beyond, *N Engl J Med*, 352 (2005): 1627–30.
67. A. Sullivan, K. Hedberg, and D. Fleming, Legalized physician-assisted suicide in Oregon: The second year, *N Engl J Med*, 342 (2000): 598–604.
68. L. Ganzini, H. Nelson, T. Schmidt, D. Kraemer, M. Delorit, and M. Lee, Physicians' experiences with the Oregon *Death with Dignity Act*, *N Engl J Med*, 342 (2000): 557–63.
69. While it is rare for health professionals to be charged and found guilty of assistance at suicide, it can happen. A family physician in Toronto prescribed a lethal dose of barbiturates to a despondent unstable patient who later took them all in a pique of despair. When the doctor was informed by friends of the patient that he had done so and was lapsing into a stupor, the doctor did nothing, advising them to do nothing also. The patient died of respiratory failure. The doctor pleaded guilty to assistance

at suicide and was sentenced to three years in jail. *R v. Dr. Genereux Ont CJ* 1998 (not reported).

70. Lord Browne-Wilkenson quoted in C. Franklin, Elm Road and Hillsborough: Tragedy, the law and medicine, *Intensive Care Med*, 19 (1993): 307–8.

71. 'Death is not an event in life . . .' L. Wittgenstein, *Tractatus Logico-Philosophicus* [1921] (London: Routledge & Kegan Paul, 1961), 147.

72. N. Brown, *Life against Death: The Psychoanalytical Meaning of History* (Middletown, CT: Wesleyan University Press, 1959), 101–6.

73. L. Snyder and D. Sulmasy, Physician-assisted suicide, *Ann Intern Med*, 135 (2001): 209–16.

Conclusion

1. R. Tamblyn, M. Abrahamowicz, D. Dauphinee, E. Wenghofer, A. Jacques, D. Klass, et al., Physician scores on a national clinical skills examination as predictors of complaints to medical regulatory authorities, *JAMA*, 298 (2007): 993–1001.

2. D. Irvine, *The Doctors' Tale: Professionalism and Public Trust* (Oxford: Radcliffe Medical Press, 2003).

3. T. Beauchamp and J. Childress, *Principles of Biomedical Ethics*, 4th edn. (New York: Oxford University Press, 1994).

4. A. Jonsen, M. Siegler, and W. Winslade, *Clinical Ethics*, 5th edn. (New York: McGraw-Hill, 2002).

5. R. Gillon (ed.), *Principles of Health Care Ethics* (Toronto: John Wiley & Sons, 1994).

6. W.R. Reich, (ed.), *Encyclopedia of Bioethics*, rev. edn. (Toronto: Simon & Schuster Macmillan, 1995).

7. J. Sugarman and D. Sulmasy, *Methods in Medical Ethics* (Washington, DC: Georgetown University Press, 2001).

8. S. Blackburn, *Think: A Compelling Introduction to Philosophy* (Oxford: Oxford University Press, 1999); S. Blackburn, *Being Good: A Short Introduction to Ethics* (London: Oxford University Press, 2001).

9. H. Frankfurt, *The Reasons of Love* (Princeton, NJ: Princeton University Press, 2004); H. Frankfurt, *The Importance of What We Care About* (Cambridge: Cambridge University Press, 2005).

10. R. Amdur and E. Bankert, *Institutional Review Board: Management and Function* (Mississauga, ON: Jones and Bartlett Publishers Canada, 2002); S. Eckstein (ed.), *Manual for Research Ethics Committees*, 6th edn. (Cambridge, UK: Cambridge University Press, 2003).

11. T. Smith, *Ethics in Medical Research: A Handbook of Good Practice* (Cambridge, UK: Cambridge University Press, 1999).

12. T. Beam and M. Sparacino (eds.), *Military Medical Ethics* (Washington, DC: Office of the Surgeon General, 2003).

13. The British Medical Association, *Medical Ethics Today: The BMA's Handbook of Ethics and Law*, 2nd edn. (London: BMJ Publishing Group, 2004).

14. J. Rawls, *Justice as Fairness: A Restatement* (Cambridge, MA: Harvard University Press, 2001).
15. A. Gawande, *Complications: A Surgeon's Notes on an Imperfect Science* (New York: Henry Holt and Company, 2002); A. Gawande, *Better: A Surgeon's Notes on Performance* (New York: Metropolitan Books, 2007).
16. R. Klitzman, *When Doctors Become Patients* (New York: Oxford University Press, 2008).
17. A. Merry and A. McCall Smith, *Errors, Medicine and the Law* (Cambridge, UK: Cambridge University Press, 2001).
18. J. Groopman, *How Doctors Think* (Boston: Houghton Mifflin, 2007).
19. P. Appelbaum, *Almost a Revolution: Mental Health Law and the Limits of Change* (New York: Oxford University Press, 1994).
20. M. Balint, *The Doctor, His Patient and the Illness*, rev. edn. (Madison, CT: International Universities Press, 1988); J. Berger, *A Fortunate Man: The Story of a Country Doctor* (New York: Pantheon Books, 1967); R. Tallis, *Hippocratic Oaths: Medicine and Its Discontents* (London: Atlantic Books, 2004).
21. E. Picard and G. Robertson, *Legal Liability of Doctors and Hospitals in Canada*, 3rd edn. (Toronto: Carswell Thomson Canada, 2007); J. Downie and E. Gibson (eds.), *Health Law at the Supreme Court of Canada* (Toronto: Irwin Law, 2007); C.A. Kent, *Medical Ethics: The State of the Law* (Toronto: LexisNexis Canada, 2005).

disclose, 182; public expectations and, 179–80; when to disclose, 181–2
estrogen replacement therapy (ERT), 35
ethics: *see* clinical ethics
ethics committee, 191–2
ethics toolbox, 29
'ethics work-up', 17–18
euthanasia, 241–2

fairness, 10, 15; *see also* justice
families: end-of-life decisions and, 238–9; informed consent and, 102–3; *see also* parents
fetal alcohol syndrome, 215
fetus: health of, 214–15; status of, 215
fitness: to practice, 69–71; to work, 65–6
Fleming v. Reid/Gallager, 129–32
force-feeding, 24–8
Frankfurt, H., 11

'gaming the system', 90–1, 196
gender: abortion and, 213; justice and, 192, 193
genetic diseases, 59–60, 214
gifts, 174–5
Gillick case, 135
guardians, 134
guidelines: no CPR orders, 234–5; practice, 200–7
gunshot-wound reporting, 66

harm, 'imminent', 151
harm and benefit, patient-based, 16
healthcare system: access to, 188–9, 195–6, 206; assisted reproduction and, 219–20; justice and, 187–206; managed, 190, 204–5, 245; negligence and, 205–6
health information: control of, 52–4
Hegel, G.W.F., 218
heteronomy, 33
Hippocratic Oath, 14, 139
Hume, David, 28
hypnotics, 42–3, 46–7

immunization, 45–6
impartiality, 199–200
incapacity: autonomy and, 32; *see also* capacity
infertility, 219–20
informed consent, 94–114; elective procedures and, 106–7, 112; exceptions to, 111–14; information to disclose and, 104–7; legal details of, 100–11; obtaining, 107–11; patient suggestibility and, 114; refusal by relatives and, 102–3; responsibility for, 103; treatment alternatives and, 107; withdrawal of, 108–10; *see also* consent
Inglefinger, F., 47
involuntary committal, 150–1
involuntary treatment, 129–34
IVF (*in vitro* fertilization), 217, 222–3

justice: definition of, 188–9; distributive, 187, 189, 191; minimal, 191–4; optimal, 191–4
justice principle, 5, 15, 20, 26, 187–206; medically necessary treatment and, 194–200

Kant, Immanuel, 4, 73, 223
Kraman, S., et al., 181

Lamer, Justice Antonio, 207, 244
law: abortion, 209-10; autonomy and, 32–3, 34, 36–8, 40–1; capacity and, 119–21; child welfare, 154; confidentiality and, 54, 67–9; drug industry and, 170; involuntary treatment and, 133–4; mental health, 148, 150–1; privacy, 62–3; public health, 64; role of, 5–6, 13; truthtelling and, 75, 81–2; *see also* courts
liability: duty to protect and, 151; *see also* negligence
lies, therapeutic, 74, 88–9; *see also* deception

litigation: informed consent and, 94; practice guidelines and, 203–4; reducing risk of, 180–1; truth and, 81
living wills, 233–4

McGregor, Colin, 68–9
Malette v. Shulman, 36–8
managed care, 190, 204–5, 245
mandatory disclosures, 63–7
Mandatory Gunshot Wound Reporting Act, 66
medically necessary treatment, 194–200
medical need/benefit, 197–8
medical records, 53–4
medico-legal death investigators, 66-7
'mental disorder': duty to protect and, 150–1
Mill, John Stuart, 4, 94
Mini-Mental State Examination (MMSE), 128, 129
minors: *see* children
Morgentaler decision, 209–10
multiple sclerosis (MS), 72–3, 75–6

'narrative medicine', 36
necessity: definition of, 195–6; *see also* medically necessary treatment
'negative transferences', 231
negligence, 177–9; approved practice and, 145; birth and, 214; limited resources and, 205–6
'negligent events', 178
negligent practice, 99–100
New Brunswick: capable-minor law in, 135
New Charter, 167–9, 172–7
Newfoundland: involuntary treatment in, 134
nihilism, therapeutic, 15–16
non-maleficence principle, 5, 15–16, 138–45, 162
no-resuscitation order, 234–5

Oken, D., 82

Ontario: capacity in, 148; involuntary treatment in, 133–4; reporting in, 66
Oregon: death in, 246–7
outcomes research, 200–2

palliative care, 242, 245, 246–7
parents: consent of, 153–61, 235; *see also* children; families
paternalism, 32, 39–40, 45, 47–8, 82; capacity and, 147–8
patient-based care, 30–49
patient-choice rationing, 202
patient-physician relationship, healthy, 173–7
patient safety, 185
Patient Self-Determination Act, 233
patient-specific factors: justice and, 193–4
patient waiver, 47–8; informed consent and, 111–12; truth and, 84–5
Peabody, F., 165
permitted disclosures, 67–9
persistent/permanent vegetative state (PVS), 241
pharmaceutical industry, 169–71
physician-assisted death, 241–8; reasons to oppose, 244–5; reasons to support, 245–6
'pillow angel', 159–60
placebos, 90
Popper, Karl, 2
Porter, Roy, 185–6
postprofessionalism, 163
practice, 'approved', 144–5
practice guidelines, 200–7; legal risk and, 203–4
Prescription Project, 170
primum non nocere, 15–16
Prince v. Massachusetts, 154
principles: ethical, 5, 8–17, 20; respect for persons, 78–81; *see also* autonomy; beneficence; justice; non-maleficence
prioritizing: justice and, 189–90
privacy, 50–71; autonomy and, 32; definition of, 52–3

About Oxford University Press

Oxford University Press (often referred to as 'OUP') is one of the oldest publishing companies in the world, as well as one of the largest. It is a department of the University of Oxford, and, like the University as a whole, OUP is devoted to the spread of knowledge: any surplus generated through its activities is directed toward the publication of works which further scholarship and education, or to encouraging and sustaining research on which these books may be based.

The Press dates its origins back to the fifteenth century. The first book to be printed in Oxford—the *Commentary on the Apostles' Creed*, attributed to St Jerome, by Theodoric Rood—was issued in 1478, barely a quarter-century after Gutenberg's invention of the printing press. Over the following century, a number of short-lived private businesses, some patronized by Oxford University, took the field, but in 1586 the University itself obtained a decree from the Star Chamber confirming its privilege to print books. That same year, Oxford University lent £100—a small fortune at that time—to a local bookseller, Joseph Barnes, to set up a press. Barnes produced many books now prized by collectors, including the first books printed at Oxford in Greek (1586) and Hebrew (1596), and Captain John Smith's *Map of Virginia* (1612). The Great Charter, secured by Archbishop Laud from King Charles I in 1632, increased the independence of the Press, entitling the University to print 'all manner of books', and approximately 300 books were printed before Barnes retired in 1617.

In 1633, the University first appointed 'delegates' to oversee printing and publishing. Records of their deliberations date back to 1668, and to this day, OUP's editorial work is overseen by delegates appointed from the University's faculty. The operations of the Press as a whole are directed by a board that includes the vice chancellor of the University and other University administrators, as well as a number of delegates and officers of the Press.

The University established its right to print the King James Authorized Version of the Bible in the seventeenth century. This 'Bible Privilege' formed the basis of a successful publishing business throughout the next two centuries and was the spur for OUP's expansion. In London, the Press established a Bible warehouse, which later grew into a major publisher of books with educational and cultural content aimed at the general reader. OUP then began to expand internationally, starting with the opening of an American office in 1896 and the Canadian branch in 1904.

Today, OUP is the world's largest university press, publishing more than 6,000 new titles a year and employing approximately 5,000 people in 50 countries. Few if any organizations publish a more diverse range of titles than Oxford, including scholarly works in all academic disciplines; Bibles; music reference works as well as sheet music; textbooks; children's books; materials for teaching English as an additional language; dictionaries and reference books; professional books in fields such as law, brain science, and medicine; academic journals; and a burgeoning online publishing program of electronic resources and publications. Oxford and New York are the two largest publishing centres within the Press, but publishing programs of significant size and scope exist the world over, in such countries as Australia, China, India, Kenya, Malaysia, Mexico, Pakistan, South Africa, and Spain, as well as in Canada.

About Oxford University Press Canada

Established in 1904, OUP's Canadian branch was the only the second overseas office to be set up (following New York in 1896). Before the twentieth century, the main suppliers of books in Canada were the Copp Clark Company, the W.J. Gage Company, and the Methodist Bookroom (eventually renamed The Ryerson Press after its founder, Egerton Ryerson). These three firms represented other lines that were later distributed directly by branches of their parent houses or by exclusive Canadian agents. Prior to 1904, Oxford books had been sold in Canada by S.G. Wilkinson, who, based in London, England, travelled across Canada as far west as Winnipeg. Wilkinson did a large trade with S.B. (Sam) Gundy, the wholesale and trade manager of the Methodist Bookroom. When OUP opened its own branch in Toronto, Gundy, already familiar with Oxford books, was invited to become its manager. The premises were at 25 Richmond Street West and, lacking an elevator of any kind, were perhaps not ideal for a publishing house!

In 1929, the branch moved to Amen House, named after Oxford's global headquarters in England and located at 480 University Avenue. After Gundy's death, the branch became closely allied with Clarke, Irwin and Company, an association that continued until 1949 when that firm moved to its own offices. In 1963, the Press moved to a new building at 70 Wynford Drive in Don Mills, a site which served it well for the next 46 years. By 2009, however, the branch had outgrown 70 Wynford. An extensive search process culminated in the move that November to a split-site configuration. The offices relocated to new premises at the Shops at Don Mills, an innovative retail/office/residential development, while the warehouse moved to a site in Brampton that not only offered more affordable rent and carrying charges but also provided a modern high-bay space much closer to major customers and Pearson International Airport.

Today OUP Canada is a major publisher of higher education, school, and English-as-a-second-language textbooks, as well as a significant trade and reference publisher. The Higher Education Division publishes both introductory and upper-level texts in such disciplines as sociology, anthropology, social work, English literature and composition, geography, history, political science, religious studies, and engineering. Its authors include many of Canada's most accomplished scholars and educators. Each year, the division publishes more than 60 new Canadian texts and 150 student and instructor supplements deriving two-thirds of its total sales from books and other learning materials written, edited, and published in Canada.

OUP Canada's first home, at 25 Richmond Street West in Toronto.